TOWARD A RATIONALITY OF EMOTIONS

TOWARD A RATIONALITY OF EMOTIONS:

AN ESSAY IN THE PHILOSOPHY OF MIND

_____

W. GEORGE TURSKI

OHIO UNIVERSITY PRESS
ATHENS

Ohio University Press, Athens, Ohio 45701
© 1994 by W. George Turski
Printed in the United States of America
All rights reserved

98 97 96 95 94   5 4 3 2 1

Ohio University Press books are printed on acid-free paper ∞

Library of Congress Cataloging-in-Publication Data

Turski, W. George.
    Toward a rationality of emotions : an essay in the philosophy of
mind / W. George Turski.
        p.   cm. — (Series in Continental thought ; 21)
    ISBN 0-8214-1075-X
    1. Emotions (Philosophy)   2. Emotions and cognition.   3. Emotions
—Sociological aspects.   4. Rationalism   I. Title.   II. Series.
B815.T   1994
128'.3—dc20   93-42936
                                                            CIP

For Maya, Kaya and Damian,
and for my parents

CONTENTS

ACKNOWLEDGMENTS

CHAPTERS FIVE AND SIX have appeared in substantially the same form in *Philosophy Today,* and Chapter Four has been published in *The Journal for the Theory of Social Behaviour.* I am grateful to the editors of both journals for granting permission to draw upon this material. Much of the research for this work was done while I was a doctoral student, generously supported by the Social Sciences and Humanities Research Council of Canada. I owe a more personal debt to David Carr for his encouragement and confidence in me, and to John McGraw for his unfailing friendship ever since he inspired me as an undergraduate to pursue studies in philosophy. Above all, I wish to thank my wife Maya: for her patience, faith, understanding, and courageous holding of the family fort together.

PREFACE

RECENTLY, WHILE BROWSING through some books at a university library, I came across a text on emotions and mental disorders. Opening to the introductory pages, I learned about a growing realization among researchers in psychology that in order to understand the underlying structure and dynamics of many psychopathologies, it is essential to understand the nature of emotions. I then checked the book's publication date to get an idea of the period to which this report applied. A truth that has so long been a property of common sense was only now dawning on some high-powered theorists of motivation and behavior; the book was merely a couple of years old.

Old ignorances and neglects sometimes die very slowly indeed. Of course, philosophers have nothing to crow about here either. As the history of philosophy amply demonstrates, emotions have not been a topic of high priority. The traditional highlighting of intellect, argument, and reason as the discipline's subject matter and the core of human nature has tended to displace interest in them. Certainly some writers considered emotions seriously, and some even exalted them as superior to reason, yet clearly the vast majority's position was negative or one of indifference. Consequently, despite increased interest over the last several decades, it remains true, I believe, that the state of systematic research on emotions is still in relative infancy—burdened by groping and tentative concept formation and by the lack of consensually agreed-upon parameters for investigating them.

There is, I believe, a lucid explanation for our current and historical confusions about emotions. Simply put, and as often noted, emotions do not fit neatly or univocally into our conception of ourselves and so easily generate ambivalences about them. Consider just a few philosophically important contexts within which their role can be specified, without, however, yielding any obvious conclusions about their nature or value. Think, for example, of being deeply hurt, missing someone, being driven by strong jealousy, being obsessed with something to the point of insanity. Add to this the apparently quite natural identification of emotions with the causes of major human shortcomings—such identification evidenced most poignantly by traditional religions' lists of sins (e.g., greed, envy). How easy it is to conclude that emotions are something we would be better off without. But then think of a human life without love, friendship, hope, or generosity. Most of us would surely recognize it as an impoverished life. From this angle, emotions appear critical for a stable, coherent, and mature selfhood, for being a good person. They sustain commitments that make this life worth living. And if we take to the ostensibly emotionless First Officer Spock of the starship *Enterprise,* that is because he expresses just enough such commitments. Indeed, we find depictions of purely rational, Frankenstein-like creatures so alien that they rightly inspire our horror.

Switching contexts, think of acquiring knowledge. What we know is in large measure a function of what we pay attention to and are interested in, and this in turn is surely a function of our emotions. Without them, we probably wouldn't know much. Often emotions will afford insight, provide advance knowledge, as when a passing thought— "I don't know what it is about him—he just gives me the creeps"— turns out to be amply justified; the guy was indeed a crook. Here in a sense one *knew* something, notwithstanding the fact that initially the object of attention had little detailed propositional content. On the other hand, this is not invariably so; our first hunches frequently lead to epistemic dead ends, perhaps better left unexpressed and in the privacy of our own thoughts. And we are all too familiar with the phenomenon of wishful belief, where what we are convinced is solid knowledge is largely a product of skewed inferences put in the service of our strongly wanting something to be so. Here our emotions were an enemy, not an ally.

Another context: the mind-body problem. Emotions obviously involve our bodies. In experiencing them, we typically feel an "organic density," for which reason it might be tempting to assimilate them theoretically to strictly somatic phenomena. But emotions also engage concepts and thinking and an infinite variety of presentations. They are *about* things and as such (i.e., as *intentional* in the technical [phenomenological] sense of the term) are as fit to be tenants of the mind as any of the entities, states, or processes that traditionally have rented there. And there is an additional difficulty here awaiting any theorist wanting to place emotions in some intrapersonal topography. Some emotions are highly "cerebral," or at least hardly bodily felt— for example, intellectual curiosity, nostalgia, perhaps aesthetic delight. Others, such as certain types of fear or anger, will register themselves quite strongly throughout the entire organism. So "where" are our emotions?

A related context, the last to be touched upon here: responsibility. Do we choose our emotions? Are we agents responsible for "having" them, or merely their passive victims? If we think, like Descartes, that we are responsible for our beliefs because the will has infinite power to assert, deny, qualify, or refrain from judgment, then perhaps we are responsible for our emotions to the extent that they are judgmentlike. Well, some are; others surely are not. Once again, the best that we can offer as an honest answer to our query is a noncommital "It all depends."

One could go on, but an obvious point has been made, and it is one that has strongly informed the content and the form of the work that follows. That point is that it is difficult to provide useful generalizations about emotions within any of the more important parameters we typically use when thinking about humans. Psychological activities do not come in neatly delineated groups, and it applies especially to emotions, I think, that they are not a "natural class" defined by some common property or exhaustively analyzable via a schema of species and difference. At the level of theory, what we think emotions are, what can be done with or about them, will be inextricably linked with the sort of phenomena we select as exemplary—the selection process being moreover significantly influenced by extratheoretical (i.e., practical, moral, political) concerns. A critical corollary (noted by Amelie Rorty) emerges here—that alternative theories of emotion will likely come complete with their own evidence, their own sustaining empirical "facts," so that when each is examined sympathetically, none will prove easily refutable. Whatever the exchanges among parties adhering to contending perspectives, they will hardly qualify as dialogue.

It is primarily for reasons relating to this situation that, while embracing an approach to emotions that can be generically characterized as "cognitive," I have refrained from open partisanship for a particular theory of emotions. I am convinced that focusing on emotions' semantic and conceptual aspects provides the best prospects for getting clear about them, and I have offered some general reasons for subscribing to this approach. In the main, however, I have been more concerned to examine what it takes in the interrelation of conceptual, historical, psychological, and sociological factors for sustaining a coherent picture about emotions in relation to some features vital for being human.

In the process of my research and reflections, I have come to appreciate greatly the fragility and contingency of our emotional makeups, including my own. I realize that some readers may find my conclusions needlessly programmatic and tentative. There is a sense, though, in which simple honesty demands just that. There may indeed be at the theoretical level a large wedge between my ideas about emotions and some other views. But notwithstanding any obvious and even large differences, I remain keenly aware that what separates some of the formative factors that have led to my position, as well as the manner of its research and presentation, from the formative factors of other perspectives, has been in many instances, I am sure, nothing but a sliver.

Human agency is such that its theories about itself contribute to the experiences these theories describe. Somewhere, somehow, we think there must be some constraints on the proliferation of our self-interpretations. In relation to emotions, and mindful that any premature closure will surely exact a price, we will need many more interpretations before any such constraints become consensually self-evident. This makes research into emotions often frustrating and difficult, and yet—precisely for the glimpse it offers on the myriad possibilities of being human—deeply rewarding.

PREFATORY NOTE

THE RECENT REEMERGENCE of theories that emphasize the semantic and conceptual aspects of emotions has also revealed questions about their rationality. There are essentially two standard senses in which emotions can be assessed for their rationality. First, emotions can be said to be categorially rational (i.e., not intrinsically arational) insofar as they presuppose our psychological capacities to be clearly conscious of distinctions, to engage and manipulate concepts, and hence to provide intentional (in the technical sense) descriptions as *reasons* for what we feel and are moved to do. For this "cognitive" rationality, we can apply the usual standards intrinsic to the processes of belief formation such as coherence, consistency, inferential validity, and appropriateness of evidence. Secondly, and derivatively of rationality as a teleological or strategic notion, emotions can be thought of as rational or irrational depending upon their function (i.e., their success or lack of it) in fulfilling certain specified human purposes.

While neither adhering to nor dismissing what these two mainstream perspectives afford, the following essay is an alternative, yet complementary project. It attempts to gain insights into emotions by programmatically examining their relation to a number of features fundamental to being human: intentionality, expression and language, sense of self, responsibility, self-deception, and value cognition and moral agency. The goal is less to fit emotions within some formulaic description of rationality and more to allow the latter's potential definition to be informed by these broadly based investigations. This reflects an underlying conviction that rationality is not a unitary property of our minds but a complex stance toward the world. It also exhibits an awareness that, as evidenced by current debates, rationality is very much a contested notion.

1

INTRODUCTION:
PAYING ATTENTION TO EMOTIONS

Philosophical discussions serious about emotions—anger, love, fear, jealousy, and so on—customarily begin by noting the indifference and contempt with which the Western intellectual tradition has on the whole treated them. Such complaints point to the deeply rooted rationalism of the tradition as the principal cause of the denigration of emotions. Accordingly, we are reminded that whenever emotions are spoken of in connection with acquiring knowledge and rationality in general, it is almost invariably to highlight the ways they perturb cognition and muddle the truth. Far from something that gives or helps to generate significance and coherence in our lives, emotions are viewed as dreaded disintegratintg factors over which we have but scant control. The contemporary signification of *pathology* (from the Greek *pathos,* "feeling") as something aberrant, abnormal, or suffered crystalizes well the judgments underlying this attitude. Or consider the intimate link between the emotion of anger and (demonic) insanity as conveyed in the expression "I am mad (as hell)."

But of course it is not the traditional preoccupation with knowing per se that is the principal villain but the defining of emotions vis-à-vis a certain construal of rationality and knowledge acquisition that sees them as far less personal than they actually are. In this restricted understanding, we tend to forget that even the most abstract forms of knowledge require curiosity and passion to know as well as a commitment to truth without which knowledge would simply cease to advance. And we pay little attention to the fact that the great intellectual movements that canonized this mind-set—the scientific revolution most notable among them—could not have been sustained without an informing set of powerful, essentially emotional understandings about the nature of human agency.

Certain qualifications notwithstanding, it is not unreasonable to point to Plato as having in large measure initiated this state of affairs. Though he expressed (in the *Phedrus* and in *Timaeus*) a sense in which the emotions can be the ally of reason, the doctrines that subsequently have had the greatest impact on thinking about emotions pertain to his localizing them in the body, which in turn he generally distrusted or even disdained. On Plato's account, the emotions are what is bestial and animal-like in us, to be ruled and controlled by the rational soul, which comprises the intellectual function and is located in the head.

The extent to which so many of us find this view natural and uncontroversial only confirms the power and longevity of the Platonic paradigm in our tradition. But it is important to note at once how little Plato's partition of the person and his localizing of psychological functions in specific parts of the human organism had to do with relevant empirical knowledge of human physiology and how on the other hand it was informed by a symbolism that had its roots in a wider cosmological framework. As James Averill (1974) tells us, Plato considered thought as a form of self-motion and as such also circular, the latter property being definitive of self-sustenance. Hence it was logical to place it within a spherical structure such as the head. Additionally, and in support, the head also imitated the spherical shape of the universe (itself besouled with rationality), being moreover placed closest to the form-populated heavens. That the passions—the name traditionally used in reference to emotions until roughly the middle of eighteenth century—as something one does not initiate but undergoes were then assigned to the body followed naturally but also necessarily. The emotions had to be placed somewhere other than where the rational (self-moving) soul was to minimize the possibility of the latter's becoming polluted by them.

While commonly accepted, these opinions were not universally endorsed. Not surprisingly for Aristotle, for example, his talent for sticking a little closer to experiential ground led him to somewhat different conclusions. Though he was well aware of the potential noxiousness of emotions and also followed Plato in dividing the human soul into a rational and an irrational part, Aristotle nevertheless argued against any sharp division between the two. What emerge from the relevant sections of his works on psychology, ethics, and the art of persuasion are quite subtle and sophisticated views that consider emotions as much more than simple noncognitive and context-free phenomena that can be subsumed under the general category of bodily perturbations. While not denying the presence of affective impulses—emotions remained always for him "enmattered"—Aristotle insisted on the centrality of factual beliefs and moral judgments in the causation and individuation of emotions, and so on the latter as clearly a manifestation of the human mind. (A further important corollary here is that emotions are not necessarily irrational or uncontrolled responses to situations. The beliefs and judgments implicated in emotions can be evaluated and justified—there is a point to or warrant for them—and this is what ultimately lies behind the familiar dictum about the capacity [of a virtuous person] for feeling the right thing, at the right time, toward a proper object and in the right proportion.)

Now, this psychology of emotions coexists in a nice ecological balance with other views of the Aristotelian corpus. In particular, it certainly does not conflict with anything Aristotle might have said about science, knowledge, or thinking; quite the opposite. First, there is the involvement of subjectivity with the objects of experience as expressed in the general "participational" model of knowledge—wherein, that is, in being informed by the same *eidos,* the mind takes part in the being of the known object. More specifically, though, and crucially, when discussing particular sciences and types of knowledge, Aristotle insists that we cannot give a "state-description" of the knower independently of considering the realm to which the objects to be known belong. Conversely, knowledge of particular domains of reality requires as its condition specific moral qualities and/or practical skills consistent with the (formal) aims of that knowledge. But whatever the level at which we exercise our intelligence, knowledge is inseparable from our powers of doing and making.

Nevertheless, for all the evenhandedness of Aristotle's philosophy, it is paradoxically also within his thought that we can locate a significant contribution to the ensuing neglect of emotions. Beyond the association of intellect with activity and emotion with passivity that he shared with Plato (and others), I have in mind the privilege accorded to *theory* as the highest form of human understanding. The critical point is that this was at once a privileging of an understanding that aims at a *disengaged* perspective (i.e., one that abstracts from our immediate wishes, desires, opinions, etc.). For once this sense of theoretical understanding is taken up by modern philosophy and considered as criterial for *all* knowledge, but now also shorn of its embedding context of qualitative ontological and psychological distinctions, the road is paved for a systematic exclusion of emotions as phenomena worthy of serious consideration in their own right. Epistemology becomes instituted as the queen discipline based on a cerebral method defined by subjectivity's conscientious reduction of itself as a concrete living and feeling being. As in Plato, the latter aspects of existence are relegated in a dualistic scheme to the less significant, even if not unequivocally dysfunctional, realm of the bodily.

Now, one assumes that the reflexive generation of absolute clarity and certitude is a *willful* and *motivated* effort requiring at least some degree of discipline and concentration. But of course the explicit formulations of epistemological methodology do not thematize these aspects of our cognitive functioning, thus ensuring that within the context of that (officially) most important of philosophical pursuits— the clarification of knowledge—emotions simply have no place. The new standards homogenize all knowledge, flattening out its previously qualitatively diverse forms wherein the role of emotions might have been explicitly acknowledged. To be sure, emotions do not disappear from philosophical scrutiny; indeed some of the more extensive treatments of the passions have been authored by the staunchest of rationalists. But these views, even when separately stated in thematically independent works, are always understood as secondary appendages and far less important than the "principal" writings on epistemology or ontology. Meanwhile, the power of epistemology as construed by the moderns becomes extremely difficult to undermine because in defining itself so thoroughly by the disengaged perspective, that epistemological project manages effectively and systematically to hide its own motivating interests. The logical truth that however neutrally articulated that construal is, we could not have given our assent to it unless we were moved in some way—unless, that is, we recognized through certain feelings the norms and values it embodies—all this gets neatly removed from our vision.

From the perspective of a historical concern in philosophy with knowledge, the above account suggests, of course in rather broad strokes, why emotions have fallen into neglect and even disrepute. Perhaps this fate, given the theoretical bent of our tradition and culture, was highly predictable or even inevitable in strictly epistemological contexts. But should emotions have fared better at the hands of moral philosophers? We are intuitively tempted to answer in the affirmative, principally on the basis of our ordinary commonsensical understanding that values are typically brought to evidence in emotion. Such an assessment, however, turns out to be false.

If Descartes is for us the obvious chief protagonist in the denigration of emotions vis-à-vis knowledge, in the context of ethics that role belongs to Kant. For it is Kant who, with the exception of respect, banishes all emotions from the moral domain on the grounds that they belong essentially to the realm of sensibility and inclination. The net result of his diremption of sensibility and pure reason—it is the latter's practical version that grounds morality—is that it treats persons in abstraction from character, effectively divorcing ethical thinking from any realistic moral *psychology* and preventing us even from seeing that the two ought to be linked.

It is thus most unfortunate that it is Kant who even to this day has turned out single-handedly to set the tone of mainstream moral theorizing. I mean the tremendous proclivity for formulating general rules and laws and the belief that morality consists principally of such, and further the conviction that even if not just reason but inclination can be the source of moral precepts, it is reason's providing the latter with appropriate form and tests that will certify them as such (see Baier 1985, chap. 12). In this context, as Annette Baier remarks, it is interesting to note the absence of a normative theory (i.e., a system of moral principles in which the less general are derived from the more general) in both Aristotle and Hume, two thinkers who took emotions seriously and developed some of the most subtle views about them. It surely is not that neither had a vision of proper human ends; quite the contrary. It is that both believed that getting there is not due to following abstract principles but more a matter of emotional cultivation as well as having adequate knowledge about our psychology on one hand and the empirical world in which we will attempt to enact whatever it is we are enjoined to enact on the other.

Yet Kant also holds an ambiguous status. If his contribution to the dismissal of emotions is both considerable and undeniable, he must also be credited with initiating the road to their potential rehabilitation. Admittedly, the formal categories of the mind placed at the center of our understanding the objective world are far from those of a fully vitalized subject. But the Kantian Copernican revolution constitutes the first, and hence perhaps the most important step toward the recovery of ourselves as concrete feeling beings. Once Kant establishes (through the original transcendental argumentation) the principle of binding and objective validity of certain insights that we can gain from the vantage point of being *inside* the processes that generate our experience, it becomes simply a matter of time before richer descriptions of human agency emerge in response to enlarged conceptions of the objective realms in which we are active. This process of the concretization of the knowing subject begins already with Hegel, but Marx and Nietzsche are perhaps its best-known nineteenth-century protagonists.

Among the various representatives of neo-Marxism, psychoanalysis, phenomenology, and existentialism who continue and extend this development into contemporary thought, and in the more specific context of concern with emotions, two names in particular deserve to be mentioned. It belongs to both Max Scheler and Martin Heidegger to have decisively relocated the locus of emphasis in epistemological questioning by setting in contemporary context a classical Greek notion, namely, that to know the world, we have to be in tune with it and hence have some sort of concrete emotional links to it. For each thinker, then, epistemology no longer starts with the problem of *certitude* of a particular knowing but begins much earlier, by addressing the issue of our *openness* for something, the conditions that make it possible that something is there at all for us.

Thus Scheler argues for a priority of acts of interest (particularly love) over against knowledge and takes this as valid in a transcendental (i.e., Kantian) sense for all objects of cognition. Here the sense of cognition is extended in line with his anthropological position that we are first and foremost loving beings before we are subjects of knowledge or volition. Just as perception of ordinary events may be said to be cognitive in a prelogical sense, so such acts as empathy and sympathy, by virtue of their intentionality and their function of providing contents, may be so described (1970).

For his part, Heidegger (1962), in a more thoroughgoing transcendental move, inquires back beyond intentionality. Not so much interested in affectivity as it contributes to revealing the mode of being of particular object domains, he locates in moods the power of opening the "world" as that wherein everything is encountered. In a conscious effort to distance himself from Descartes and much of philosophical tradition, Heidegger renounces certitude, clarity, and distinctness, as well as the ability for critical doubt, as properties criterial for knowing. Cognition need not be identified with the more restricted understanding of rationality as a process of weighing evidence by appeals to general principles and standards of inference. The new norm is the broadest possible disclosure of self and world (Blankenburg 1972).

Whatever the differences in the scope of their investigations, Scheler and Heidegger can both be seen as expressing a powerful truth: that we ignore the emotional aspects of existence at the peril of restricting the domains within which we are cognitively and existentially active. Nevertheless, it is clear that this warning has had marginal impact regarding mainstream philosophy's concern with emotions; to put it gently, the latter's rehabilitation is at best in infancy. Of course, the topic is not dormant, and there has been, relative to the past, increased interest in it. (For one, the existentialist appropriation of the obvious intentionality, or aboutness, of emotions has highlighted the transcendence of subjectivity into a worldly anchor and thus promoted thinking about emotions as something more than brute and ineffable subjective states. And some credit must also be given to psychoanalysis; though in theory it steadfastly clings to the orthodox view of emotion as an enemy of reason, it assumes in practice an essential connection between the two because without this assumption its notion of a "talking cure" would be wholly unintelligible.) Still, as Morwenna Griffiths (1988) points out, journal literature on emotions is scant, and books on emotion are not widely read by philosophers or their students, who are rarely assigned readings on emotion, even in those thinkers who have had a great deal to say about the passions. It is the *other* works of Aristotle, Descartes, or Hume—to take the most obvious examples—that receive almost exclusive attention.

Thus I believe that the customary complaint referred to at the outset deserves to be reiterated even more forcefully, especially in light of the distressing dryness and lack of explicit concern for emotions by most participants in the various contemporary "rationality debates." It is particularly disappointing to find this characteristic in the writings of the likes of Habermas, Gadamer, Arendt, philosophers who make much of disavowing the modern epistemological construal and aim precisely to overcome the resultant empty (procedural) conception of rationality as merely a calculation of means toward reason-transcendent goals—that is, as "instrumental reason." In this context, Agnes Heller's (1982) objection (to the effect that in the identification of the structure of personality with cognition, language, and interaction, the Habermasian man ends up with no body, no needs, and no feelings) seems entirely justified. To be sure, in the shift of focus from Cartesian to dialogical subjectivity, the by now notorious linguistic turn adopted by all has accomplished much to concretize the self. Further efforts are needed, however, to vitalize it; the persistent if muted cries from the bureaucratized wilderness to get in touch with our feelings cannot be altogether dismissed as mere expressions of narcissism. On the contrary, they are often legitimate expressions of concern for the identity of the self we in the West have forged for ourselves, a self whose sense involves both a pull toward privacy and an emphasis on the fulfillment of feelings, drives, and aspirations each of us allegedly finds (and is enjoined to cultivate) in oneself. (No doubt, at the terminus of the logic of such an identity, we get incoherent about ourselves and the usual proposed remedy to find ourselves by moving away, and disowning our embedding community turns out to be precisely the disease for which it purports to be the cure. But this should not detract from the fact that however distorting, contingent, and historically specific, that is still *our* identity, one we are not in a position to refashion or discard at will.)

Be that as it may, the implicit message of Habermas and others appears to be that yes, we need to enlarge our conception of reason, but there are limits. One senses that even if we are less ignorant about the emotions today, a lingering suspicion of them prevents us from engaging them seriously. Now, this resistance, I suggest, is both un-warranted and perhaps even detrimental to the very goals someone like Habermas espouses for his inquiry. A persistent theme of his has been to expose the various forms of ideology insofar as these play a role in our capacities to articulate generalizable interests. But in this context I can hardly think of a more suitable target than the entire set of notions that predominantly inform our understanding of the emo-tional sphere. Surely if anything has had a directly detrimental effect on our capacity to articulate generalizable interests, it is the idea that what we as a culture have made synonymous with the fulfillment of the good life—the latter claim being underscored by the burgeoning psychotherapeutic industry—is beyond any rational and objective (i.e., intersubjective) assessment because it purportedly occurs without any mediation by the larger groups to which we belong and the pat-terns of meaning they embody.

The recalcitrance to engage emotions seriously is all the more puzzling because a common strategy of many of those attempting to rescue reason from irrelevance vis-à-vis our moral and engaged life is to appeal to the Aristotelian notion of *phronesis,* or practical judg-ment. The latter is seen as a paradigm of a rationality capable of as-sessing particular ends, a rationality that therefore involves more than a discriminate application of general rules in pursuit of reason-transcen-dent goals. Now, admittedly *phronesis,* insofar as it is acquired through teaching or systematic instruction (as opposed to habitual exercise), is in Aristotle's scheme an intellectual virtue. But any rigid distinction between the latter and the virtues of character that are essentially emotional and dispositional in nature breaks down because the right dispositions are as much required for the proper development of practical intelligence as is the latter for the transformation of naturally given dispositions into authentic ones (i.e., virtues of character) (Mac-Intyre 1984, ch. 12). Moreover, virtues are dispositions not only to act in particular ways but also to feel in particular ways, so that *phronesis* ends up for Aristotle intimately linked to the experience of the right emotion, toward the right object, on the right occasion, and in the right proportion. Conversely, emotions in this view become more or less intelligent ways of being in the world over which we can exercise a measure of guidance and control. They are also (at least in part) socially constituted or mediated because *phronesis* essentially demands a public space for its cultivation.

Why this link in Aristotle between emotions, intelligence, and sociality has been historically neglected and remains so to this day without generating a more serious consideration of affectivity is a matter of both traditional prejudices and more specific factors. For the more recent period, the setting of emotions by mainstream psychology within the evolutionary context of biological adaptation—a move inspired by Darwin's (1896) seminal work on emotional expression—has without doubt played a most significant role. This has confirmed, as it were, all those views that reduced emotions to the biological level. Without going into further details, what I think is important is to recognize in Aristotle a view I believe eminently worthwhile, if not necessary, to resuscitate—that there is a meaningful sense in which we can talk about something like a "rationality of emotions." A caveat is in order, though: across all disciplines that may presently invoke rationality and/or emotion to account for our actions and behavior, it would be difficult to find a pair of categories for which there exists less consensus about what they actually comprise.

For those who take emotions to involve beliefs (an increasing group to which Aristotle clearly belongs, as his treating of certain emotions in the *Rhetoric* shows), there is initially a fairly straightforward and unproblematic, if minimal, sense in which emotions can be said to be categorially rational (i.e., not *non*rational). This is defined by the emotions' presupposition of our psychological capacities to be clearly conscious of distinctions, to engage and manipulate concepts, and hence to provide *reasons* (i.e., intentional descriptions) for what we do or feel (Calhoun and Solomon 1984, 31). Here we can apply the usual standards intrinsic to the processes of concept formation and articulation—namely, coherence, consistency, and inferential validity—but must also add, to escape the charge of being vacuous, evaluative criteria that deal with completeness of evidence on whose basis we hold particular beliefs. Armed with this apparatus, we can thus go on to charge with (degrees of) irrationality those emotions at odds with our (avowed) beliefs, those whose beliefs are inconsistent with other beliefs, those whose beliefs were acquired in a manner generally not conducive to obtaining true beliefs, or any combination of these, so that the bottom line is that the reasons offered for feeling a certain way are simply found inadequate.

Now, this is a useful but limited approach. For often we are at pains to come up with the adequate grounding reasons for an emotion and yet are reluctant to qualify it straightforwardly as irrational.

We feel it contains a measure of insight, and therefore should not be dismissed too quickly. (This may be because of a dogmatic decision that however inarticulated or unfounded, the emotion will always be, so to speak, its own arbiter—a kind of headless romanticism, one might say. But equally well, it may be because such insights have turned out in the past to be true, so we heed our experience.) Yet another possibility may be that an apparently groundless emotion is just too strongly felt or endures for too long, thus convincing us that it must make sense within some larger yet unrecognizable pattern, that there is indeed greater systematicity and coherence to our emotional lives than we are accustomed to think. Then too, there is the danger that in our rush to propositionalize every emotion that comes our way (for the purposes of this sort of analysis anyway), we will miss their *experiential* content; the judgment arrived at about the quantum of reason a particular emotion possesses will be vacuous, will tell us little about the *life* in which that emotion occurs. Nor will the judgment speak to any socially grounded notion of appropriateness of experiencing it.

Thus we might consider a broader, explicitly teleological conception of rationality wherein emotions can be thought of as rational or irrational depending upon their function (i.e., their success or lack of it) in fulfilling certain human ends or purposes. Now, this second sense of rationality of emotions can also be found adumbrated in Aristotle. For us, however, it turns out to be quite problematic.

The Aristotelian individual is a being with a telos defined by the exercise of those virtues necessary for the conduct of the good life, the highest form of which is the contemplation of things divine. We could then say that the emotions that promote these virtues—being the latter's necessary (though not sufficient) conditions—are functionally rational while those that frustrate them are clearly not. Now, the individual becomes intelligible on account of his role and status as a member of a particular community, the polis. Indeed the city-state is what humanizes agents, for to be human and a *zoon politikon* are identical. The virtues and their corresponding grounding emotions thus find their home not just in the life of individuals but in the affairs of the city because the latter is the unique social form in which alone they can be fully cultivated and made articulate (Gastaldi, 1987). We can see, then, that the emotions, through their direct links to virtues, can be assessed not only for their logic but also that they are in an important sense socially constituted, public, and open to appraisal rather than some private and internal mental or bodily states, a qualification that the ancients would likely find in any case unintelligible. Moreover, such opennenss to appraisal implies both that the individual can be held (to a lesser or greater extent) responsible for his emotions and that these are in principle educable.

In contrast to the partiality of so many theories of emotions, ordinary language usage reveals a dimension of passivity with which we may experience our emotions and a more existentialist attitude in which they can be qualifyingly said to be a matter of choice. To be "overcome" by anger, love, or jealously does not strike a dissonant note, and at the extreme, such experiences are socially acknowledged through legal doctrines that absolve one from guilt for an act by reason of being so overcome. On the other hand, we standardly condemn or praise individuals—and thus impute responsibility—in respect of their having a certain emotion, its intensity, or both, as in "He should not have been (*so*) angry." We have a sense here—often quite strong and articulate however "private" and culturally discounted as perhaps a mere preference—about the appropriateness or inappropriateness of a given emotion for the particular context, or its value or disvalue in relation to a certain normative conception of personality.

For Aristotle, such an evaluative stance vis-à-vis our emotions is of course eminently rational, the "logic" of emotions being assessed in relation to ever wider but coherent metaphysical horizons. Moreover, it is entirely unproblematic because Aristotle assumes a sense of what in anthropological terms can be called common culture, a system of shared meanings, beliefs, and practices that orient the lives of individuals. The continual use of the first-person plural in his moral arguments acknowledges that he is expressing not merely an individual opinion but is rather articulating what is implicit in the thought, speech, and action of a community of which he is but one member and accidental spokesman (MacIntyre, 147–48).

But can this be sustained in light of our radically different conceptions of subjectivity and the realities of cultural pluralism? For in the modern period we define ourselves no longer in relation to a cosmic order but as subjects who possess an internal view of the world along with innate drives and purposes. What were once quasi-public phenomena have been relegated to the private—hence viewed as inaccessible—realm of endogenous motivation. Left without the metaphysical scaffolding that made this formerly entirely natural, is it possible for us once again to bring our emotions into the ambit of explicit assessment and objective understanding?

Certainly no intelligent answer to this question can even be attempted in abstraction from specifying just what sort of phenomena emotions are. And here we encounter significant difficulties that are camouflaged and glossed over because of the homogenizing quality of the concept of the emotion as well as various emotion concepts themselves. Once we move beyond language and vocabulary, the diversity of conditions and states historically taken as emotions argues strongly against their being grouped into some "natural" class and easily distinguishable from such other traditional tenants of the psyche as motives, attitudes, cognitions, desires. Even within a single emotion-type, the difference in etiology and function of states that belong to that type (e.g., rage and indignation as species of anger) may put in question whether the latter should be grouped together in just that fashion. And there is little relief in sight because the traditional classificatory distinctions (e.g., active-passive, voluntary-involuntary, psychological-behavioral) are themselves among the hottest potatoes of philosophical psychology. Summarizing this situation, Amelie Rorty (1980, 23) is led to a rather daunting conclusion: presently a proper account of emotions requires nothing short of a revision of the entire map of psychological processes, activities, and their complex interrelations.

But Rorty herself believes it is too early for such an enterprise, requiring as it does inter- and intradisciplinary consensus on terminology and identification of relevant issues—a consensus the present absence of which ought to inform our efforts as consciously provisional, a "heuristics without ontology" (120). But to speak in this idiom is to suggest at once that the task of defining "emotion" is just as much, perhaps more, a matter of self-conscious or explicit interpretation as of combining the relevant empirical research. I say explicit because interpretation has entered "postempiricist" science in a big way, having been acknowledged as an integral part of all empirical research, so that this qualification may seem redundant. But the explicit is meant here in a strong sense to capture what I take to be the outstanding differentiating characteristic of the human species. The thesis resonates principally in contemporary hermeneutics: we are beings whose agency is modified through varying conceptions of ourselves and our agency.

There is, then, a legitimate sense in which emotions (if one agrees that they are at least in part constitutive of human agency) are of our own making. What we make of them bears on the structure of our experiencing them and determines the range of stances we adopt toward them. To make use of a familiar fable, we are not after piecing together all the different perspectives on the elephant, which is allegedly there and awaiting discovery but which each of us sees only imperfectly. The adoption of a hermeneutical stance precludes assigning to emotions such an entitative status. It is *we* who have the task of creating the elephant as well as remembering ourselves as those who have done so.

Suppose, however, that agreement is reached on just what emotions "fundamentally" are—for example, bodily states the causality of which is explicable in experience-independent, physicalist terms (perhaps this is the level at which objectivity could most easily be achieved); contrary to expectations, interpretation would still be indispensible. For we would be under an obligation to show the significance of this finding within a broader framework, that is, circumscribe the emotions' function in relation to ascending levels of the human organism that in the end terminate in the question, "What is the telos of mind?" Even if emotions are biological phenomena, what exactly does that reductive account explain? We can see a parallel here, for example, with genetic psychology's attempt to link intelligence and biological functioning wherein the latter is said in some loose sense to determine the former. But the enterprise depends not just on identifying certain biological structures and properties but on correlating those with others that pertain to full development, or what might be called successful human maturity. And here interpretation enters inescapably. Are the formal intellectual operations Piaget (1971) identifies really those that constitute maturity? Are they universal or, as has often been argued recently, reflecting only ethnocentric prejudices rooted in the values of a white, middle-class, theoretically oriented milieu? None of this is either given or obvious but has to be interpretively negotiated. Interpretation is thus not optional; it cannot be dispensed with.

That said, I too shall be concerned with a certain interpretation of emotions. What follows is a brief statement of it, along with an explication of the principal commitments that underlie it. This will also shed some light on exactly what it is that I intend by a "rationality" of emotions.

I consider emotions to be modalities of mind or personal postures that *thematize* the sense of our *engagement* with(in) the world, where that sense typically (though not always, given the phenomenon of ambivalence) reveals itself as a style of partiality—for or against, broadly construed—vis-à-vis the objects we are involved with. A number of features are implicit in this somewhat broad definition.

First, the metaphoric notion of posture is an attempt to circumvent the different forms of dualism that frequent thinking about emotions—most obviously, that of mind versus body and action versus passion. For a posture, like most ordinary emotional experiences, is what precisely straddles the line between the two realms. It is, to use Merleau-Ponty's (1962, 188) apt description of emotion, neither bodily nor intelligent but rather wholly bodily *and* wholly intelligent. We recognize a given physical configuration as a posture by virtue of the *intent* it embodies, its quality of aiming at some privileged (expressive) outcome and so of being an incipient *action;* no intent or body, no posture. This duality also means that postures are nicely ambiguous with respect to the active-passive distinction. Some are consciously adopted; others, spontaneous but still carrying intent, as when we talk of having a "relaxed posture."

Second, postures are—as I want to insist emotions are—always contextualized. It is because I see the sun and the shadows that I grasp the raised hand as a stance of shading one's eyes as opposed to one of fending off a blow. A third parallel can be drawn because posture is something predicated of the whole person; so with emotion as a vital experiencing which is not tangential but is capable of permeating the depth and breadth of (embodied) existence. And so, relatedly, emotions are postures that pertain to engagement; they are concrete ways of being in the world, each emotion being a different mode of *having* a world.

But the central term in the above definition is *thematize.* While incorporating some of the connotations associated with *posture,* it extends *emotion* in ways the most important of which can be stated as follows: intrinsic to emotions is a certain reflectivity whose explication shows that whatever else emotions are and however spontaneously we customarily experience them, they are essentially grounded in *reasons* that express the terms of our engagement with the world. I have in mind here the type of awareness that parallels what Herder (1966) described in his analysis of the semantic function of language. (The comparison is especially apt, I think, in view of how *un*reflective and spontaneous an activity the use of language normally is.) For example, it is only because I implicitly grasp a certain object under its aspect of shape (and not, say, color) that I can immediately identify it *as* a geometrical figure and apply to it the appropriate vocable—for example, circle or square—shape being the relevant property dimension underlying the concept of geometrical figures and allowing for recognizing, in a strong sense, such figures. Emotions, I claim, are like that. It is only because I grasp a certain situation under the aspects that constitute it as an offense to me—its property dimensions so to speak—that I take my indignation to be the natural and appropriate response to it. An alternative way of stating the claim is that certain *descriptions,* in the sense of understandings, are both required for, and constitutive of, the experience of emotions.

In the sense outlined above, thematization is obviously intrinsically symbolic, conceptual, and related to language. Less obviously, but critically, the linkage to explicable reasons suggests that the explanation of emotions must be couched in the vocabulary of intentions, values, beliefs, interpretations. But another, perhaps still less obvious implication of this thesis is that emotions can be plausibly, if not best, construed as cultural acquisitions determined primarily by the concepts and the circumstances of a particular culture. Biology is secondary.

To say the least, such views sound counterintuitive. So strongly are we individually and collectively attached to thinking of emotions as intruders from an inherited biological past that we will often discount experiences that put this in doubt. Even in those highly integrative and integrated states where "feeling" and "thinking" are indistinguishable—when, that is, emotion is experientially and concretely an affective *cognition*—we are bound to suspect that no matter what its conceptual and cultural components are, it is at bottom still nothing more than just a (bodily) feeling. But does one not at least on occasion experience feelings—for example, about justice or fairness—that as much as any mathematical proof are conceptually sophisticated and grounded in reasons, reasons that can moreover compel commitment to those values as unambiguously as one is compelled to accept the conclusion of a valid syllogism?

Of course, many emotions can be quite strongly felt; indeed we typically take those as paradigmatic (anger, fear, and sexual arousal being the leading candidates of traditional emotion research). They can preoccupy us as well as disrupt or skew against our will the more deliberative and ideational processes associated with the intellect and at the extreme even interfere with normal physiological functioning. Just this is what gives apparent plausibility to the emotion-as-atavistic-bodily-response view, seducing us to plump for reductive biological explanations and to hold them up as the total picture. What more, then, other than a phenomenology of such integrative states as I have just referred to above, can be offered to the skeptic who refuses to reassess that mainstream view?

First, putting biological factors in the background is by no means intended to dismiss them as unimportant. (Any basic textbook in endocrinology should quickly cure anyone of such a dismissal.) It is, rather, consciously employed to mark off the *relative* autonomy of emotions, in the specialized sense as defined through the notion of thematization, vis-à-vis the biological level. This requires some support that can be provided by distinguishing two dimensions of affectivity that are especially prone to sowing confusion because they can be the source of very strongly felt experiences but are nevertheless apart from the sense of emotion defended here.

With the category *drives* I wish to designate all those biologically determined tendencies the fulfillment of which is indispensable for individual and species preservation. Some obvious candidates are the need for food and water, elimination, periodic rest, for attachment and contact (without the latter, infants almost invariably fall into ill health and even die), and sex. Drives become differentiated from one another very early in infant development, and although some evidently require a higher level of maturation and manifest themselves later than others (e.g., the sexual drive), they are all innate. All share the characteristic of not being a response to extrinsic factors but originating spontaneously in the organism. Their intensity is not diminished by habit, nor are they interchangeable, in the sense that a satisfaction of one drive could replace the satisfaction of another. With the exception to the sex drive, none can be successfully repressed over a long term without engendering serious pathology.[1]

Of course, the innate character of drives entails no denial of the culturally distinctive ways of organizing for their satisfaction. What and how one eats, where one eliminates, with whom one is sexually involved, are all regulated by as diverse norms as there are different cultures. Indeed we rarely see drives in their nonsocialized expressions except in the most extreme deprivating circumstances where the cultural component pertaining to the manner of their satisfactions drops completely out of the picture. Hence to speak of "pure" drives is an abstraction. But this fact, on the other hand, should not lead to a conclusion that drives are culture-relative. As a result of environmental factors, there may have developed in certain cultures a greater emphasis on one drive than another, as reflected perhaps in a more elaborate social organization intended to satisfy it. But only food (i.e., a substance with specific nutritive values) will satisfy our hunger, and this is not open to interpretation.

The second range of affective experiences we should distinguish are what may be called *standard affective reactions*. I have in mind here such expressive phenomena as rage, startlement, fright, disgust, crying, smiling, and laughing, all of which are relational in the sense of being tied to an extrinsic stimulus; their origin is not intraorganismic. Now, I have typified them as standard because, like drives, they appear to extend across all cultures. This claim to universality is strengthened by the plausibility of an evolution-grounded explanation for (at least some of) these phenomena wherein they are considered "remnants" of instinctual acts aiming at survival. Thus, to take rage as an example, Darwin (1896) argued that such features of it as bared teeth, urge to strike, and trembling were the lasting symptoms of the seizure of prey intended to be destroyed. Disgust can also be reasonably linked to the instinctual action of vomiting, the expectoration "appearing" in the features of an affective reaction without its actual occurrence (Heller 1979, 71). And little elaboration is needed for the various expressions of fright—the "fight or flight" response, as Walter Cannon (1929) called it—as maneuvers clearly aiming to preserve bodily integrity.

Once again it is necessary to insist on the abstract nature of these distinctions. The reactions described do not normally occur in any pure form but are infused with extrabiological factors that constantly modulate them. But taking such influences into account as well as differences in individuals' sensitivity thresholds, the possibility of describing some of the eliciting conditions in observer-independent or extensionalist terms—or what amounts to the same, the existence of some objects or conditions that universally evoke the response—legitimates the explanation of these phenomena in physiologico-biological terms. The examples that back this up are fairly obvious. We know that anything that sensorily overwhelms or disorients us (e.g., a sudden loud noise, darkness) will frighten us. Rage is a response to attack or severe bodily constraint. For disgust, excrement seems to evoke that reaction universally.

In a sense, both drives (insofar as they incite to action) and standard affective responses are our most basic or primitive stances in the world. And clearly emotions can incorporate them. Romantic love, whose component of attachment is frequently matched, especially in men, by equally powerful sexual urges, is an excellent case in point. We can find another confirmation of this idea in the inability to love those who were severely deprived of strong human attachments in childhood. But the claim is that even though emotions are built on drives and affective reactions—in this regard, certain of Freud's typifications of adult (especially pathological) emotional life in relation to different bodily functions are particularly brilliant—in no instance can they be reduced to them. At most, biology only contributes elements to and sets limits upon the symbolic-conceptual constitution of emotions. Stated differently, I am insisting that whatever their value, it is not to be assessed in terms of any direct common measure with the more obvious ends of drives and standard affective reactions. Taking seriously the notion of thematization as the hallmark of emotions precludes any such assimilation. In contrast to these affective phenomena, emotions are essentially *interpretive* stances.

From here, the notion that emotions are best construed as cultural acquisitions could be argued in a more or less "transcendental" fashion, that is, by showing that as modalities of mind involving concepts, they presuppose symbolism and language use, hence culture. But the thesis can be given a more standardly empirical support that extends beyond that created by focusing on certain salient features in our experience. What exactly is pursued here?

Reviewing a number of rival accounts pertaining to the growth of culture and the evolution of mind, Clifford Geertz (1973, chap. 2) questions particularly the adequacy of what he calls the "critical point theory." According to the latter, our capacity to acquire and develop culture was a matter of a sudden all-or-nothing type of occurrence in the phylogeny of the primates. This view is in turn embedded in a more extensive belief—that the growth of culture in itself has been inconsequential for mental evolution.

By reconsidering the time scale employed to discriminate the stages of evolutionary development and using some widely accepted data of physical anthropology on australopithecine hominids, Geertz seriously undermines the view he is questioning. He argues convincingly that rudimentary culture in the form of simple toolmaking and a system of communication more complex than that of apes but less advanced than true speech can be predicated of our ancestors at a time when their brain size was roughly one-third ours. From this follows a most important conclusion: the greater part of human cortical expansion has followed and not preceded the "beginning" of culture, and therefore there are no a priori reasons not to suspect that cultural accumulation interacted with and played an active role in the shaping of the final stages of our biological development (67). Indeed the synchronic, rather than serial, emergence of such specifically human physiological characteristics as a completely encephelated nervous system and higher cultural accomplishments like the creation of symbols strongly suggests just such a thesis. But then, this implies that our nervous system is not just an enabling condition for the acquisition of culture but that the latter is indispensable for that system's functioning, in the sense of requiring the accessibility of public symbolic structures to build up its own autonomous, ongoing pattern of activity. As Geertz poetically puts it, "A cultureless human being would probably turn out to be not an intrinsically talented though unfulfilled ape, but a wholly mindless and consequently unworkable monstrosity" (Geertz 1973, 68).

If correct, these views have profound consequences. For our concerns, the explosion of the bogus dichotomy between biological heritage and culture radically undercuts the orthodox disjunction between emotion and cognition as separate processes, each with roots on one side but not the other of that dichotomy. On the picture here presented, our capacity to experience shame turns out to be just as culturally informed as the ability to employ *modus ponens* reasoning is biologically grounded. There is no phylogenetic priority of emotions over cognition; the former are not biologically more primitive than intellectual capacities. Even if it is true, if something of a paradox to contemporary ears, that only a highly "emotional" creature (i.e., one with very sophisticated neural capacities for feeling and sensitivity of various afferent and efferent impulses) could have developed the talent of abstract thought (Langer 1962, 73), what I have marked out as the sphere of emotions proper must have a priori emerged only subsequent to that initial development. That we are the most emotional as well as the most rational of animals is surely due to the complex interaction between "thought" and "emotion," and not because we have somehow grown each of these capacities by excluding the other—that is impossible. Nor are there, one might add following Pribram's (1980) complementary arguments against the viability of localizing emotional and cognitive functions in "older" or "newer" parts of the brain, neuroanatomical grounds on which these distinctions in their radical expression could be sustained. (If emotions engage the entire brain as a *system,* as it appears they do, is it not arbitrary and prejudicial to attribute causal functions to one as opposed to another part of it?)

But the anthropological arguments cut deeper. For they substantiate in an empirical mode what has been argued from an ethical perspective by every committed existentialist and by many who defend an interpretive approach to the study of human reality. That we are self-completing animals, agents of our own realization who "create out of our general capacity for the construction of symbolic models the specific capabilities that define us"—all this is not some idealistic fancy. It is a complex fact about our concrete existential predicament that is brought on by the extreme generality, diffuseness, and variability of our innate response capacities. Our behavior is extrememly plastic and not strictly but only very broadly controlled by genetic programs, the latter setting the overall psychophysical context within which specific activities are organized by the resources of culture (Geertz 1973, 217–18).

By now I must appear to have strayed too far from the primary concern with emotions and their rationality. But I think not. I believe the notion of thematization as constitutive of emotions has brought all this onto the agenda as legitimate supporting argumentation. But it has also implicitly revealed a major difficulty: the absence of an apparent single explanatory finality that would cover all emotions.

From various sources, a number of candidates have been proposed to fill this role. Thus the social-constructivists usually argue that emotions are transitory social roles that serve the integration and propagation of values that constitute culture (for samples of this general view, see Harré 1986); however, they seem to ignore individual psychodynamics. This lack might be seen to be corrected by Robert Solomon's (1976) position that all emotions serve to maintain our self-esteem, but Solomon, commited to the first-person perspective, abstracts too much from the social dimension and sees emotions principally as subjective strategies. There are also the more evolution-oriented views—for example, Ronald de Sousa's (1987)—in which emotions function as essential organizers for a being that has many options for action not dictated by automatic responses and is not governed by a fully determining rationality either. But this just states a truth of such generality that I am unsure of its greater significance. Besides, it is uncertain whether we can consider emotions directly from the perspective of having survival value; for all we know, they could be just "pleiotropic by-products of other organic processes that do increase reproductive fitness . . . (in themselves disfunctional) yet tolerated by natural selection because they are linked to other phenomena whose positive contributions more than justify this cost" (Elster 1985, 379).

Now, all the views just mentioned, even if partial or perhaps obvious, contain plausible truths in them. Still, it remains an open question whether they can be coherently stated under the auspices of a single account. My hunch is that such a theory might encounter too many exceptions to be explanatorily useful and so will be faced with the prospect of qualifying itself to extinction. The mentioned vexations about the possibility of grouping emotions into a natural class can be seen as applicable here as well. Just as we are presently being forced to reconsider and then subsequently to "create" anew the elephant called emotion, so, too, the answer to the question about the teleology of emotions will be linked in significant part to answering an essentially ethical-political question: what is it that *we want* our emotions to "do" for us?

Hence I propose to relocate the gravity of the questioning about emotional rationality away from a concern that emphasizes either establishing what emotions are "really" for or (whatever they are) whether they fit into some established formulaic notion of rationality to just clarifying a number of dimensions I take to be germane to thinking broadly and constructively about emotions, and whose clarification is therefore vital for perspicuous judgements about them.[2] In the end, rationality is neither some uniform psychological property nor a single method or procedure but a complex and multidimensional stance of persons vis-à-vis the world. This is not a denial of the importance of the former sorts of endeavor; surely part of what it means to see emotions perspicuously is to attempt to specify their function, even if this necessitates at times a measure of speculation. But such specification will make sense only within a broader context that encompasses both the means and the ends talked about as well as the terms in which the two are related to each other. For example, to ascertain that emotions serve self-esteem, we must first encompass the relationship between self and emotion, just as to argue that they are in some sense public, we should first outline how that holds for the general category of mental phenomena.

What follows, then, is not a single continuous argument progressing in an orderly way from a set of premises to a clear conclusion. Nor do I aim to set forth a theory of emotions, though I am quite at ease to accept that what I am advocating is a variant of a theoretical approach generically known as cognitive. I offer instead a series of quasi-independent investigations, a sort of Hegelian gathering of perspectives whose overall unity is secured by the common focus on emotions. In this context, the "rationalizing" of emotions means simply the enrichment of our understanding of them by the cumulative insights thus obtained. A number of my investigations are naturally intended to address (and to challenge when necessary) certain notions that are quite specific and central to how we ordinarily think about emotions (e.g., their privacy). Others pertain to issues that are implicit in those ordinary assumptions, issues that any philosophical account must dig up and examine if it is to have any hope of getting clearer about the bigger picture of human agency. Yet no claim is made on behalf of any particular investigation that it is pivotal, or that taken together they exhaust the range of relevant perspectives or concerns through which emotions might be profitably investigated.

Because I believe the relevance of examining emotions in relation to such critical features of being human as intentionality, expression and language, sense of self, and responsibility will be self-evident, I shall take the liberty to dispense with the customary provision of an outline of each chapter that at once gives the latter's raison d'être. In general, the essay is methodologically informed by a conviction that the explanation and study of emotions can no longer be adequately done solely in terms of psychological attributes of *individuals*. In the various discussions that follow, I have thus tried to incorporate as much as possible a social aspect, though perhaps not always carrying this to the extent to which it would be desirable.

I cannot overemphasize the fact that this work is programmatic and that the views that follow are provisional and contestable. They are, of course, neither definitive nor constitutive of the only approach to emotions—just one that explicitly acknowledges the hermeneutical dimension of human reality and is thus conscious of its own fragility. When it comes to emotions, especially, any objectivism is untenable. The validity of the proposed approach in relation to the claim about perspicuity cannot be measured with a yardstick and in relation to some immutable state of affairs. It lies rather in the kind of personal understanding it provides and interpersonal practice it hopes to engender. Any "proof" will be found not so much in the pudding as in our continuing to eat it.

This may yet turn out to be considerably more difficult than we suspect. Beyond those lucky few whose lives are indeed significantly altered by reflection, it would be naive to expect insight on these matters to flourish at large. There are powerful social and psychological pressures (not to mention the baggage of our common philosophical heritage) that each of us carries in his or her self-understanding and that conspire to privatize experience and deny us an understanding of it in broader terms.

I shall end here with just one very significant example. In relation to what I believe an adequate understanding of emotions entails, there is hardly a more contrary and insidious notion than the idea that psychological states are (ontological) *particulars* that attach to individuals in abstraction from their social setting, much as pains and twinges do. To be sure, our use of language for designative purposes makes some of these reifications inescapable, especially when combined with our naturally strong attachment to the *reality* of the contents of our minds. But there is also an argument that this assumption about our mental life is powerfully anchored in, and sustained by, the psychosexual development of males mothered by women in a patriarchal society (Scheman, 1983). If such indeed is the case, collectively we may have some distance to go and plenty of work to do before attaining emotional rationality.

To those discouraged by such prospects it can only be replied that cultural rationalist prejudices notwithstanding, emotions are not optional and neither therefore is our obligation to seek clarity about them. Some schizophrenics, apparently terrified of (and as protection against) not being able to experience any emotion, will inflict great physical pain on themselves in a desperate effort to generate some sense of vitality and life (Gaylin 1986, 208). We should not have to witness such horrors to be convinced that emotions figure centrally in infusing our lives with meaning and are thus deserving of our attention. "Who needs a heart if a heart can be broken?!" laments Tina Turner in a recent popular song. Whatever interpretation one wishes to give to this expression, the one intimating that the "heart" is in any way optional is surely to be excluded. And if meaning is understood generically as engagement, where else ought we look for it but in the personal stances that thematize it?

2

CONSCIOUSNESS:
INTENTIONALITY *AND* DISPOSITION

While admitting significant limitations in our present ability to frame useful generalizations about emotions (if we are fortunate to have defined them at all in the first place) and so relatedly guarding against offering a view of them that gains its coherence through forced abstraction from the descriptive ground, we must nonetheless make some attempt at circumscription to get any research going. Can we point, then, to some basic (in the sense of pervasive) phenomenon or facet of human existence that, given sufficient care and a decreased level of abstraction, can be described without prejudice to further articulation of its essence? We should be able to do so; certainly to admit the need for drastic reconceptualizations in philosophical psychology, and even further to acknowledge that any particular conceptualization in this realm will be significantly constitutive of the phenomena as experienced, is not in principle incompatible with offering some constraining (though perhaps only provisional) constants as possible theoretical starting points.

The experience of the world that continuously reveals itself to us is essentially infused with an affective tone. Our situations are never amenable to strictly neutral descriptions bereft of any emotional *meaning* or *significance*. It is this fundamental assumption that grounds a consideration of emotions primarily from the standpoint of their intentionality—that is, from the standpoint that takes them as essentially or noncontingently connected to the objects of our world. We must note at once that the latter are understood here in the broadest possible sense, to include not just perceptual objects and situations but also thoughts, ideas, beliefs, imaginings, and that the ontological status of these objects is not at issue because what counts for the subject is these objects as they are meant by him or her.

This noncontingency is to be understood in a dual sense. First, emotions as directed acts are *necessarily* of, or about, something; one cannot experience an emotion without taking hold of at least some features of an object that serves as the referent to which the emotion points in going beyond itself. Second, emotions are specified or defined as the emotions they are by the (types of) objects to which they are directed. Fear is of the "threatening" or the "dangerous" as pride is of "something that relates to ourselves" and worry is about the "potentially harmful"—it being, it would appear, logically impossible to be aware that one has a particular emotion without being aware of its particular object (i.e., one characterized in a particular way). Another example: if an object of my experience is an already realized possibility, it would be incoherent to say that my experience is one of hope; conversely, the condition of my hoping is my directedness to something that is yet to come. The "logic" of hope is constituted by the mind's orientation toward a possible future event.

Inspired by the tradition initiated by Brentano and Husserl, wherein it was always recognized that emotions are and ought to be treated as genuinely psychological or mental phenomena, the insistence on the intentionality of emotions has by now become a standard feature of most philosophical accounts of emotions. In line with the spirit of most of these analyses, I want to suggest at once that no nonintentional account of emotions will give us the means to make much sense of them, or, what amounts to the same, that insofar as "feelings," taken as physiological or visceral attendants to or "symptoms" of emotions, can be employed in analyzing emotion, feeling and emotion cannot be pried apart. The judgment here is that the rival Cartesian-inspired theories that treat emotions as little more than hormonal flows have by now been sufficiently and justly discredited and that the traditional notions of feeling are far too impoverished to contribute anything philosophically interesting to our understanding of emotions. At the same time, the more sophisticated "component" views of emotions have not fared much better. To take a case in point, for all its insight and subtlety, Hume's (1888, bk. 2, pt. 1) account of emotions provides an excellent illustration of the hopelessness of attempting to link emotions as internal impressions with their putative objects along causal-atomistic and associationist lines. Once separated, a Herculean effort is required to put together again the various features of an emotion (for Hume, principally impressions and ideas), an effort that in Hume borders on incoherence. Without denying that bodily feelings are typically or even always present in emotions, the notion of intentionality as mutual codetermination of act and object obviates this confusion and presents in comprehensible terms how an emotion is "about" something, namely, *its* object. The notion appears indispensable.[1]

My worrying, then, refers me to (is about) something in a way that my throbs, tickles, nauseas, or headaches clearly do not. This is the usual supporting argument, classically formulated by Kenny (1963), that points up the intentionality of emotions and by implication safeguards their integrity as mental. Another argument for the nonidentity of emotions and feelings as sensations is that whereas we can have an emotion without being fully aware of it (i.e., an unconscious emotion with regard to which we can subsequently experience a genuine revelation), this is not so with feelings; an unfelt feeling is a contradiction. But this argument also presents a challenge to the notion of intentionality as a pillar of understanding emotions because it appears to undercut the stated necessity of mutual implication of emotion and object. For it may be argued that the experiences of what we normally typify as moods or dispositions—for example, a dread without a specific object or a "pointless" depression whose (many) objects fail somehow to fit under a description that would be a clear reason or warrant for eliciting that depression—are essentially objectless and hence nonintentional.

There are important implications to be drawn here, especially for a view of consciousness, but the invalidation of the notion of intentionality in the realm of emotions (and perhaps finding recourse in a rival physicalist description) is not one of them. For by definition, the condition of *any* experience of consciousness is that it be directed toward something, and the significance of such diffuse experiences as anxiety is not so much a lack of object as a *felt absence of an object.* That is, the meaning of such an emotion is to a large degree generated by an inability to find a (rational) focus; inescapably, in dread I fear "something" because "the empty slot where the object of fear should be is an essential phenomenological feature of this experience" (Taylor 1985, 48). The experience may be of no particular thing, but not of "nothing." Rather, what one experiences are characteristics that the object must have in order for that emotion to be what it is. For dread, whatever its object, the latter must have the characteristics of posing a danger or threat.

Far from leading to the abandonment of the thesis of intentionality, the alleged counterexamples turn out to amplify it, but also to enlarge it beyond a strict correlativism of act and distinct-object suggested by the bald statement that emotions are about objects. At the same time, this set of considerations leads in another direction. It allows us subsequently to deal with an influential distinction pervasive in theorizing about emotions—emotions as *occurrent* states or episodes against emotions as dispositions.

The following provides some background on how and why the distinction arises. In describing someone as angry, for example, we can refer to the actual displays of anger on his part (the raised fist, the shouting, etc.), this being the occurrent sense of "angry," or we can intend this dispositionally, that is, as a term of character that indicates the person's proneness to acts of anger. Now, for the theorists who make use of this distinction, it is the displays that count as the emotions proper, their evident worry being that without it, the concept of emotion becomes just too general in scope; hence vacuous. Accordingly, they prefer to keep that concept more centered on bodily feelings or upsets, convinced that the latter is what distinguishes emotions from other mental states. But these feelings are usually (under)described as of the same variety as the more autonomic physiological responses such as throbs, flushes, increased pulse rate. Since these are clearly non-intentional, the problem (as in Hume) becomes how to square them with the professed intentionality of what presents itself phenomenologically as a *unitary* experience. The standard saving response is to argue that the (apparent) intentionality of emotion-as-feeling is really a borrowed intentionality, that is, that the intentionality "within" emotion really belongs to another intentional state (e.g., belief), which in turn has caused the feeling or bodily upset.

But the nature of this causal link remains unspecified. Typically we may be offered superficial linguistically grounded justifications by reference to such locutions as "His realizing the danger *made* him tense up," where nothing, however, guarantees that the causality imputed to the intentional state in fact exists. And so the relationship between emotions as intentional acts and experienced feelings is as obscure as in any other dualism. Emotions end up as thoughts with feelings tacked onto them or vice versa. If one insists on their intentionality, they are emasculated to mere beliefs as feelings drop out of the picture. On the other hand, if one insists (equally legitimately) that something is also felt, then by virtue of the impoverished sense of feelings emotion-as-felt becomes located in the effect of some intentional state rather than in the intentional state itself. With intentionality out of the picture, emotion becomes just . . . feeling.

The emphasis on occurrent states as at least partially definitive of emotions thus assumes an untenable dualism. But this is in a way a

secondary problem, one arising provided the distinction with dispositions gets off the ground in the first place. And it is this latter proposition
that seems questionable. First, the distinction discounts the emotionality of moods or "colorings" of consciousness and such "calm" passions
as intellectual curiosity, aesthetic appreciation, long-term commitments
to a cause, and the like, experiences that for the most part are not episodic and strongly felt bodily but nevertheless, I want to insist, are
full-fledged emotional experiences. They bind and engage us in the
world in determinate ways and are not to be parceled off (as they
usually are) under some vague category like "attitudes." Curiously, it
is never considered how much energy and effort we can expend or
how much hardship and physical harm we can endure when influenced by some of those calm passions. Clearly, they are as capable of
moving us in the sense of influencing our bodily condition and possessing motivational force as any of the more immediately "vigorous"
emotions such as fear or anger.

Second, the distinction also discounts the sense in which specific
tendencies to act in a certain way toward objects of emotions are often
legitimately used, indeed are essential, to define those emotions that
are inadequately specified by the type of object to which they are directed and whose act-object correlations have thus inevitably an analytical, vacuous ring to them. It is because certain objects are typically
threatening and hence referring us to the harmful that we readily understand that they inspire and specify our fear. On the other hand, it is
far less taken for granted what the typical objects of anger, love, or
hate might be since often and not unexceptionally it is the same
parameters (e.g., the animate) that will delineate the characteristics of
the objects of all three. Save for some very broad parameters, then,
there are no characteristics that an object of love typically has (we are
inclined to say the "lovable," but this tells us nothing), so that the
burden of defining that emotion falls on referring to how we are disposed to act toward its object. (Of course, from the phenomenological standpoint just about anything can be an object of fear. But we are
speaking here about that which elicits the normal, consensually agreed-
upon and readily understandable reactions that do not require additional contextual description to be comprehended. It is normal for
guns to inspire fear; not so for marshmallows. When the latter does
occasion this unusual response, we require further information. Is the
subject a diabetic?)

Now, at a certain point the attempt to highlight emotions as occurrent states and their diremption from dispositions begins to look
not just problematic but forced, an attempt to establish in experience
more than can be delivered on the basis of what is basically, I think, a

very abstract distinction. At times, in fact, it borders on incoherence. William Lyons, for example, argues that "a claim that someone has a disposition labelled 'x' does not imply that there must be occurrences also labelled 'x' " (1980, 55). This sounds right as an antibehaviorist manifesto, for there is much more to an emotion than just physiological or behavioral manifestations. But then this skimpy formulation leaves completely unanswered on what ground it can meaningfully be said that one has such a disposition. Does not the notion of disposition to have certain experiences necessarily entail a reference to those experiences? (To carry this to its logical conclusion, in the unrestricted sense in which Lyons uses the notion, it can be validly, if vacuously, said that each of us is disposed to anything.) Surely more can be said on behalf of dispositions; whatever it may mean to have one must minimally be to *experience* something. Here it appears as if a disposition were some affectless state that gets its name from a purely contingent relation to what suddenly and inexplicably follows it. How underdescribed this notion remains only confirms its abstract nature.

It is possible at last to come to the point of what must surely by now seem an unnecessary digression. I have deliberately engaged at length the view that treats emotions predominantly as episodes or occurrences because I believe it is uncomfortably close to the discredited position that emotions are just feelings and because the contrast it draws on is ultimately untenable, carries little force. In opposition, and notwithstanding certain scientistic prejudices that hold up cool and detached rationality as a human ideal—one needs only to consider how fiercely and irrationally the proponents of such a view are capable of defending it to see it for the pretense that it is— I want to insist that ("this side of the grave") there is no such state or condition as complete absence of emotion. On the view I am proposing, even something like a seemingly passionless and undemonstrative sense of security one may have is to be considered an emotion. For it is that sense that literally *moves* us to remain calm in trying circumstances. We are always, as Heidegger would say, in the grip of some mood. And the difference between moods or dispositions and emotions is not one of belonging to different categories. The two are continuous with and supportive of each other and distinguished in the final analysis— and this brings us back to the theme of intentionality—by nothing more than the degree of specificity of their objects.

Why, then, is intentionality usually taken as insufficient by itself to do the job of specifying emotions in the first place? Why do the latter have to be abstracted from the unity of lived experience and singled out as episodes or occurrences with more or less explicit references to bodily conditions? Because corresponding to the underdeveloped sense of feelings there persists implicitly in much theorizing about emotions what I would call an "angelic" notion of intentionality that abstracts completely from our sense as *embodied* agents. The notion of intentionality may indeed be accepted by many as the indispensable successor to and replacement of the classical empiricist view that construed perception and cognition on the model of contact between material objects. For humans, "objects" are clearly more than an ensemble of primary or secondary qualities (i.e., their material properties), and it surely belongs to Husserl's tremendous achievements to have shown this by reinterpreting perception through an analytical framework traditionally employed for examining the more clearly "conceptual" modes of mind such as judging, asserting, believing, denying (Solomon 1977, 173). But the complementary notion—something that was always implicit in Husserl's program but that he himself, by reason of the ambiguity of his break from empiricism on one hand and a commitment to Kantian transcendentalism on the other, could not articulate clearly—namely, that behaviour is *internally* related to perception and conception, has escaped the attention it deserves. On this view, perceptual and behavioural space are *one,* for it is our behavioral know-how that enters into what we see, and this is what endows the phenomenal field with meaning or significance (Taylor 1959, 95). Thus I am capable of perceiving something as a cube only because my capacity to amble around it and "verify" its many-sidedness is an intrinsic component of my perception; without it, none of the sides I actually see could appresent or "announce" any other sides. Closer to emotions, a situation signifies danger and inspires fear because it threatens to overwhelm my abilities to continue my normal existence, to counter the danger or avoid it altogether. In both cases, my behavioral know-how infuses my perception, and if need be, I can thematize my intended though not yet discharged movements as an embodied agent that constitute that know-how.

Here we enter the territory initially indicated in broad terms by Heidegger and later rendered in greater detail by Merleau-Ponty. It is the practical concerns that constitute our primordial insertion in the world. The latter reveals itself in the first instance not as something to be thought or represented, and from which we thus have a measure of distance, but as a continuous series of tasks to be done, projects to be fulfilled, actions to be taken. In Merleau-Ponty's elegant summary, "Consciousness is in the first place not a matter of 'I think that' but of 'I can' " (1962, 173). Here something is significant, has meaning, by virtue of appearing in the context of our actual or projected action (or our being acted upon that has a bearing on our action); the "I think that" is possible on the foundation provided by the broadest possible sense of the "I can." (Not insignificantly, and pointing toward a notion of consciousness as *exertion* and *effortful* directedness, *intendere* [from which intention and intentionality derive] meant in classical Latin a "stretching out" or a "straining towards." Much the same point can be made in strictly linguistic terms. There is a close link between intentionality in its technical sense of requiring objects to appear under particular descriptions and intention in the normal understanding of intending to act. The choice of description at least partly determines the range of premises available to us from which to infer possible outcomes and that thus underlie intending to do anything [Harré 1984, 116].)

Existential phenomenology did not, of course, have a monopoly on these sorts of insights. Similar and equally important conclusions about consciousness had been reached earlier by Gestalt psychology, in particular by those representatives of it who worked in Leipzig (the leading names here are Felix Krueger, Wilhelm Stern, and Philipp Lersch). A brief look at them,[2] prefaced by some relevant remarks about Husserl, proves most useful.

For Husserl, as is well known, emotions generally were at best of marginal concern. Like Descartes, he certainly took the *cogitata* in a broad sense and so granted intentional correlates not just to thinking and perceiving but to judgments and volitions as well as emotions. In this he also followed a thesis proposed earlier by Brentano but elaborated the intentionality of an emotion in terms of a dual structure of an underlying founding intention that gives the presented (perceptual) object and the founded intention that accounts for the object-as-felt (Husserl 1970, 570). Unlike Scheler, who was later to argue for logically prior and independent emotion-based intuitive acts whose felt objects are values, Husserl suggested that the presented object can stand on its own but that the felt object is inseparable from the presented one and is intelligible only by virtue of this link. How feeling somehow attaches itself to the perceived given is not entirely clear save for what was intimated by Husserl's general use of a "vectorial" approach (Schrag 1969, 83) in the explication of the origin of meaning. But even for instances of what would conventionally be called emotional intuition, he nevertheless insisted on a primacy of perception where the paradigm case is that of the clearly specified datum that stands in (polar) opposition to the intending consciousness and is grasped with evidence.

There are reasons for this view. The underlying model unmistakably present here is that of knowing as *seeing,* and so are its connotations of a subjectivity distancing itself from its object. At the same time, Husserl is working under the programmatic and methodological exigencies of the transcendental reduction which is theoretically based on the assumption that we have an immediate first-person knowledge of the essential features and states of our minds, and this in abstraction from any empirically derived beliefs about them or the objects to which they are directed. Moreover, Husserl's (especially early) phenomenological analyses, as purely structural, are formal and static; the ego or subject being no more than a characterless identity pole to which all intentional acts are referred. Not surprisingly, then, there persists in them a complementary Cartesianism of delineating essences or evidential structures that offer themselves to a subject who (in trying to become a pure viewer pursuing a pure science of consciousness) soberly reduces his or her contribution to nothing.[3] What finally emerges from the primacy of perception as Husserl construes it is a theoretical model of psychic events as a "stream of consciousness" wherein the contents of such a stream are continuous and linked clearly objectifiable experiences (i.e., one thought or content of consciousness arising from the previous experience and leading to another, etc.). Husserl is apparently quite concerned about this continuance, so much so that he proposes that the "stream" is in fact the a priori form of consciousness.

There are doubts, however, whether this picture of a linear continuance of the stream of consciousness is a faithful description of our prethematic experience. For example, there is Stephan Strasser's humorous comment, "The much-praised stream of consciousness seeps away continually into the sane, in order soon to rise again from mysterious underground sources" (1977, 90). It also turns out to be the target of the Gestaltists from Leipzig.

As against Husserl, and also in contrast to their Berlin counterparts (Wolfgang Kohler, Max Wertheimer) who investigated almost exclusively psychic act-patterns that were sharply bounded and clearly segmented, the Leipzigers took note of the fact that in the developmental process of consciousness, distinct experiential wholes are a rather *late* arrival that presupposes much that is vague and diffuse. Moreover, even if it holds for mature adults that the totality of their experience develops into a plurality of more or less circumscribed complexes of parts, this experiential perspicuity is always a *relative* one. For a feature of such affective experiences as an enduring high excitement or fatigue, or an absorbing dedication to something is that the clearly defined object or goal arises out of the totality of the lived field only if attention allows it to do so. A similar observation holds for such preintentional "dis-ease" or "pressure" experiences, as when one is disturbed by a conviction of having forgotten something without knowing quite what. These and other parallel observations, then, were what led the Leipzig group to guide their agenda from the outset by one principal interest: the connection between objectivating acts and affectivity.

It was Krueger who first articulated this link, arguing that "separate sensations, perceptions, relations, even acts of remembering, distinct thoughts, decisive acts of the will—in short, all the articulations of experience split themselves off in one brief moment from a diffuse felt directedness . . . (by which, moreover) *they remain always functionally governed*" (Strasser 1977, 91). Later, from a more personalist perspective, Stern complemented what he considered in Krueger a still too objectivist orientation (i.e., one excessively focused on the object-pole of experience) by insisting on the sense in which emotions as living experiences close to the person constitute her unique, irreplaceable, and intimate center. For Stern, *all* experience consists of a peculiar dialectic between apprehension of external objects, states of affairs, persons, and so on, on one hand and self-experience on the other. While progressive rationalization of experienced objects—that is, stricter differentiation and articulation—withdraws and in a way estranges us from the world, it is feeling as emotional intentionality, and more accurately its *bipolarity*, that both embeds us back in that world and integrates individual states into the totality of personal experience. In emotion, the objective meanings of the world are personally appropriated in a process of "melting" or "introception" (Strasser 1977, 92). Finally, Lersch, taking into consideration the views of Krueger and Stern, proposed a strata theory that typified and hierarchized the various levels of emotion-related experience.

This is, of course, at best a sketchy picture of the combined results of the Leipzigers' research. Nevertheless, through their focus on what one could call the twilight zones of consciousness, wherein experience has an identifiable totalizing tone or quality but is not yet segmented into discrete units or are sharp lines drawn between the self and the objects it experiences, we can appreciate a critical and salient feature of consciousness. What we see here and what is absent in the "correlativism" of early Husserl (and, I submit, never quite compensated for even in the more dynamic genetic descriptions of intentionality in such later writings as the *Crisis*) is that consciousness is not only intentional in the usual (primary) understanding as directed and capable of (re)presenting the world but also *dispositional* in the original sense that can be extracted from the Latin *disponere*, as relating to an arranging or setting in order. Thus to suggest that consciousness has a tendency or is disposed toward its content is to emphasize its *active* function of relating or connecting that cannot be construed as a simple pointing, referring, or indicating (Schrag 1969, 85). On this view, meaning arises neither ex nihilo nor through an intentional "arrow" fired by a transcendental subjectivity at its object nor through some cerebral process of representation but through consciousness's relating one content to another. (An important implication here is that if perception minimally presupposes a structural relation between figure, ground, and experiencing subject, then it is disposition, as that which configures these three terms, rather than perception, at least as construed by Husserl, that lies at the basis of our experience.)

From an admittedly quite different perspective and motivated by different concerns, this picture of consciousness as dispositional or relational surely joins much that subsequently appears under the various headings of existential phenomenology. In particular, it makes accessible in far less forbidding terms Heidegger's central claim for an ontological interpretation of moods as an attunement with the world wherein self and world reveal themselves to be an indivisible complex, a *unitary* phenomenon. It also anticipates Sartre's thesis about emotions as ways of *living* in the world and much of what Merleau-Ponty says about the intentionality of the lived-body. More generally, though, yet critically for understanding emotions, it entrenches the case for a holistic (and concrete) conception of consciousness whose original experience is a totality that only subsequently is *dissociated* by and through the lived-body into individual units. In this perspective, "felt, willed, and conceptual meanings mix and mingle in primordial world experience; [f]eelings vitalize concepts, concepts organize feelings, and both concepts and feelings are colored with volitional dispositions" (Schrag 1969, 90). The traditional dichotomies between thought, emotion, and volition simply break down in favor of a more fluid transition between these phenomenologically different modes of intentionality. The multipartite self of the old faculty psychology and any fast division into what is inner and outer, subjective and objective, self and other, mind and body, is definitively put to rest.

The importance of this analysis of consciousness lies in its provision of a badly needed perspective on a number of issues raised earlier. (It will also stand us in good stead later.) First, it should be clear how easily the experiential interwovenness just spoken of escapes us if we think of subjectivity and mind as either a synthesizer of originally differentiated psychic facts or merely a referential point for its manifold objects that come and go in streamlike fashion, and consequently how we are ready to parcel off and dirempt the various modes of our conscious existence only to attempt clumsily to recombine them when we wish to capture adequately the holistic nature of emotional experiencing. The integrative conception of consciousness that I am insisting on in combining the notions of intentionality (in its primary understanding as description-bound directedness) and disposition makes no allowance for an emotional intuition as some autonomous quasi faculty. Intentionality is a unitary feature of (dispositional) consciousness whose experientially different forms become coarticulated through felt, willed, and noetic meanings. There are no "pure" emotional objects that do not involve, at least to some extent, conception, evaluation, and volition; by definition, they are complex objects. (At the same time, the "proximity" of different forms of intentionality points to the difficulty of their adequate distinction and the consequent opposite temptation to *identify* emotions with beliefs, desires, etc.)

Second, the pervasiveness of disposition solidifies the suggestion that there is no such state or condition as complete absence of affect. Our original contact with the world is a vitally lived one, and this persists as an underlying dimension of *all* experience. Moreover, the *felt* echoes of the world that infuse and "direct" the progressive development of more analytically fixed, abstract knowledge must be experiences of an active embodied consciousness. And this in turn strengthens the critique of what I called the "angelic" view of intentionality (i.e., a view that neglects our sense of embodiment and behavioral know-how in accounting for the generation of meaning) while at the same time amplifying the important features of self-involvement and partiality vis-à-vis objects noted in the generic interpretation of emotions proposed in the last chapter.

If intentionality is a generic term for conscious relatedness to the world, the specific nature of emotional intentionality lies in its focus on the self's engagement. It highlights certain of the objects that we encounter as in some sense important to us, that is, as focal points of our concerns in the world. And it is precisely this sense of engagement of one's self that distinguishes thought and affect not as separate mental acts or processes but as two different forms of awareness. Typically, and to some extent always, emotional experiencing involves bodily feeling. The latter can be thematized as *partially* constitutive of the experience even in instances of calm engagement or when we are so absorbed in the object of the emotion that little is felt, where feeling arrives, so to speak, "after" the experience. However, and this must be strongly emphasized to avoid the impression of conceding to the conventional view, all this is not because emotions are essentially bodily feelings, but because *all* intentionality entails behavioral know-how and the forms of intentionality that engage embodied agents in the world and signal what is of concern to them will naturally "register" themselves in more or less explicit fashion as something bodily felt.[4] The truth that emotions are predominantly if not essentially thought-formed experiences and that the important differences among them are conceptual remains intact. Aristotle, it seems, had it right when he suggested in *De Anima* that bodily change stands to directed thought as "matter" to "form" (Skillen 1983, 310). In emotion, we are moved as incarnately conscious whole beings where feelings are present, but it is thoughts that are most salient. To overemphasize feelings amounts simply to committing the fallacy of misplaced concreteness.

But what exactly do we feel in emotional experiencing? While rejecting the episodic approaches that emphasize physiological upsets as definitive of emotions, we ought, at least as a conciliatory move, provide some answer here, especially with the admission that we typically do feel something in emotion. Now, initially I had been highly critical of the sense of feelings that draws more or less straightforwardly from our experiences of sensations (i.e., pains, throbs, tickles, etc.). I suggested that this (physiological) sense of feelings was just too impoverished to contribute anything significant to our understanding of emotions. Subsequently, in the discussion of embodiment and intentionality, I introduced the notion of behavioral know-how as the latter's condition. To draw this out, I mentioned that such know-how is constitutive of perception, and the notion seemed also applicable in emotional contexts. Something imposes itself as dangerous and inspires fear because it threatens to overwhelm my capacities to avoid it or to counteract its influence; it puts in jeopardy the integrity of my ordinary existence. And this I can feel in intended but undischarged bodily movements that make up my sense of embodied agency. But fear, at least in its usual sense that refers us primarily to contexts of threat to bodily integrity, arguably belongs to the least complex of emotions. Thus a question may be raised whether it can legitimately serve as a paradigmatic example from which one can draw general conclusions about emotional experiencing. What about jealousy, respect, or anger? Vis-à-vis these emotions, all of which presuppose a high level of cognitive and symbolic mediation as well as social interaction, the idea of feeling behavioral know-how appears somewhat thin. What we feel "feels" somehow richer, more sophisticated, than projected tendencies and motor skills that the notion principally connotes.

I think we can meet this objection, and maintain the validity of the original thesis, if we consider the bodily changes attendant on emotions as tendencies and motor events that determine their *expression,* so that what we feel in emotions are the "expressive sets" of our bodies (de Sousa 1980, 287). This redefinition has the merit of retaining the general link of meaning-intention with mobility and behavior (the primary sense of embodied agency) most evident for relatively "simple" emotions like fear while also giving full scope to the feelings involved in those emotions that are conceptually complex and thus entail a high level of linguistic development and competence. The involvement of the body in the latter cases is of course obvious in a trivial sense; the body is also the medium of linguistic expression. More importantly, though, the linguistically formulated expressive tendencies in emotion are no less tied to our projects and actions than the motor skills that determine movement. Since J. L. Austin, especially, we have come to appreciate to what extent language is a form of *action;* it defines the stances we take vis-à-vis ourselves and others and symbolically projects what we might otherwise physically do. And as Merleau-Ponty has shown, even its most abstract expression finds its ultimate roots in perception and what we initially started out with: behavioral know-how. It can be seen at once that the proposed sense of feelings as tied to behavior, action, and expression has nothing to do with what is conventionally grouped under sensations. Under a microscope, a sinking feeling in my abdomen caused by rough seas may appear identical to the one brought on by news of the death of a close friend. Experientially, though, the two *cannot* be the same. The former is a more or less "brute" fact, the latter a focal point of the range of expressive (hence intention-backed) bodily tendencies that are integral to the appearance of a meaning unity (a sense of loss, outrage, an "it isn't so" denial, etc.) that defines the experience. Here indeed, emotion and feeling are neither distinguishable nor independently specifiable.

A number of significant methodological issues come to light at this point. For one, we are now in a good position to appreciate the complementarity of different and apparently unrelated strands of phenomenologically inspired theorizing about emotions and the grain of truth contained in each approach. That theorizing, Robert Sweeney (1975) tells us, follows roughly a dialectical pattern of development wherein we find altering emphasis on each term of engagement we suggested emotions to be. On the one hand, there are analyses such as Husserl's, Scheler's, and (with qualifications) Heidegger's that focus on the intentional or "object-related" aspect of emotions and hence construe emotions primarily as a type of cognition. On the other hand, in the theories of von Hildebrand, Michel Henry especially, and (with qualifications) Sartre, much more attention is paid to emotions' interiorizing, self-affecting aspect. In this latter perspective, emotions are principally reactions or responses, and this is also the starting point of those attempts that focus on emotions' consequences for behavior and hence describe them as motives. It appears that what prompts a decision in favor of either the cognitive or the response, experience-oriented model is usually an underlying ontological or a priori commitment regarding the extent of the passivity of emotions, a key traditional parameter in thinking about them.

Now, we can see that not considering what the opposite side emphasizes would surely be imprudent for even the most ardent advocates of either orientation. The very constitution of the sense of partiality that moves us in emotional awareness requires being engaged with(in) the world. The value aspects of objects are not some independent Platonic essences; their constitution is intimately linked to our projects and hence to embodied agency. No hard split can exist between cognition and our being affected. Similarly, the self-affecting, interiorizing, or response aspects of emotions are conditional upon a cognition of valued objects, the experience of self-affectation coming to be only through the mediating factor of an outer-directedness. The response model cannot claim to be more experience-oriented or superior on the basis of an alleged immediacy of the experience it attempts to describe. At bottom, the "cognitive" and "experiential" approaches turn out to be two sides of the same coin. This is just what is so valid, for example, in Sartre's (1948) theory.[5] His notion of emotions as "magical transformations" of our world is meant to convey them as projections of new value structures that are essentially changes in the intentional direction of consciousness, and more precisely, in the latter's embodied relationship to the world. In emotion, the world changes its qualities because in altering my intentions and behavior, I alter my relation with the world. That Sartre ultimately degrades emotions, seeing them as inferior modes of consciousness, and takes a somewhat instrumentalist stance toward the body is here beside the point. What matters is that he insists on the holistic and integrative character of emotions as structures of consciousness through which we concretely *live* in, and are bound to, the world and that the key to this is embodiment.

In this perspective, an emotion is a kind of bridge between self and world where the directedness toward the latter is also at once a situating of the subject—something pointed up even at the abstract level of thought in the futility of attempting to separate our conceptions of the objects of anger, fear, love, from our conceptions of *our-*

selves in provocative, fearful, or loving situations (Scruton 1987). Discounting either pole leads to losing what is most significant about emotions and is likely to issue in a view of them as not much more than concatenations of ontologically different components. The various meanings of the objects of emotion are (as much as those of more strictly perceptual acts) neither "in our minds" nor "in the world"; they arise only through our concretely lived *interaction* with the world, from which interaction they cannot be abstracted. Indeed, I think we are permitted here a generalization concerning emotions in relation to that all-pervasive and often destructive subjective-objective dichotomy: *whatever* one wishes to put in each rubric of the distinction, the emotions cannot be adequately analyzed in terms of either precisely because they are, to borrow Ronald de Sousa's (1978) apt metaphor, "on the frontier" of the subjective and the objective.

In line with this dictum, let me mention three further, more specific "directives." All are related and made particularly salient by the idea that consciousness is dispositional. First, there is an urgent need to develop metaphors that highlight consciousness' relational and organizing features and that would thus make it that much harder for us to lose sight of the experiential interwovenness (of concepts, feelings, volitions, mind, body, subject, object, etc.) so critical for emotions. Colin Wilson (1972), for example, speaks of consciousness as "web-like," and Schrag (1969) sees experience as a "dynamic field." These holistically informed characterizations add to consciousness a sense of depth, fluidity, and involvement that is badly needed in traditional formulations dominated by the metaphor of vision and its experience-segmenting and mind-distancing influence. It is metaphors such as these that should provide the background for any thinking about emotions.

Second, the expanded picture of consciousness gives reason for caution about employing too freely the notion of intentionality, especially in its primary sense as directedness to objects. The point has been made by Solomon (1979) that the notion, especially as it appears in early phenomenology (and paradigmatically present in what I have called Husserl's act-object correlativism), retains the atomism and dualism it purports to overcome. Put differently, such standard schemas as "act" and "object" (or "*noesis*" and "*noema*") or bald talk of "aboutness" undermine (or at least do not sufficiently convey) the sense of mutual codetermination of self and object. That sense, in the case of emotions especially, has to be asserted in strongest possible terms, failing which we risk reverting back to the idea of emotions as some purely inner episodes on the one hand while missing the essential experiential or psychological properties of (emotional) objects on the other. Given this, the "object" is best regarded as no more than a "shorthand" that denotes a focal point of something that is nothing less than a way of experiencing. (Analogous strictures can be seen to apply to attempts to reconstruct emotions solely on the model provided by linguistic analysis, i.e., as an account of the logical structure of emotion terms and/or propositional attitudes. For logical analyses that concentrate on terms take them as significations of clearly defined or delimited [and in this sense "closed"] concepts with known intension and extension. Whereas the meaning *of* an emotion as a synthetic experiential whole reveals essentially a multilevel or plurivocal [and hence "open"] structure for which a term is indeed nothing but a shorthand denotation, a best candidate, so to speak; its logical analysis is therefore bound to fall far short of adequately capturing the experienced emotion. Moreover, if what is essential about emotions and their objects is the experienced self-involvement, a personal reference, this reference is precisely what is lost in the transition from an intentional "I am proud *of* [something]" to the propositional "I am proud *that* [something is the case]," a reconstruction that in any case proves impossible for instances of emotion verbs; for example, "I love Jane" [Solomon 1979, 26]).

This leads to the third and methodologically perhaps most important point, once again implied directly by the dispositional dimension of consciousness: for an adequate grasp of emotions, our task must ultimately shift from phenomenological description to hermeneutical understanding. This is already accomplished in large measure in the transition from transcendental to existential phenomenology. To be sure, the detour through the object retains significance as a useful point of departure, but only that. For the articulated object cannot be absolutized since it is a focal point of only one of the many possible configurations of experience (and ultimately many forms of life) that involve that "same" (public) object. From this angle, emotions implicate a general theory of interpretation.[6]

Finally, and to conclude the present discussion, I want to revert to a somewhat more standard analysis of what emotions are. I am concerned that my repeated insistence on the holistic nature of consciousness and experience not be read as some sort of "panemotionalism." With the aim of becoming more specific about emotions, what follows is a brief look at some strategies that view them in relation to other conventionally recognized modalities of mind.

In light of their having motivational force, perhaps the most obvious would be the attempt to assimilate emotions to desires. Now, desires are simply defined by what they dispose us to. And since the partiality vis-à-vis objects that marks our sense of engagement with them in emotions assumes certain dispositions or inclinations, it is easy to conclude that emotions just *are* desires too. But emotions, as Charles Taylor (1970, 723) points out, over and above being defined by what they dispose to through their immediate objects, are also related to *other* dispositions into which we gain insight precisely by the way we are partial to a given object. For example, our aspiration to dignity and integrity becomes most visible in our sense of its loss (i.e., through guilt), as our desire for privacy may be learned through embarrassment. Put differently, what inspires emotions is the apparently immediate object, but as it is embedded within those broader desires or aspirations that underlie our partiality for that object. To come back to the language just used in the discussion of Sartre, emotions thematize the (type of) relatedness to objects. And in fact it is often difficult to differentiate them from desires because the broader embedding aspirations remain in the background, overshadowed by the immediacy of our responses to the object. Thus an emotion like fear can easily be seen as a (negative) desire because the dispositions to avoid the threatening object predominate the experience to the exclusion of our recognizing the founding positive need for existential integrity. Another "vigorous" emotion, anger, is often misconstrued as a simple desire to punish. But clearly that desire can be founded only on its relation to some moral order that we aspire to maintain and on the basis of which we assess the gravity of the transgression to be rectified. On the other hand, some emotions (e.g., joy, contentment) are problematic for assimilation with desires not so much because they relate to founding background aspirations as because they are without a predominant, focused desire—where it is unclear what it is one is disposed to in the first place—and this is another reason not to identify emotions with desires. To be sure, at least some desire appears to be integral to emotions, and by virtue of their motivational power, desires and emotions may even be seen as different species of the same genus. But for the reasons elaborated above, emotions appear to be more complex mental states than desires and ought to be approached as such.

When we shift our focus further from the phenomenologically inspired literature and take our cue from the logic of emotion words, it is plausible to argue that they form part of the vocabulary of appraisal and criticism, so that emotion ascriptions logically entail ascriptions of evaluative and factual judgements or beliefs (see Bedford 1962). (It would be incoherent, for example, to claim that one is overjoyed at something that is simultaneously insisted on as a matter of indifference.) At first this move looks suspiciously intellectualist. But there are some good reasons for at least a guarded introduction into emotion theory of the notion of judgments in general and evaluative judgments in particular.

One consideration in favor of this approach is the frequent interchangeability of the verbs *to feel, to think,* and *to believe.* To say that one thinks, believes, or feels something to be the case often amounts to the same thing—that one is convinced about its being the case. A more substantive reason for taking this option is that for many an emotion, changes of belief will often cancel or alter that emotion. I do not continue to fear something I learn is harmless or remain angry with my child for a misdeed it turns out she did not commit, just as a differing assessment of one's responsibility may turn an embarrassing situation into a shameful one. And of course reasonings and inferences, processes that judgments and beliefs assume, are often crucial for how we obtain the evidence that sustains or cancels our emotions or how we first assess an object of an emotion as an instance of what we take it to be.

Beliefs, then, appear implicated in emotions in more than just an accidental sense. And in fact there is a strong temptation to pass beyond language use into an ontological thesis that emotions *are* beliefs, especially where there is involvement of those judgments we experience as straightforwardly evaluative. But this should not be surprising. First, among different (types of) judgments, evaluative ones present themselves as vividly as emotions as a species of "seeing as": intentional acts defined by the objects to which they are directed. Second, emotions are the acts wherein values are typically brought to evidence. In general, what we feel about various objects indicates how we value them, and this must be so because the sense of partiality for or against objects of our engagements makes it clear that evaluation is at the heart of emotions. It is only because I take an omission in a financial statement as a "fraud" as opposed to "an honest mistake" that I become angry.

Nevertheless, even if evaluation is integral to emotions (as was the case with desire), it does not appear that emotions can be *unqualifiedly* identified with evaluations. We can hold evaluative beliefs in a more or less detached manner and without much sense of the self-involvement crucial for emotions. Conceivably, this objection could be overcome by arguing that analytically evaluations are self-involved, that the notion of value presupposes an engaged valuing self without which there simply are no values. But there is a further problem, of emotions often not being *reliably* evaluative, that is, instances where what we feel strongly about is different from what is conventionally taken to be the case or what we would value in light of our more considered judgments. Put differently, even if our beliefs about something normally go hand in hand with how we feel about it—indeed to the point where we can say that typical beliefs are what specifies a typical emotion—the capacity for resisting the claims of what we take as reality remains our emotional lives' most outstanding and fascinating feature. Sometimes the conservation of our emotions is such that our avowed beliefs play little, if any, role in influencing them. The world stubbornly continues to appear to us in a certain way in spite of our *sincere* convictions that it cannot be, or isn't, so; we are apparently quite capable of sustaining emotions without holding the beliefs that are normally relevant to them.

There is a long "cognitivist" tradition, stretching back to Aristotle and more recently arising from the reaction against William James's (1884) neo-Cartesian thesis that emotions are just perceptions of bodily feelings, that considers beliefs as *the* cognitive element, in the absence of which the identification of emotions is almost impossible. Many of the claims for belief's role in emotion are indeed consistent with, if not complementary to, the arguments that emotions are essentially and necessarily directed toward objects. But for any view that takes judgments and beliefs in their customary understanding as articulated (or articulable) propositions, the indisputably real phenomenon of emotional conservation will present an insurmountable paradox when emotions are identified with beliefs or beliefs are unqualifiedly considered constituents of emotions: the conscious upholding of contrary or even contradictory beliefs.[7]

On any account of human agency, this is clearly unacceptable. Indeed, the suggestion that emotions are simply beliefs appears as unwarranted as any radical diremption of the two that ensues in an unbridgeable gap between our doxic and emotional lives. If that is the case, though, what should we see emotions as?

I believe that the most plausible answer lies in in a direction that construes emotions as organized patterns of attention and focus whose meaningful aspects do not lie in clear and fully articulated propositions but arise from a complex and tacitly held interpretive scheme that pervades *all* our experience (see Rorty 1980, de Sousa 1980, Calhoun 1984). In this view, it can still be maintained that emotions are specified by their objects, with the proviso that the latter are understood not as exhaustive descriptions but more as compressed denotations for something much larger that lies behind them. Likewise, emotions can be said to be judgments or beliefs in Kant's sense of constitutive judgments (or systems of such [Solomon 1976]), or like Kuhnian paradigms: synthetic experiential wholes in terms of which we see the world. To adopt de Sousa's (1980) excellent analogy, emotions set up the questions that articulated propositions are the answers to. Recalling now the discussion of the dispositional dimension of consciousness, there are obvious affinities with this construal. At the very least, we can appreciate that it is not abstract. Far from being just a useful theoretical construct, it turns out to reflect nothing less than a fundamental feature of consciousness. Indeed, emotions so construed seem to offer a better window on consciousness than its other modes.

To return once again to the concept of intentionality, what ensues in the wake of its original formulation by Husserl is tremendous gains in faithfulness to human experience as well as opening up vast and rich fields for investigating that experience, gains that are consequent to the passage from third-person or objectivist accounts to first-person descriptions. The consideration of the dispositional feature of consciousness further amplifies the idea that when it comes to emotions, this emphasis on subjectivity should be retained and even further consolidated if any sense is to be made of them. (It is still *my* consciousness that configures experience.)

But inherent in this emphasis is a danger of subjectivism, and the point can be made technically yet simply: intentionality as configuring directedness of consciousness is after all not a relation between one entity and another but a feature or property of *one* entity. The challenge thus posed is clear. The experience of individuals, the meanings, to which the first-person accounts of emotions refer must somehow be brought into the public realm.

3

THE "LINGUISTIC TURN": EXPERIENCE AND EXPRESSION

Our first move is to dispose of the widespread and deeply ingrained rationalist notion that imputes absolute truth value to introspection or the perception of our "inner" states. The implicit contrast here is with ordinary perception, which ever since Descartes's notorious examples in his *Meditations* we accept as easily subject to all sorts of error. But assuming that there is nothing like a mind-state that is not (simultaneously) grounded in a brain-state,[1] introspection is just as dependent on and conditioned by the physiological apparatus of our bodies, and so just as subject to deception, as the perception of the "outer" world. Linguistically, of course, we mark out the difference between the two forms of error as *illusions* and *delusions,* respectively. But both are clearly based on an appeal to some standard conditons of existence. Just as a color of something can be verified only in standard lighting conditions with our visual sense intact, so a psychological state is deemed authentic only if it occurs within what we take as normal physiological functioning. Hence our discounting of attributions of psychological experience when we are not sober, extremely tired, or in some other such state.

Of course, the range of factors influencing our mental states (with obvious consequences for our assessment of them) need not be limited, as Freud so brilliantly showed, to physiology. Certain developmentally significant experiences of early childhood can be linked in lawlike generalizations with subsequent emotions and fixations, so that it makes sense to think of the former as causing the latter. But this just amplifies the point that the purported absolute truth value inhering in the knowledge of our psychological states cannot be maintained on the grounds of an immediacy that does not in fact exist. However counterintuitive it appears (at least in our culture), and though it is not the case *normally*, in principle it is possible that others may know us better than we know ourselves. Indeed, this is assumed by most schools of psychotherapy, regardless of their particular orientation, although for some (e.g., metaphysical behaviorism), the assumption is obviously unrelated to anything like a mind or psychological states. Even if infrequently, we can be seriously mistaken or confused about what it is we feel (e.g., "Am I angry or hurt?") and/or about the actual causes of a particular emotion—especially that the latter, as opposed to the (intentional) objects, do not figure in those experiences. The notion that our minds are perfectly transparent to us and that knowledge of our mental states is incorrigible has more to do with a prejudicial understanding of what constitutes subjectivity, objectivity, and evidence than with anything that can be unequivocally confirmed by actual experience.

Now, in some respects this argument anticipates much that follows here since my strategy will be to undercut as much as possible the entire inner-outer distinction. Perhaps it is stated in unduly dualistic terms. But then, especially since Descartes's identification of subjectivity with self-enclosed thought, later amplified by Rousseau's "affective" introspectionism and continuing to the present, it has overwhelmingly been the view that emotions are something deeply private, known veridically only by the individual who experiences them, at once incommunicable and inaccessible to others. Thus in light of this prevailing opinion—and few of us can claim to have completely extricated ourselves from it—it seems appropriate to meet immediately and on their own ground some of the principal assumptions of the dualist stance that motivates that opinion. Of course, I have not yet shown that emotions are communicable. But since the arguments for incorrigibility and incommunicability really represent two sides of the same metaphysical view of mind, to see how the former arguments fail cannot but throw some light on why the latter also fail, though at this stage this link is admittedly not clear.

Among the key observations that Alfred Schutz (1962) makes in his analyses of the social world is that the traditional theories of mind underestimate the difficulties of self-perception while overestimating the problems of our apprehending the experiences of others. In their attempts to account for intersubjectivity, these theories appeal to convoluted inferential and analogical argumentation and the theory of empathy. All of them fail, however, either presupposing in their premises the "other" whose very existence they are attempting to prove or, unable to transcend their solipsistic starting assumptions, only elaborating a serial multiplicity of the same "I," but not a community of diverse subjects.

Schutz's arguments are essentially those stated much earlier by Max Scheler, who was among the first to propose that community life (the we-experience) precedes all individuated life, that self-consciousness is in fact both a late phylogenetic and a late ontogenetic development. (The former claim may be largely speculative and subject to dispute, the latter is amply confirmed by psychological studies in child development.) It matters little to us today that Scheler ultimately grounds the we-experience in an unacceptable metaphysical thesis of a common psychic stream. What is crucial is the way he subverts the starting assumption of the orthodox accounts of intersubjectivity—that thought or experience is some hermetically sealed entity to be inferred from external properties and movements—by positing an insoluble link between experience and expression. In the process he also radically alters the meaning of "internal perception."

On Scheler's account, the classical theories lock subjectivity in its own psychic prison because they fail to understand the role of the lived-body as a selector and analyst for the possible contents of *all* human experience and not merely sense perception. Thus such contents as those of our thoughts, emotions, or intentions never arise in some pristine immediacy. They emerge in consciousness only insofar as they posit some variation of our lived-bodies and more specifically only insofar as they discharge themselves in "intended movements or at least in expressive tendencies" (Scheler 1970, 246). So true is this, in fact, that if an expression of an emotion is blocked, this invariably tends to repress it simultaneously as an "internal" experience. On this view, there is no inexpressible experience. The latter option, as Don Ihde (1969) comments, points in the direction of some form of mysticism that terminates in silence, only to be invariably betrayed by the numerous ways of describing that silence. On the other hand, to insist on expression without meaning or experience logically culminates in mechanism, that is, in the nonintentionality of a machine—with the proviso that the latter's dimension as an extension of human creative intentionality and experience is wholly ignored and forgotten. For us, then, to experience something, to have a consciousness of it in the sense of being clear about what that something is, requires a *medium* of expression. At the same time and by definition, an intention underlies any expression. Experience and expression are constitutive of each other.

The revolutionary potential of this insight for conclusively undermining the specifically modern conceptions of subjectivity, experience, language, and expression has by now been amply detailed and demonstrated. (Which is not to deny the powerful, self-alienating hold of these conceptions on contemporary consciousness and the way they unfortunately play themselves out in natural, personal-social, and political domains.) Clearly, all of what the modern and Enlightenment thinkers took as comprising an inaccessible, private realm acquires on this view a necessarily external dimension, and in fact the whole inner-outer distinction (often also stated as that between subject and object), at least in any strong sense, begins to break down completely. This is not to suggest that this distinction can be definitively discarded but only that it can be sufficiently undercut so as to deny the entities to which its terms refer different metaphysical status. The terms are reflective of a bipolarity that exists within any experience as two divergent tendencies and not as absolute dichotomies (Schrag 1969, chap. 4). Thus it makes more sense to define internal perception (if one still wishes to maintain this terminology) in relation to its typical object—meaning, or perhaps, better, "the object as meant"—rather than in reference to the latter's putative spatial location.

To claim that expression is essential for experience is of course to deny the modern view that it is a bodily movement from which we somehow infer intent. Strictly speaking, a gesture or expression does not *indicate* a meaning; it is meaning in all of its diverse forms, that is embodied by and found *in* the expression, not separate from it. In this context, some ordinary expressions are indeed telling. As love "resides in the kiss and the embrace," so grief is "written across" an anguished face, and anger is manifest in the pounding fist or that sardonic remark. In recently popularized terms, the message here cannot be divorced from its medium, because the latter organizes (serves as an organ for) the former, and there is little point in attempting to decide whether the sense of these expressions is metaphorical or empirical. Perhaps the best way to state this is that they are metaphorically formulated empirical truths, empirical precisely because we live "through" them; they are descriptions of the form of our psychological life. To link expression to experience on the model of the (problematic) relation of sign and signified object is (in line with the ontology of thinghood, the spectator theory of knowledge and the words-as-instruments theory of language) to presuppose that experiences and their expressions have some kind of entitative status, that they are *things* of one sort or/and another (Schrag 1969, 72). This presupposition is simply illegitimate.

Scheler's insights into the nature of human expression and its link to experience went on to receive a much more detailed and exhaustive treatment by later phenomenologists, in particular by Merleau-

Ponty. They also resurface, albeit in a quite different form and on a different basis, in the later Wittgenstein's arguments against private ostensive definitions and insistence that the explication of meaning must ultimately end in a reference to forms of life. But Scheler was also heir to a long expressivist tradition the modern roots of which can be traced to the romantic reaction against the Enlightenment conceptions of meaning and language.

What unites the seventeenth-century nominalism of Hobbes and Locke and the latter attempts to give a naturalistic account of the origin of language (Condillac) is the assumption that the aim of a theory of knowledge is to provide descriptions that accurately and unambiguously *represent* the empirical world. (As Hobbes put it, "Truth consisteth in the right ordering of names in our affirmations" [Hobbes 1948, 21], leaving little doubt at the same time that he understood the criterion of this right ordering as some form of straightforward correspondence to the physical universe.) The motivation here is to overcome the projections or anthropomorphisms imputed to earlier semiological cosmologies that see the universe as a meaningful order and thus also to fall in line with the burgeoning viewpoint of natural science. In this context, words become useful *instruments* whose primary role is to connect concepts with things, so that what emerges from this linguistic instrumentalism is a highly designative view of meaning (Taylor 1985, 250). Words acquire meaning by virtue of standing for or signifying things, and a theory of meaning is an account of the process of framing representations, an account of designation.

Against this view, expressivist thinkers like Herder and von Humboldt protested that it presupposes just what it is attempting to prove and moreover that it unjustifiably degrades expression in general and the activity of speech in particular. They bracketed the claim that words are essentially signs whose primary function is referential and took note of linguistic consciousness itself—that is, that we have the capacity to employ words as signs to begin with and that this semantic function is precisely what needs to be explained and not assumed. In their perspective, language is no longer just an assemblage of signs but the medium and vehicle, a life-form, of consciousness itself. Thought is abandoned as the explanatory cradle that generates meaning through designation; in its stead, speech is seen as the primary activity within which any lexicon is constantly generated and modified. Here thought, desire, or feeling are not just mental givens but a reflection of a single life process whose differentiation into a multifaceted interiority is a matter of accomplishment and not simply a priori postulation. Thus, to experience something, to be able to *identify* its features, is essentially conditional upon our capacity for progressive articulation of that something through language (Taylor 1985, chap. 10).

To restate our previous (general) thesis, then, this time as it applies to the primary medium of human expression: language and experience are a paired phenomenon wherein language is constitutive of experience, and vice versa. In Don Ihde's creative formulation, the two are "the paired foci of the single ellipse of subjectivity" (Ihde 1969, 52). In this perspective, meaning arises not through designation or through language's relation to something else but *in* the expressive process itself. Expression makes something manifest to ourselves (and others) by embodying it; it is a *realization* of what one intends. That there is always a certain, indeed at times extreme degree of noncoincidence between our experience of something and our encompassing it in language does not by itself justify absolutizing this difference through an ontological diremption of the two. The fleeting thought still requires language to be anchored for a deeper consideration, and any experience "demands" its own minimal description, even if we can say no more about it than that it is "ineffable." Conversely, even for an expression whose richness or complexity initially overwhelms our understanding of it so that it must be explicated in terms of other mediating expressions, some grasp of its animating intention is essential for it to be recognized as an expression. (Of course, the thesis of mutual implication of language and experience in the constitution of each must be understood as obtaining given only a certain level of ontogenetic development. The existence in children of literally prelinguistic thought and preintellectual speech suggests that speech and thought have different roots, merging only at a certain moment of ontogenesis, after which they develop together under reciprocal influence [see Vygotsky 1986]. This latter view seems further supported by the fact that for adults, pathologies in one of these functions do not automatically signal disintegration in the other.)

We readily recognize in the above discussion of expressivism the central premise of the philosophy of reflection—that the life of the mind consists in a dialectical process of externalizing itself in objectivations or expressions and at the same time returning to itself in the reflection on these externalizations. Thus to know—at least in the primary understanding of knowing as entailing the use of concepts, which are absent in such other forms of knowledge as exercising a skill or "knowing how"—is inseparably bound up with the capacity to say. After a period of disregard, these Hegelian notions return toward the end of the nineteenth century in the context of Dilthey's focus on meaning as the proper object of human sciences. This in turn leads to

Heidegger's contemporary understanding of language wherein language becomes definitive of our humanity. For it is language that effects a clearing for, and a disclosure of, being. It "names" and differentiates, transforming our inchoate sense of being-in-the-world by bringing into focus, and thus making known or present for us, features of reality that were previously indistinguishable. In this fashion Heidegger's understanding of language (as well as Merleau-Ponty's later emphasis on *parole* as a condition of objectification) also recovers what the classics already knew: language and speech cannot be understood instrumentally (i.e., as finished products for our use) because they are in the first instance an existential projection of the self "into" the world, an organismic and developmental *activity* that engages us to the core. Indeed, the notion of the inseparability of thought or experience and discourse is reflected in the very fact that *logos* (from the Greek *legein,* "to say"), in addition to its meanings as "word," "thought," "knowledge," and "reasoned account," also referred to the words actually used in such an account (Taylor 1985, 217). The same insight is contained in Merleau-Ponty's declaration that "speech does not translate ready-made thought, *but accomplishes it*" (Merleau-Ponty 1962, 178), as in the biblical claim that "in the beginning was the Word." Apparently even God could not dispense with language as a medium of creative power through which he enacted his willed vision. The etymology of *person* points in a similar direction. Beyond the usual association with possessing reason, having roles, being a character—all specifically human capacities—what is foundational to these is our capacity for speech. For a person is in the first instance that being "through" (*per*) whom "speech" or "sound" (*sonus*) is introduced into the world.

But why this lengthy exegesis on experience-meaning and expression-language? In one sense, the effort is obvious since as covered by the general claim that experience and language are constitutive of each other, emotions too must be seen as strongly tied to language. And in fact if one looks at the development of contemporary philosophical and psychological theorizing about emotions, there has been a historical development toward a recognition of this fact. But the point about linking language and emotions cuts deeper than is apparent. For our understanding of emotions, I want to claim, in large measure must be "linguistic," but in the sense of being essentially tied to the understanding of the medium of language. And this is where so much contemporary theorizing, even if it accords language an important role, shows itself as woefully inadequate. But this requires some background explanation.

In this context, William James's neo-Cartesian position elaborated toward the end of nineteenth century serves as a most useful point of departure. Insisting that a concept of emotion without reference to physiological changes is inconceivable, James (1884) argued that emotions are essentially just perceptions of specifiable bodily feelings. Take away the quickened pulse and the involuntary visceral and muscular constrictions, and our fear of a menacing bear becomes merely a cool intellectual recognition of its presence. Hence fear *is* (our perception of) these physiological changes. To be sure, James drew a conclusion most of us find extreme, yet the commonsense observation that gave rise to it continues to inform powerfully a particular view of emotions that remains prevalent in our culture: whatever else an emotion may be, it is still primarily a bodily feeling.

Now, this view is open to a set of serious objections that stem principally from its neglect of intentionality, and I shall mention only what seems to me the most important one. The objection turns on the issue of differentiating emotions. For if the principal criterion of emotional experiencing is physiological disturbance, then the theory is unable to account for the entire spectrum of our emotional life. It necessarily discounts subtle and physiologically "quiet" emotions such as aesthetic enjoyment, but more important, it is also unable to differentiate emotions from nonemotions and from one another. On James's premises, the feeling consequent to meeting a menacing bear is entirely equivalent to a physiologically identical feeling that may have been drug-induced or caused by a disease; without reference to anything else (e.g., behavior, cognition), both must be considered emotions and on equal footing. (Here the question of what remains of an emotion if one abstracts from attendant physiological disturbances is turned around. To take fear, for example, what remains of it without a perception-evaluation of danger? In the absence of the latter, rapid breathing and increased pulse rate can just as easily be interpreted as a symptom of illness.)

Not surprisingly, then, James remains unspecific about how events and objects in the environment produce the physiological disturbances he calls emotions, and he is even more vague about how we can identify and distinguish among different emotions just on the basis of the physiological changes associated with them. And this is the focal point of Walter Cannon's (1971) important critique of James's theory. In a series of experiments, Cannon showed that even if visceral changes always accompany emotions, the *same* visceral changes occur in very *different* emotional states and in nonemotional states. Thus they cannot be a good basis for differentiating emotions. Moreover, Cannon suggested that the visceral processes are not a strong source of sensation to begin with, so that even with distinct changes in visceral structures, it is unlikely that such changes would always be reflected in emotions.

Despite major flaws and powerful counterarguments, the Jamesian thesis has continued to exert significant influence, in large measure no doubt because its primary emphasis on physiology renders emotions amenable to objective quantiative measurement, methodologically so attractive for experimentally oriented psychologies. Consequently much effort has been expended in the attempt *not* to reject its basic orientation. We can see this if we move further along the spectrum in the direction initiated by Cannon, whose conclusions can be seen as the starting point for Stanley Schachter and Jerome Singer. In the early 1960s, this pair of Harvard psychologists conducted what remain (especially for academic psychology and sociology but less so for philosophy and anthropology) among the most influential and best-known psychophysiological experiments concerning emotions. The latter were intended to provide an empirical basis for a more "cognitive" theory with which Schachter and Singer wished to supplement James's thesis. The experiments involved administering subjects injections of adrenalin, then providing different subjects with different social scenarios. The key finding of this procedure was that although they experienced strong physiological changes, the subjects did not consider themselves in a specific emotional state until they were provided with "suitable cognitions." Only in "dangerous" circumstances was fear aroused; only in an "offensive" situation did subjects report feeling angry. What Schachter and Singer concluded from this was that an emotion may be a bodily state of arousal but that there must be other features present if we are to account for the diversity of emotions and our recognition of that diversity (Schachter and Singer 1962).

Thus emerges a two-component view of emotion. There is still the Jamesian physiological arousal, but it is now coupled with a cognitive ingredient that according to the two psychologists consists of "labeling" or naming these feelings in accordance with cognitions attending the situation. As for how we know which label to attach to a feeling, given a number of possible attendant cognitions, it is suggested that our physiological arousal upon perceiving, for example, a figure with a gun in a dark alley is labeled fear because the arousal is interpreted through one's knowledge about dark alleys and guns.

At first glance, this story appears plausible and attractive, accommodating the popular understanding of emotions as private inner events while addressing, seemingly head-on, the emotion-differentiation issue that so radically undermines James's thesis. But even if one accepts that it is a cognitive factor that sets emotions apart, as Schachter and Singer argue, their account of how this comes about is wholly implausible. For upon encountering a figure with a gun in a dark alley, one could just as well be excited from a sense of adventure. In short, how can these circumstances be interpreted as "dangerous," as the proper context of fear, unless they are *lived* (or have been in the past) as "fearful"? That is, unless there is an a priori reference to the emotion as constitutive of the (original) experience of encountering someone in the alley, the only constraints placed on the "labeling" of the consequent physical arousal are our imagination and creativity. The feeling-label connection remains contingent.

To be sure, here language plays a crucial role, as the whole notion of labeling intimates, and this is certainly a move in the right direction. But the picture remains Jamesian. It was Sartre (1948) who railed against all such accounts of emotions for making them nothing but epiphenomena (rather than structures) of consciousness and for deemphasizing the role of consciousness in general. And the situation with Schachter and Singer is not much better. For analogous to Sartre's point, which centers around neglect of intentionality and placing emotions "out" of consciousness, whatever an emotion is, here it is still a (bodily) feeling extraneous to the expressive realm in general and the linguistic sphere in particular; the latter limps behind as a provider of concepts and labels. As residual dualists, Schachter and Singer also end up with an illegitimate breakup of emotion as a unitary experience.

We can see why. For corresponding to the strong interest in physiological changes there is a thoroughgoing designationist-instrumentalist picture of language in their scheme, the two features working in tandem, and this is what accounts for the powerful and widespread influence of that scheme and what, given the untenability of the underlying premise about language, dooms it. Yet how exactly do the features referred to work in tandem? And for what reasons, other than the crucial and already mentioned contingency of the feeling-label relation, is this a failure? The answer puts in clear relief why something like the expressivist position on language, where language is constitutive of emotions in a strong sense, must be upheld when we theorize about them.

It is significant and not by accident that in most dualist-type accounts, especially those inspired by empiricism, such physiologically involved personal states as anger or fear are frequently taken as paradigmatic emotions. Fear in particular is favored because it is often occasioned by a situation that seemingly involves no interpretation.

Most feelings of impending bodily harm appear to be of this nature; no redescription of the intentional object is likely to alter significantly our sense of danger and potential harm. So precisely because of this disinvolvement of subjectivity in the constitution of its object, fear becomes for us a brute datum, an independent and objective entity not all that different (on the empiricist reading) from a perceptual object. But if that indeed is its status, there is no further problem. For we have found a fit candidate to be pointed at and designated by language, which in turn explains for the empiricist how we come to possess *fear* as an everyday empirical concept. Understanding the latter process renders intelligible how objectivism and linguistic instrumentalism complement each other.

Of course, the expressivist could object, invoking the thesis of the general constitutive function of language in experience, that even for brute fears a minimal articulation is presupposed delineating the properties that make an object menacing and so enables us to recognize it from among others. Still, those fears are so much like reflex reactions that it is tempting to think the objection could be overcome via a stimulus-response type of model wherein we instinctively "know" something to be dangerous or harmful and are just "wired" to respond in a certain way, that is, to have a specific feeling.

But even if we concede this (in any event doubtful) possibility for the physically harmful, a reductive account of this sort is wholly untenable for the entire range of mental postures that can be called—just because the concerns and purposes that underlie them are unstatable in physicalist-objectivist, third-person terms—the specifically human emotions: pride, hope, shame, charity, respect, envy, resentment. That is, once we move beyond the realm of those values that are relevant for us primarily in virtue of our being living organisms, it becomes impossible to ignore the involvement of subjectivity in the constitution of objects of emotions of this range. The latter are inextricably bound to and depend in a strong sense on our sense of worth as persons. But this sense is just what constitutes our insertion within a *moral* community, and language enters the picture because it is *the* medium that enables us to make discriminations (of value) that are foundational to such a community. It is difficult, if not impossible, to conceive how we could concretely experience something like "justice" or "freedom" in an evaluative and not merely inclinational way— that is, as matters that inherently involve a recognition and application of standards—unless the complex range of social practices, actions, and ends invoked in their name is intersubjectively articulated and differentiated.

Language is thus absolutely essential for experiencing the specifically human emotions. In contrast to the physically harmful, the descriptions we offer here are radical determinants of the objective sense of the situation we find ourselves in and the stances we adopt. But then our deep implication in sustaining or altering that sense prohibits thinking of language in this context along designationist lines. The requisite independence of the object from the description just does not exist. Using Frege's terminology, we could say that what the referent turns out to be is dependent on the sense in which it is expressed—that is, the mode in which it is presented. So the reading of language here must be expressivist, indeed doubly so. For it is not only that language brings a situation or an object into focus, enabling one to experience them in an explicit way, it is also the descriptions we offer of *ourselves,* our self-understandings, that are constitutive of the very nature of the emotions in question. The latter turn out to be through and through "ideological," each infused with a set of mutually implicating assumptions and expectations about the world and oneself as well as the relatedness of one to the other.

It cannot be understated, I think how important the view adumbrated above is for a concern with emotions. The implications are vital and many, and I will attempt to point out only what seem the most important ones. First, though, I would like to make more explicit some points of connection with the substantive issues raised in the last chapter.

In a quite general way, it is clear that many of the issues raised through a concern with language run parallel to those that surfaced in the discussion of consciousness and intentionality, and in fact the exegesis on expression and language is basically a further elaboration of the conditions of intentionality in general and those of its forms that I have referred to as the specifically human emotions in particular. Thus the latter, to be experienced at all, require articulated descriptions and distinctions, and these in turn (and contrary to a possibility left open by linguistic instrumentalism) cannot be arbitrary. This particular requirement is obviously an extension of, and is underlied by, the notion of intentionality as an essential or formal relatedness of consciousness to (its) various objects.

But the link between an expressivist conception of language and intentionality can be seen at a still more general level, in the following way. If, as the expressivist suggests, language is an activity or form of behavior through which meaning arises, this dovetails neatly with the phenomenological view that learning empirical concepts, including obviously those of emotions, is a matter of explicating a unity of significance through learning new behavior or acquiring a new capacity such as the use of words. In other words, considering language as part of a continuum of *gestures* (i.e., a modality of action), as for example Merleau-Ponty (1962) does, makes of it an instance (to be sure a special one) of the important general thesis explicated in the last chapter, that of behavioral know-how as constitutive of and implicitly dwelling in meaning.

A further point of convergence with earlier discussions concerns the methodological necessity of using an interpretive approach in studying emotions. I had proposed that emotions are those mental modalities that thematize involvement in the world through a sense of partiality vis-à-vis objects and that for a number of reasons relating to their phenomenal features it is best to describe these modalities as patterns of attention rather than articulated judgments or propositions. The "object" of an emotion was then considered a sort of shorthand description or focal point that nevertheless could never exhaustively capture the lived experience within which it was embedded, and this in turn is what requires our turn to an interpretive approach. The "same" public object can be a focal point of many possible configurations of experiencing. But this is just the conclusion urged on us by the expressivist view that our emotions acquire form through our attempts to articulate the sense of the situation that moves us. For the linguistic bringing into focus of a sense is something that can be done more or less adequately—it can distort or provide greater insight—even though it lacks the univocal criteria of success provided by the designationist pointing toward an independent and objective entity. But then, just because there are no such criteria, articulation turns out to be an essentially interpretive activity; it makes something initially unclear intelligible yet open to revision and further articulation because the process of "making sense" is not perfectly transparent to us. In short, interpretation strongly invites—one is tempted to say entails—reinterpretation (Taylor 1985, chap. 2). Thus Nietzsche's dictum to the effect that there are no facts, only interpretations.

I now turn to the implications for thinking about emotions that follow more strictly from the discussions of the present chapter. Perhaps the most important—because it extricates emotions from their traditional domain in the solitary individual and sets up the possibility of placing them within sociocultural and historical *contexts*—relates to the expressivist emphasis on speech. For this emphasis means that conversation (as opposed to the written word) is to be considered in some sense primary, and this is but another way of saying that language founds public space; it transforms something that is initially a private matter into something that is for (or before) *us*. Expressions manifest our emotions and put us in the presence of the emotions of others. Through the link to a common medium of expression, emotions thus become in a very general and perfectly understandable sense public phenomena. Indeed, the constitutive function of expression is precisely what allows one to suggest that for any given community there must be essential or logical connections between particular emotions and corresponding expressions. Without some such intersubjectivly shared "grammar," our knowing what others feel as well as feigning and deception become incomprehensible. To be sure, we can hide our emotions, remain expressionless. But this is a matter of effort and learning that from a developmental perspective is clearly a late arrival, not an initial given.

But any potential "logic" of emotions is not restricted to regulating just the above-mentioned possibilities. Rather, the links to language and ultimately a moral order suggest that we can assess emotions for their appropriateness in light of a vision of the world that inheres in the collective imagination of a community or culture. We can thus speak of the "truth" of emotions not in the sense that they adequately reflect some independent reality but that they cohere with life itself. From this angle, we can also appreciate Iris Murdoch's (1970) insistence that literature ought to belong to the most essential and fundamental activities of human culture. It is an education in how to picture and understand human situations, an uncovering of a "truth to life" (see McCormick 1985, Scruton 1980). It implies that "an emotion . . . which everyone can now perceive in himself must once have been wrested by some 'poet' from the fearful inarticulacy of our inner life for this clear perception of it to be possible" (Scheler 1970, 253). In creating new and richer forms of expression, an author extends the scope of our possible self-awareness. He or she opens up our apprehension of the world by breaking through to experiences and objects that have hitherto been obscured by rules and conventions embedded in everyday usage of language.

We have arrived here at a most radical consideration put on the agenda by expressivism, namely, that the development of new modes of expression permits us to have new emotions that by virtue of an added reflective dimension have greater depth, subtlety, and power. As Taylor puts it, "The language user can feel not only anger but indignation, not only love but admiration" (1985, 233). Through speech, the language our emotions are embedded in is continually recreated, altered, reshaped; there is a generation of meanings that are genuinely new even if they are never autonomous in the sense that they must, however minimally, draw on the rest of language or a given term's previous usage. (At the same time, it must be understood that the very factors that drive this creative dynamic of emotion institution preclude the idea that a "logic" or "truth" in this domain is an absolute. For the latter are elicited from the lives of, and negotiated among, concrete historical individuals, none of whom ever share completely the same environment, genetic makeup, potentialities for action, or self-interpretations. The expressive transformation in the activity of language require taking a full account of the *actors* behind them.)

The development or acquisition of emotions, then, is not simply a matter of labeling inner states or genetically based threshold sensitivities, as "getting in touch" with our emotions is not a process of discovery. They are creative acts. In fact, the idea of learning an emotion is ultimately unintelligible on the designationist view of language (there is nothing to learn, it's all within us), as is another major corollary of expressivism—that different individuals and different cultures may have radically different emotional repertoires. For this corollary runs directly against the psychologistic model of emotions as internal episodes without any constitutive connections to ascriptions or behavior, hence without context and independent of social convention. Are we not all, the standard prejudice somewhat schizophrenically runs, basically the same, even if experience is subjective and only privately accessible to the individual who has it? What about "basic" or "universal" emotions?

Now admittedly, the notion of basic emotions is difficult to give up, so absorbed are we by the traditional view. We just take it for granted that somehow what we feel in anger, fear, or love must be pretty much what a Japanese or a Hindu feels in these states, that indeed there is a set of specific "feels" that are definitive of the experience of these emotions. This idea appears plausible since after all, the anatomical requirements for smiling, crying, eye-widening, adopting defensive or threatening postures, involve specific muscle systems, physiological pathways, and somatic tensions distributed in definite ways. Thus the phenomenal quality of an emotion is certainly (at least in part) determined by the physical requirements for its *typical* expression (Harré 1984, 124). But then we learn that when "angry," a Japanese smiles, the Westerner pounds his fist or stomps his foot, and the Utka Eskimo does not even have "anger" as a descriptive category; he or she just doesn't get angry in any sense familiar to us (Briggs 1970). In short, once we move beyond certain reflex responses relevant for us as living organisms (e.g., eye blinks, the startle pattern, covering one's head with hands) into the realm of language, interpretation, and social convention, there are no universal expressions but only ones typical of a given culture.[2] And this amounts to saying that the cross-culturally encountered differences of behavior and expression can be plausibly seen as reflecting differences in the experience of emotions themselves.

At the very least, we should insist that any claims to universality must be established empirically and not legislated beforehand. There are no "natural signs" or "natural feels" because the anatomical organization of our bodies produces no correspondence between specific gesture and given "states of mind" (Merleau-Ponty 1962, 189–90). (Of course, members of the *same* culture, having acquired a given emotion within similar action contexts will likely experience the same "feelings" [though how can this be verified?], and we may surmise this to be particularly true of those cultures that like the Maori, use specific anatomical ascriptions rather than reasons, "objects," "causes," or strictly psychological categories to identify their emotions; for example, "My liver is tiny" in place of "I am sad" [Harré 1984, 125–26].)

Finally, it is clearly the case that the emotional repertoires of different cultures vary enormously, the absence among the Utkas of what we would certainly regard as a universal emotion being a case in point. It is also evident, as the demise and emergence of different emotion categories suggests, that an emotional repertoire of the same culture may undergo alteration. To mention just two examples: for us, romantic love is an emergent emotion, but accidie, with the demise of its sustaining medieval moral-religious context, has become obsolete. As for emotional diversity, as a general rule, it can be said that the more extensive the vocabulary a culture possesses, the richer, more varied, and differentiated will be the emotional life of its members.

The stated concern of the current discussion has been to evade a subjectivism of emotions and to bring them into the public, intersubjective domain. I have attempted to do so by invoking some themes in the phenomenology of the lived-body and by linking emotions to language. I suggested in turn that the latter must be given what was called an expressivist reading. This seems to be the necessary though often neglected premise behind claims that emotions are (at least in part) socially constructed and informed by culture-specific "feeling rules" (see Harré 1986, Hochschild 1979). Wittgensteinians might insist that I am addressing a pseudoproblem since for them, mental predicates are from the beginning assumed to be cashable only in terms of the social conventions and practices in which they function. But having started out from the phenomenological perspective, thereby commiting myself to the relevance of the first-person standpoint and the internal features of mental states for the explication of meaning, something like the present exegesis seems to have been necessary. Without abandoning my phenomenological roots, then, I hope to have said enough about how something like "feeling rules" for "private" experiences is possible to begin with. From this general position, I want now to go on to examine the more specific ways in which emotions are acquired as well as embedded in and structured by language.

4

EMOTIONS AND LANGUAGE: THE FORMATION OF EMOTIONAL SENSE

✦

Of the several methodologically different approaches to emotion in Aristotle, the one of greatest interest for our present purposes is found in the *Rhetoric*. In contrast to the biologically inspired metaphysics of psychological states in *De Anima* or the evaluative context of his *Ethics,* in the *Rhetoric* Aristotle gives us a definition-grounding descriptive account that also examines the emotions' etiology in terms of the several component *meanings* that constitute them. Among the diverse "passions," anger is assigned a most prominent place and correspondingly receives a very sophisticated analysis.

Anger, Aristotle tells us, is "a distressed desire for conspicuous vengeance in return for a conspicuous and unjustifiable contempt of one's person or friends" (Calhoun and Solomon 1984, 44). Further, on the appetitive side, we may derive pleasure from contemplating or carrying out the revenge. And listing some important circumstances that may bear on the intensity of one's anger, Aristotle mentions that it is likely to vary in accordance with the status of the individuals involved. Significantly, this group comprises both the direct participants in and the observers of the situation constituting the offense. Thus we are likely to be more angered by an insult from a subordinate than from a superior, and we shall suffer especially perhaps if this occurs in the presence of other subordinates. On the other hand, indifference to the offender or the witnesses will tend to mitigate or minimize our anger.[1]

This description clearly acknowledges the emotions' experientially felt (bodily) dimension. More importantly, however, it emphasizes that norms and beliefs that pertain essentially to the *moral* order within which individuals are inserted—beliefs about general welfare, wrongness of contempt and maintenance of worth, status, wealth, and power; assessments of character—are constitutive of emotions themselves. Anger, and by implication other emotions, Aristotle suggests, is a *contextual* phenomenon; it is not merely a sudden release of some repressed psychic quantity or an intrusive force from our biological depths but above all a moral reproach and a response to a transgression.[2] Anger and other emotions arise essentially within a social and political framework; the requisite shared norms and common understandings preclude rendering an account of emotions in purely infrapsychological terms.[3]

The intent behind this brief outline of the Aristotelian thesis is threefold. First, it urges on us the necessity of accounting for emotions in terms pertaining to the moral orders within which they are experienced. Second, the outline is meant to amplify one of the principal contentions of the last chapter—the critical role the social medium of language plays in our experiencing emotions. That role is tacitly assumed in the sense that it is simply very difficult (and perhaps even impossible) to conceive how in the absence of language the various "distinctions of worth" and shared understandings Aristotle alludes to as requisite for "anger" could be effected. Moreover, if this irreducibly social and cultural aspect holds for such an ostensibly basic emotion as anger, it surely does equally (if not even more) for the complex phenomena of pride, shame, charity, or hope. Finally, the Aristotelian account forces on the agenda a latent developmental question. For intuitively we feel, and most of us would surely want to insist, that infants and small children experience emotions. They certainly behave "emotionally"! Yet their relatively undifferentiated expressive repertoires and lack of linguistic skills to make the requisite experience-constitutive distinctions would seem to necessitate a denial, or at least a qualification, of this piece of conventional wisdom. Whatever anger may be for a small human being, it cannot be the full-fledged experience defined by Aristotle. What we thus need is some description of early affective life and an indication of how we get from there to the level presupposed by Aristotle's analysis. I shall begin with this last point and work my way back to the other two.

Contrary to both popular belief and what appears to the untrained eye, the behavior of an infant is not a random or unpatterned sequence of events. Rather, it is highly structured to serve functionally appropriate biological ends. The structure reveals itself as a chain of extremely brief but quite distinct episodes, in practice taking the form of potential *gestures* that in spite of their brief duration, are nevertheless very highly organized as sequences of coordinated actions (Newson 1979, 209). Now, it is this structure that the primary caregivers (usually mothers) map onto insofar as they interpret an infant's reactions by a process of what Newson so appropriately calls "adultomorphism." That is, the baby is assumed to possess from birth definite "wishes," "intentions," and "feelings," both communicable and demanding of respect, and whose interpretation stands to be confirmed or corrected by the baby's subsequent response when these states are initially acted upon to accommodate it (211–12).

From this stage on, a continuous and very subtle interactive process of mutual adjustments develops wherein, however, it is the caregiver who supplements the psychological attributes of the infant by providing the meaning structure for its acts, accordingly influencing or even inducing them. Thus, presenting attractive objects will typically elicit a reach, and certain sounds or gestures may be repetitively "modeled" for the child until he or she imitates them (Kaye 1982, 193). Just this seems to happen, for instance, when eye contact is established with an infant and the adult replies to a perceived smile with a smile and says "hello," thus teaching that baby the practical meaning of looking at other people, that is, "the ways that personal recognition is expressed and what happens when the other person 'takes it up' " (Shotter 1976, 27). Or, should a mother decide that her baby is on a particular occasion "curious," she can promote that mode by simply noting the direction of the child's look. She thereby makes and maintains something to be a visual object for the child for a longer period and thus also influences the temporal structure of the activity (27).

At this stage, none of the child's recognizable "intentions" are in any meaningful sense either autonomous or strictly private. Rather, in being cogenerated, they are very much shared intentions.[4] And it is only gradually that the caregiver's supplemental and reinforcing actions and the onset of language lead experience to a fully differentiated and self-indexed form and the child advances beyond being a mere "apprentice" who has little idea of the overall point of his or her activity. A person, an intentional agent, emerges as a consequence of being treated as a person. Experience has now been broken up into more definite temporal intervals with defined beginning and end points and with recognizable *motor anticipations.* The latter point in particular seems critical. For it is these anticipations that largely underlie the sense of engagement that is the enabling condition for the temporally (re)organized sequences of events to have emotional meanings integrated with them.

It is against this broader underlying picture of early development in which psychological attributes, and in particular intentionality (in a dual sense of intentions as well as defined object-directed experiencing), emerge through the dyadically structured process of psychological symbiosis described above that a specific instance of it can now be best addressed. I have in mind the acquisition of emotions through the medium of "paradigm scenarios." Originally formulated by Ronald de Sousa (1980), the latter theoretical construct has gained increasing currency in recent writings on emotions. It is especially useful to those concerned to show the roots of emotions in socialization processes, at the same time not being prejudicial for the more conventional psychological approaches that focus on intrapersonal dynamics. Briefly, the claim is that we originally acquire our emotions in prototypical *interactional* situations wherein (at least for our first emotions) the sense of our primitive engagement with the environment as experienced in instinctual and reflex-type responses is given a differentiated form and meaning, an identity, through our receiving early in life a *name* for it. To stay with anger as an example, we learn to recognize it as a distinct experience when a basic response to a situation such as aggression has been taken up by others and identified for us (according to mutually shared conventional understandings prevalent in our culture) as an expression of that emotion. But these basic suggestions demand further elaboration to appreciate their more important implications.

First, the situations in question are prototypical or paradigmatic, in a dual sense: descriptive and prescriptive. On one hand, they are prototypical in the strict sense of being the developmentally original occasions in terms of which certain constitutive features of an emotion are learned and subsequent experiences of a similar sort are configured and (re)identified by the individual. This does not mean that such occasions are necessarily confined to early childhood. Though the latter is clearly the life stage in which much and perhaps most of our emotional repertoire is acquired and therefore also the developmental period to which these notions are most applicable, emotions are *emergent* phenomena whose onset cannot in principle be restricted to it. Also, in addition to requiring linguistic skills, emotions presuppose different levels of psychological and biological maturation. Admittedly, the notion that childhood is a separate phase of the life cycle with specific needs and desires, and that children have different modes of reasoning and reduced capacities for moral judgments than adults, is an idea of great historical and cultural variability. Thus we have to be careful about the periodization of development that may inform potential inquiries whether there are some emotions into which we are commonly or perhaps even universally socialized. But this much can be uncontroversially said: as no "moral" responses are possible before a child has acquired a sense of integrity of objects (it is roughly at the age of one and a half that he or she first becomes puzzled at a dismembered doll, sensing that it is not as it *ought* to be), so the development of certain sexually grounded emotions comes later and sophisticated aesthetic discernment later still. Here the general heuristic is that these later emotions, as conceptually more sophisticated, will be progressively more thought-dependent.

Correspondingly, then, there are a multiplicity and range of linguistically structured situations informed by conventional understanding of personal development that can be plausibly considered paradigmatic for learning different emotions and (or even) for learning differences within the same emotion type. Indeed, it would be difficult to conceive how typical attitudes constitutive, for example, of various stages of love in our culture (play and possessiveness for childhood; fantasy, sexuality, and intensity for adolescence; responsibility and commitment for mature adulthood) could be acquired all at once. To be sure, there are strong overlaps between adult and childhood emotionality—in the case of love, principally the underlying desire for togetherness; but there are also sufficiently great differences that suggest it might be more profitable to treat these various "family-resembling" modes of love and their genesis as (at least analytically) separate. Besides, even if age-related emotion ascriptions turn out to be wholly historically specific social constructs, this does not mean that such specifications can play no role in self-experience and individual psychological development. On the contrary, insofar as they arise from and invoke a background of varying moral assessments bearing on the individual's sense of worth and responsibility, such ascriptions must be critical to that development.

The repeated reference to culturally shared and conventional understandings as that which informs the prototypical emotion-learning situations leads in turn to a consideration of their normative aspect. For clearly the "normality" of the original response, which is what allows it to be typified as an (intention-backed) expression of a particular emotion, is a *relational* property. It is assessed with reference to an object that is considered a plausible and characteristic candidate for eliciting that particular response and in the absence of which we are likely to question the legitimacy of the emotion, perhaps looking for abnormalities in its formation or even denying its existence altogether.[5] This is not so evident in our dealings with newborns and small infants, where we accept that just about any stimulus can bring on a range of different and even opposite reactions. But we begin to badger our young citizens fairly early in life into expressing (and consequently experiencing) appropriate feelings for particular objects, at particular times, at a particular age: "You're not afraid of *that!*" "That's not something to be angry about," "Boys don't cry," "You're (not) *really* sad (happy, curious), are(n't) you (?)." These are among the least subtle, and but a tiny sample, of the huge stock of expressions whose seeming absence of direct perlocutionary intent is belied by their potential for informing character and emotions. Moreover, all this comes in addition to the influence of our own strictly behavioral reactions in situations where we are copresent, reactions the infant is often likely to take up and imitate. This tacit behavioral influence must also be included under the normative aspects—what we *ought* to experience as a response—of the prototypical emotion-learning situation.

But perhaps more significant considerations accrue to the characterizing of emotion-learning situations as "scenarios." The value of this idea, especially given our traditional dualist predilections to prize "meaning" and "feeling" apart, lies precisely in its capturing the fact that what gets identified in emotion formation is emphatically neither a simple feeling nor an abstract proposition about the world but a *form of activity,* a sense of engagement with that world. And the receiving of a name for that sense is not a passive acceptance of a conventional term but more like an intention-animated entering, or a coming to inhabit, a certain description. As de Sousa insists, it is only in the context of a scenario that a reflexive response can become incorporated into an emotion as the latter's expression (1980, 285–86), which is also to say that emotions have essentially a temporal and dramatic structure. The scenario is a behavioral gestalt composed (among other things, but most importantly) of actual and potential intentions to *act,* which even at the rudimentary levels can be seen as a sort of prototypical social drama. Its plot at once defines the agent's role, feelings, and reactions characteristic of the emotion as just that way of existing—as just that way, to put it in the idiom of intentionality, of being directed to something in the world.

Here we can see clearly that any concomitant emotional "feelings" will not be ontologically independent of the physical and verbal actions through which the emotion is expressed, since they are in fact constituted by the latter (Armon-Jones 1985, 2). (This picture of emotions, incidentally, is very much in line with the Wittgensteinian claims that emotion concepts, and mental predicates in general, cannot be learned by ostensive reference to some internally introspected private states whose expressions are allegedly forms of self-reports. Physiological feelings as potentially specifiable quasi-independent "entities," while typically present, especially when we focus on the bodily aspects of an emotion, remain something that essentially plays no part in the process of learning emotion concepts.) We also gain an appreciably better understanding of the contention that it is impossible to experience, and nonsensical to claim to have, an emotion (e.g., guilt) for only a brief instant. Abandoning any such episodic view of emotion, we can, in light of emotions' dramatic character, suggest something radically opposite—that in principle there is no limit to the duration of an emotion, while a full explication of its range in a given life may require nothing short of writing a sizable novel.

I have been mainly concentrating on the early stages of emotional development where the dramatic content of emotions is necessarily restricted by underdeveloped motor and perceptual skills, limited linguistic and conceptual complexity, and the simple lack of cumulative life experience. We should now perhaps more accurately say, in refinement of the conventional intuitions about infant emotionality that got us onto the developmental exegesis in the first place, that infants really experience quasi emotions or protoemotions, emotions that are typically truncated because they have a limited temporal horizon (in both future and past dimensions). Hence they will often appear to be lived all-at-once, occurring at random and without reason, and precisely for that reason will be considered, on popular views, as paradigms of emotionality. Needless to say, infants' capacities for normatively appropriate responses to a broader range of situations, given limited learning, will also be restricted.

The situation rapidly changes as we are presented with more detailed scenarios that build on and amplify, but also modulate and transcend, those first and most immediately lived learning situations. The unmediated experiential sense progressively gains parameters and structure through associations of images, verbal "icons," simple stories, fairy tales, and myths. It becomes richer still and more refined through art and more complex narratives. Not everywhere is this process uniform; there are vast differences among cultures in schemes of value, literacy, communicative practices, and the practical means through which learning occurs and information is disseminated. For example, the capacity of a medium like television to highlight and emphasize (i.e., *real*-ize) content, its storytelling mode, and its limitless range of contexts that can be explored combine to exert an enormously powerful influence in emotional learning, in reinforcing standard attitudes but also in examining uncommon emotional experiences. This is so especially when exposure is prolonged and comes very early in life, as happens for so many of our children (see Dorr 1985).

How something gets articulated, highlighted, and thus incorporated into a sense of engagement will surely vary then across cultures. This is not incompatible with expecting something like a family resemblance among emotions, just because what we take as pride, shame, fear, or anger embody schemes of value without which, in ordinary circumstances, societies could not exist as moral orders—could not, that is, exist as *societies* in any meaningful sense of that term. But if we reject an all too quick universalizing of any emotion on grounds of common biological inheritance and affirm that the concrete social setting embodied in learning scenarios is a constituent of what it is to experience an emotion, and if we assume a certain holism about our mental life so that the meaning and lived qualities of any emotion cannot be prized apart from its "geographical" location (i.e., the way it is demarcated from and related to other emotions as well as other dimensions of life), this suggests that emotions are experientially far more idiosyncratic than has generally been conceded. Thus, arguably, the cross-culturally encountered differences of beliefs, expression, and behavior plausibly amount to differences in emotions themselves. Even the guarded form of universalism as expressed by the "family-resemblance" formulation will require tighter definitions along with detailed empirical data to escape the charge of being merely conceptual and thus vacuous.[6] The key here, which the notion of learning through scenarios brings to light, is that even if people everywhere shared formally identical beliefs, their emotional lives would differ precisely because the content of their emotions is not reducible to (mere) propositions.[7]

Taking the above considerations together, I think they suffice to intimate that ultimately the account of transformations of experiential sense into emotions will need to be embedded not just in a full-blown theory of motivation but will also require a comprehension of societal evolution. The problems here are enormous because of the scope of the investigations to be pursued and how to integrate them, but also because the scientific status of some of our most important theories of motivation, such as those of Freud, is itself in question. The debate has just not been settled about the ambiguity of whether they are essentially "empirical" or "interpretive," or more precisely, if they are "interpretive," in what terms their results should be assessed to be "empirical." A related aspect of this issue is our increasing sensitivity to any theory's practical assumptions and consequences as well as the role of rhetoric in its development and acceptance. This is why it has become not unusual to ask whether a Freud or a Piaget presents us with no more than historically specific social-political manifestos.

It is beyond my current knowledge to even begin to address these complexities, so I shall turn to a more modest endeavor. Its starting point is our having arrived at the stage of our sense of engagement as turning into an incipient emotion through an embeddedness in a linguistically informed action context, or scenario. Putting this foundational idea in more commonsense terms, the basic claim here is that to learn and experience an emotion is essentially to live out a certain story. It is also part of my claim that that story will be predominantly, if not essentially, metaphorical in nature.

Now, I take the move to consider emotions narratively to be sufficiently backed up jointly by the already-defended expressivist conception of language as constitutive of experience and by the dramatic character of emotions as conveyed through the notion of scenarios. The move is also in line with a growing sentiment in the human sciences wherein narrative is seen as a basic structural feature of the very fact of having an experience or performing an action (for a review, see Polkinghorne 1988). And although such significant narrativist approaches as those of David Carr (1986) and Paul Ricoeur (1984) gain their principal and immediate inspiration from the structural similarities between narrative and the temporal dimension of consciousness and lived experience as described by Husserl and Heidegger respectively, their views also presuppose, and ultimately rest on, something like the expressivist notion of language.

As for the metaphoricity of emotion-forming stories, this claim also requires some defense. For it has been customary, especially in positivist circles, to denigrate metaphor as a frivolous and inessential "figure of speech" that lacks genuine meaning by virtue of its incapacities to connect with facts and transmit knowledge (Cohen 1979). Or, if it does have meaning, this is thought reducible to some set of literal propositions from which metaphorical meanings are derivative in the first place. Without going into details of the historical vicissitudes of metaphor, it suffices to say that this view has been seriously undermined by the growing collapse of objectivism (see Bernstein 1983). The latter's notion of truth and reference, as well as the concomitant designationist assumptions about language and the consequent alternatives dichotomously on offer, have simply become untenable. We have no absolute or univocal descriptions of reality on the one hand, yet we must assume to be somehow anchored in that reality on the other. Thus it becomes false to think that language must be either transparent, not impeding direct contact with reality (there is no such contact, so language cannot be a true "picture" of it), or principally a distorting screen that projects experience out of its own categories and prevents us from getting in touch with what is real (were that the case, how could we know we are so deceived?). It is obvious that both options wholly trivialize language and completely miss its appresentational (in Husserl's sense of the term) nature. Once again, the viability of the expressivist conception of language as something that "allows reality to show forth in experience" (Polkinghorne 1988, 26) shows itself up. Accordingly, then, I am very sympathetic to the notion that metaphor is not just a figure of speech or an ornament to some ostensibly basic literal meanings but a "pervasive (and) indispensable structure of human understanding by means of which we figuratively comprehend our world . . . a central projective operation by which we establish semantic connections" (Johnson 1987, xx, 192). The point is essentially a variation on Kant's view that it is the *imagination* (and the schemas generated by it) that is responsible for the temporal setting of empirical intuitions and hence the key to our ability to order our experience and make sense of what surrounds us.[8]

Now, I take the applicability of this general thesis (of metaphor's central role in understanding) to emotions to be in turn essentially an elaboration of Bruno Snell's argument that we "cannot speak about the mind at all without falling back on metaphor" (1982, vi). Snell too insists that metaphor is involved at every level of human comprehension, and in brilliant fashion shows how the first identifications by the Greeks of mental processes were effected by a metaphorical use of the vocabulary of sensation, especially sight. The use of *eidos, eidetic, ideation, theory,* and the more directly "optical" *reflect, speculate, focus, insight, outlook, perspective,* in our talk about thinking make abundantly *clear* the extent to which thinking was (and continues to be) considered as a kind of seeing—a tendency somewhat mitigated by the Roman-inspired introduction of agricultural or "touch" terms and through which we obtain *grasping, observing, apprehending, recollecting,* and the like (Edie 1976, 174).

Of course, we do not recognize this terminology as metaphorical precisely because its long-term common usage has moved these words above the threshold of any ambiguity. They have become literal terms designating real processes, without the power to call up images that once inhered in them. No doubt, the stability of this terminology is also related to its reflecting, at least in "intellectual" cultures, a pervasive, uniform, and easily delineable type of experience. Is not "man is a rational-thinking animal" the single most powerful notion historically informing our self-understanding, wherein any differences between specific views of what constitutes thinking are transcended by an underlying theme that it is an attempt to create coherence and clarity out of chaos and confusion? But the interminable historical vexations over what constitutes its definition are vivid proof that for emotional experiencing, the situation is quite different. We should not be surprised. The idiosyncratic nature of a developing sense of engagement as rooted in different scenarios and involving individualized capacities for action, the development beginning very early in life and thus relatedly deeply penetrating the self, all conspire to ensure that emotions especially will require metaphor for their full articulation and sophistication. In the absence of being as clear and consensually agreed-upon experiences as abstract thinking, and because the point of an emotional articulation is not to designate an objective entity but to *intimate* and give parameters to a lived *sense,* the primary means by which this achievement appears possible will be by subsuming that sense under some other domain of experience that is already more elaborated and structured, at once more familiar and better understood.[9]

We are now in a position to appreciate a strong claim for the existence of culture-specific metaphors that do not just name emotions but in a certain way "explain and diagnose them" (Solomon 1984, 241). They embody a system of implicatures and activities that specify how we organize our emotional experiences and how these fit in with the rest of our existence. In this context, there seems little doubt that what has become known as the "hydraulic metaphor" has had a most powerful informing role in contemporary self-understanding of emotions. The metaphor presents emotions on the analogy of a force or liquid that subject to laws governing volume and pressure, fills us and spills over. Again, anger proves the most illustrative example, especially as it has been treated in experientialist linguistics.

The work to be drawn on here is Lakoff and Kovesces' (1983) investigations into cognitive-conceptual structures that underlie conventional English expressions and descriptions of anger. The authors show that what appears as randomness among many colloquialisms soon gives way to an inferential systematicity that is prefigured in the first instance by anger's uniform reification. The type of entity anger is considered and the natural laws we believe as governing that entity's behavior then become the source domain of both structural ontological comparisons and knowledge of what it is like to experience it and what we are likely to do under its influence. Hence we grant that those who have "lost their cool" are "simmering" or "stewing," or whose "blood is boiling" are undergoing a similar type of experience the prolongation and/or intensification of which will have typical symptoms and consequences. Thus, one feels one's gorge "rising" as the anger "wells up" within one. Reaching the limit point, we are said to be "bursting with anger," barely "containing" our rage or perhaps still managing to keep the anger "suppressed" and "bottled up" inside. But soon we are likely to "let off steam," "blow up," or "explode," with such explosions being mapped onto a variety of physical processes or entities such as volcanoes (he "erupted"), pistons (he "blew a gasket"), electricity (I "blew a fuse"), bombs (that really "set him off"), urination (they were "pissed off"). The natural consequence of these events is the disintegration of the constitutive parts of the entity in question. So I "blew my stack," "flipped my lid," or perhaps "hit the ceiling," potentially even to "go through the roof." As is natural in explosions, what was inside came out. Hence smoke "poured out of my ears;" were I a woman, others would say I was "having kittens."

Here we have the hydraulic metaphor in all of its pristine glory. Anger is essentially treated as if it were a liquid that when heated rises, puts pressure on its container (one's body), eventually bursting it or overflowing. Of course, the hydraulic metaphor is not exclusive, just currently the most pervasive. But there are others. We may, for example, refer to anger principally under its "temperature" aspect. Talk about "inflammatory remarks," "doing a slow burn," being "burned up" or "consumed" by anger, sees the latter as fire. To "go out of one's mind," get "hysterical," or be "driven nuts" reflect anger as insanity. Anger can also be a wild beast; one possesses a "ferocious" temper that can be "unleashed" and issue in aggressive behavior as in "bristling," "ruffling feathers," or more ominously, "looking daggers" at another.

Throughout these diverse formulations there is a unifying theme of understanding anger as a negative and potentially dangerous emotion, one that leads to loss of self-control, impairs our normal functioning, and for those reasons is also often felt as a burden to be struggled with. It can thus be metaphorically conceptualized without contradiction in terms of several different source domains that analogously embody these features. Also, common to these predominantly *entitative* understandings is a certain dualism of self and nonself that makes them coextensive as well, with yet different accounts—for example, the homuncular personification of emotions in the medieval passion plays or animistic culture's view of anger as being overcome by foreign spirits. For all the commonalities, however, there is a substantial difference between the hydraulic metaphor as we in the West have employed it and other ways of understanding the emotions.

This last claim admits, but stands independent of, recognizing the metaphor's almost universal pervasiveness. Aside from having a long ancestry in our culture, the current anthropological record notes here rather few exceptions. In particular, it seems that the central "ingredients" of heat and pressure appear not just in English but in non-

Indo-European languages such as Chinese and Hungarian (Lakoff 1987, 408) and that this in turn can be correlated with recent studies in the physiology of affective response that note increased heart rate and skin temperature in instances of anger. The concept's metaphorical elaboration thus seems widely grounded in an insight people have into their own physiology (407).

Still, only in the modern West has the hydraulic metaphor been formulated against the background of dualism *and* mechanism as metaphysical features of personhood. Only with us have the abstract superordinate concepts of science associated with forces, limits, intensity, and control, to such an extent displaced their older, experience-rich, commonsensical analogues to inform perhaps the major part of our ontology of emotions, and anger in particular. And to this corresponds an unprecedented conflation of emotions and sensations under *affects* (that favorite umbrella term of academic psychology), as well as a severing of emotions from the sphere of personal agency and responsibility and social context. To appreciate this point (and the more general one about how powerfully a metaphor can structure an emotional experience and what we should do about it), one needs only to note the widespread beliefs about the *necessity* and *inevitability* of "ventilating" our anger. Typically, any advice to "channel" it is made on functionalist grounds and not because of any moral strictures that being angry and expressing it is undesirable or inappropriate.

Here we owe much to Descartes, who precipitated this development, and to a host of subsequent others too numerous to list. Even Hume, for all his considerably higher estimation of the passions, contributed—his undeniable emphasis on the social context of emotions such as pride and shame being radically undermined by the empiricist reading of them as sensationlike entities (impressions), self-enclosed and unrelated to anything else. More recently, and notwithstanding the diametrical opposition to the Cartesian view of mind, Freud's thought has had an enormous impact in this respect. Whatever revisions in orientation toward psychological processes—whether motivation was a matter of modulation of strictly libidinal drive or consequent of the conflict between the life and death instincts or less emphasis was put on causal-deterministic mechanisms and more on interpretation and intentionality—the language of hydraulics of (early) Freud remained intact to the end (Solomon 1976, chap. 6). And without assessing the validity of the claim on the basis of Freud's theoretical writings, it seems undeniable that at the level of popular culture, his thought has been akin to, to paraphrase Rollo May, a systematic training in irresponsibility. One could add an analogous remark for behaviorism, but also for all functionalist and exclusively systems-theoretic approaches to human behavior and motivation. It is certainly worth noting that the hydraulic metaphor's zenith of elaboration, usage, and underlying denial of self-accountability (in all dimensions of that self) runs parallel with the widespread influence of all these theoretical movements.

But what, then, of the embedding of emotions within the moral order, of having a socially informed view of the rules and distinctions of worth that provide the context of what inspires a particular emotion? Has it become marginalized to the point of having no significance? Not so. In fact, the moral context is very much present, if somewhat displaced and not directly visible. For is it not the case that the now open battle over the applicability of science in understanding humans is precisely a *moral* battle that subsumes all of mind and intentionality, even if some of the experiences that have this crucial feature have been learned to be felt mechanically and as quasi-autonomous?[10] Thus even when thoroughly scientistic and seemingly neutral, our thought about emotions is pervaded by an underlying moral tension that draws its force from this larger context whose critical terms, when spelled out, would pertain to such notions as responsibility, freedom, dignity. Admittedly, usually our current everyday talk about emotions is a mixture of both normative-intentional categories and scientific and commonsensical hydraulic-mechanistic notions. For this reason, it may be tempting to argue, particularly where the former apparently structure the conscious emotional experience, that the latter are innocuous and insignificant. Such a conclusion, however, would be far from what is really the case.

Lakoff again shows this. In a disturbing dissection of the "logic" of lust (1987, 409–15) he unveils a network of metaphors and conceptual entailments linking sex, violence, and anger in the articulation of the experience of sexuality of Americans that constitutes an understanding wherein rape can be construed as a coherent or "rational" response of a sexually frustrated man. It is precisely when sexuality is thought of in terms of a physical force (as in "electricity," "magnetism," "attraction"), when its object is an opponent wielding that power (she's "devastating," a "knockout"), and when its exercise is a matter of "conquests" and "surrender" that such a man may experience a woman's (flaunting her) attractiveness as a provocation. He may in fact, especially when the consummation of sexual desire is socially or individually denied, find it offensive. He sees himself as humiliated and angered by this abuse of (sexual) *power;* he has been stimulated and denied satisfaction, and forced to control himself, feels diminished as a human being. Reddress, according now to the moral code anchored and embodied in the standard scenario for anger in our culture, calls for retribution in kind (i.e., for the counter-exercise of similar power). The woman thus physically "gets what she deserves." He is no doubt helped by a conviction that all this is beyond his control, a belief amplified by the fact that lust's ontology (i.e., the entities, predicates, and events required) has much in common with that of anger. As in anger, the conceptualization of sexual desire in terms of animality (he's a real "stud"), heat (she's an old "flame"), insanity (he's "crazy" about her), and machinery (I'm really "turned on") logically issues in a denial of controllability, self-initiation, and self-accountability.

This picture of experiencing an emotion seems far-fetched, perhaps fantastic, or at best marginal until we learn that it is an abstract of a real narrative, an actual interview response of a mild-mannered librarian who while disavowing ever acting on his frustrated desires in this manner, found the kind of rationale it expressed frighteningly understandable and easy to accept for other men. Of course, it is far-fetched to suggest that ordinary language is by itself the pathogenic factor here. And yet, in light of phenomenology's strictures that experiential acts and their contents cannot be completely separated or abstracted from each other, it is difficult to reject outright the conclusion that such language, insofar as it enters our reasoning, contributes to the pathology. The thesis here is not the hard determinism of experience by language of Whorf and Sapir. Rather, as in Vygotsky (1986), one's linguistic resources are seen as *facilitating* some ways of thinking and feeling as opposed to others.

I have at best made but a small dent in the issue of the (trans)formation of emotional sense. In this context, no doubt much more can be done by looking at literature, poetry, and drama, the expressive modes that address emotions more directly. But whether it is a single metaphor that captures an emotion or a more extended storylike account, it is critical that our focus be fixed on the underlying links that inform their use in psychological understanding and explanations—that is, why these linguistic forms are taken to apply in these contexts, in just those ways and combinations, and with that informtional content. Those links will inescapably point to the embeddedness of all "emotion talk" in a morally pregnant "life premise" comprising a notion of human agency and a correlative worldview.

From this perspective, the disappearance of an emotion term from a lexicon will typically indicate the passing of the emotion associated with it, not because the term has expired but because the relevant moral significances inspiring the emotion can no longer be sustained.

This is exactly, for example, how accidie disappeared from the psychology of postmedieval man. Frequently discussed in medieval psychological treatises, its cause was seen to lie in a failure to fulfill one's duty or obligation. Its closest contemporary analogues appear to be guilt and shame. What was different about it, however, was that dereliction, especially of a religious kind, led to neither guilt nor shame but to a kind of sadness or gloom colored by meaninglessness and lethargy. This particular response becomes in turn intelligible in light of the relationship that existed between accidie and the Catholic moral order wherein failure of duty meant a loss of intimacy with God (hence the appropriateness of gloom and lack of meaning). But with the onset of Protestantism, duty (and its failure) develops much more as a function of (inter)personal relations. As a consequence, accidie eventually disappears from the emotional register of western Europeans (Harré and Finlay-Jones 1986).

Still, it is not obvious that the correlation between the existence of a term and a corresponding experience can lead to any sort of an invariable principle. While the Utka Eskimos do not appear to get angry in any sense familiar to us (see Briggs 1970) and this correlates with an absence of anger terminology, the mild-mannered Tahitians, apparently having forty-seven words relating to anger, are said to "hypercognize" it (Heelas 1986). There is thus a similarity of psychological manner despite vastly different linguistic resources "organizing" it. Or we could point to shared, and on the surface similar, emotion stories circulating in a single culture wherein, however, men and women experience the "same" emotion differently. Such is suggested by some recent narrative-oriented feminist research. Both Gilligan's (1982) work on moral theory and women's development and Belenky and associates' (1986) work on feminine ways of knowing show that the underlying premise of women's self-experience pertains much more to connectedness to others than to individualism, rights, and competition, as seems to be the case for most Western males. Hence a man will typically experience such an emotion as anger as indignation, while a woman's anger will be less moralistic, perhaps closer to a guilt-laden frustration (de Sousa 1980, 291).[11] In jealousy, notwithstanding the homonymy of the term for men and women, the experience for men will be far more an expression of asserting property rights. The acuteness with which men experience such rights in this context, if one accepts certain psychoanalytic themes, apparently stems from the relative distance from the maternal and feminine as sources of empowerment (292).

There may also be emotional meanings embedded in stories that following the Stoics in their extirpation of the passions, lead to a denial of the value of even having (certain) emotions. On Martha Nussbaum's (1988a) reading, some of Samuel Beckett's work engages in just this type of emotional deconstruction. His characters inhabiting a world of Christian-moral ethos of Original Sin, whatever constitutes their love is toned by a sense of guilt and disgust for the body that in the final analysis proves that emotion (in the form it is concretely experienced in its specific moral-cultural setting) is an obstacle to human life and something we might be better off without. Here the unveiling of the various narratives constitutive of emotional experience is critically subsumed within another narrative of a broader scope. Here too, why the various narratives link up into particular constellations and whether it is desirable or even possible to alter or discard such constellations is inescapably informed by foundational considerations about not just the nature of emotions but human agency itself.

As we have progressed in the exploration of the linguistic structuring of emotions, talk of agency and selfhood has increasingly, but necessarily, acquired prominence. That point can be grasped, first of all, conceptually. If emotions are mental stances that thematize the self's engagements in the world, then self is nothing other than an integral complement, descriptively, and a central component, existentially, of every structure of lived emotional experience we may attempt objectively to understand and describe. But in any event, our investigation has forced on us in a quite natural way the necessity of considering it more explicitly. To that consideration, therefore, I now turn.

5

THE FEELING SELF

"For my part, when I enter most intimately into what I call *myself,* I always stumble on some particular perception or other, of heat or cold, light or shade, love or hatred, pain or pleasure. I never can catch *myself* at any time without a perception, and never can observe anything but the perception." That famous statement belongs of course to David Hume (1888, 252), and it is a claim that no discussions of mind and selfhood since Hume could afford to be dismissive about. The claim must be engaged and dealt with, if only implicitly.

What Hume was reacting to and at once challenging was a long-standing tradition that assumed at the heart of human experience something permanent, typically a soul or a self, whose principal quality of resisting change throughout the flux of (its) experiences thereby ensured our identity. Here the opponents were quite diverse, as were the conceptual strategies intended to secure the self's permanence. Most immediately (and even if abstracting from the notion of substance, still very much in Cartesian spirit), there was Locke's effort to establish necessary and sufficient conditions for personal identity by the dual employment of memory and self-consciousness. That effort followed Descartes's pivotal turning inward and the suggestion that self-identity rests on our awareness of being the same thinking substance. And earlier still we find the Scholastic doctrine of the person as a *substantia rationalis individua.*

Hume does not deny that we have a notion, an idea, or a sense of self. Rather, working within the constraints of his radical empiricism wherein all experience exhaustively divides into particular and separable impressions and ideas, he fails to find among the latter anything lending itself to stability and permanence, which is the manner in which the self is alleged to exist. In short, because there is neither valid rational proof nor sufficient empirical evidence, our conventional prephilosophical assumption of just such a self is not suitably generated; the "self," Hume concludes, is a fiction.

To the extent that he accepted the idiom of self-reflection (as in attempting to "catch himself") and insofar as self-consciousness and sense of identity are coordinate with and mutually implicative of each other, Hume's denial of the very self he was at once examining and thus positing was a flat self-contradiction. This has often been remarked. For although Hume was certainly correct to insist that the self was not an entity to be found in our experience, especially as long as it was considered on a par with other objects, the very character of many first-person assertions as nonempirical statements (in the sense that there are no conditions under which they *could* be false; for example, "I am here") ought to have forewarned him that he was looking in the wrong place or drawing (negative) empirical conclusions where none, in principle, could be made—and where indeed the force of such statements, as Descartes clearly saw in establishing his egology, was such that for ourselves, our selfhood could never be questioned without indubitably (re)asserting itself as some form of positivity.

There were other serious problems with Hume's argument. Most notably, and while essentially agreeing with the great skeptic that the self could not be in any usual sense an object *of* experience, Kant pointed out that all the discrete Humean perceptions require a unified consciousness if experience is to be possible and that that consciousness must be self-identical if such different relations among impressions and ideas as association, comparability, and succession are to obtain, as Hume (along with common sense) insists they do. Indeed, the very distinction between variability and permanence in experience could not even get off the ground if we were existentially anchored in nothing but variability (as, analogously in perception, the divide between illusion or dream and reality could not be coherently thought were we [permanently] on the dream side of that division).

Without doubt, Hume was keenly aware of at least some of these difficulties. There is, for example, his apparent contradiction of his bundle theory of self and mind with the insistence (in the appendix of the *Treatise*) on some type of unity of awareness, since neither impressions nor ideas have an existence distinct from the mind and those that constitute the bundle "self" all appear as distinctly mine, that is, as bound within and present to *my* mind. Here we find Hume also tacitly relaxing what corresponds to the atomism of experience, namely, his strict unworkable notion of identity wherein the slightest alteration of an object—in this instance the mind as locus of differing contents—"absolutely destroys" its identity.

Similar considerations can be applied to Hume's admission of memory as a real (i.e., nonfictional) phenomenon and our reflexive awareness of memory presupposed in all qualitative comparisons of the latter with other modes of experiencing (e.g., imagination) insofar as this entails an awareness of being the same subject that remembers an experience and presently has a thought about that remembering and hence just *is* part of the very concept of the numerical identity of selves (Margolis 1988, 38).

The point here is not to present Hume as a defender of the self but to appreciate the fact that however much his extreme empiricism dictated his reflections on the mind and self as pronounced in the official and popularly accepted Humean theses, when he relaxes his theoretical strait jacket and gets closer to experience, he has great difficulties maintaining his position and appears actually to concede the necessity of a "self," at least in the minimal function of assigning experience to a suitable entity and fixing such ascription in a possessive and predicative manner (31).

But more importantly perhaps, as Margolis argues, the point is also to recognize that Hume's arguments about the fictitious identity of the self cannot so easily serve as analogues for many of the current strategies that attempt to eliminate reference to selves, in particular those that do this in terms of a materialism that tries to replace numerical identity of the self by reference to the continuity of psychological "events." The latter position means to bypass the first-person intentional stance as somehow constitutive of the identity of the self in favor of *impersonal* descriptions of experience that are claimed to be exhaustive in abstraction from any ("possessive") indexing of that experience to (its) subject.

In contemporary philosophy, it is P. F. Strawson who formulates perhaps the strongest conceptual arguments against the viability of such a "no-ownership" thesis. No-ownership is usually claimed to be valid on the grounds that our belief in a self or person[1] who has various experiences is just wrong or confused, in the sense of being consequent of an illegitimate sense of possession. As we can truly "own" only things that are logically transferable, this cannot be the sense of ownership for a subject whose sole function is to be an owner for experiences, who arises in a strictly conceptual manner as a logical presupposition of ordinarily expressed "having" ideas, feelings, and who therefore cannot *own* in any but a logically *nontransferable* sense of that term. But since this is absurd, or there is no such sense, the subject could only have come in because of a confusion and so must be eliminated altogether (Strawson 1959, 96). However, if the replacement effort, having dispensed with selves or persons, suggests that the unique causal position of a certain physical body is sufficient for the ascription of experiences to ourselves, this, Strawson insists, is logically incoherent. For this strategy must be referring to "some class of experiences of the members of which it is in fact contingently true that they are all dependent on body B [and] [t]he defining characteristic of this class is in fact that they are 'my experiences' or 'the experiences of some person', where the idea of possession expressed by 'my' and 'of' is the one [being called] into question" (97). In short, the very identification of experiences, however one wishes subsequently to deal with them on a theoretical level (and hence including, or perhaps especially, those to be impersonally described, i.e., as belonging to just a body), logically requires the use of " 'my' or any expression with similar possessive force." They must be "experiences *had by a certain person* . . . [particulars that] *owe* their identity as particulars to the identity of the person whose states or experiences they are" (97). Experience and the "having" of it (by me or some other person) are thus coordinate notions reflecting the noncontingency of the link between a subject and his or her experiences.

It is important to remember that Strawson is not offering a phenomenological description of the self but is concerned with a *logical* explanation of the concept of self as it appears in ordinary use of language. To be sure, it is only phenomenological evidence gained in reflection, self-ascription, and other experiences that highlight my "I-ness" and self-possession that can fulfill and give weight to this concept. But to the extent that our ordinary idiom about selves and persons can be asserted as not just valid but perhaps inescapable, and moreover is shown to be so in abstraction from any metaphysical commitments with regard to the actual "stuff" that constitutes selves or persons, we are entitled to treat the self as a quasi-transcendental "salience" of our experiential life and not as some vestige of "folk psychology" awaiting replacement pending the arrival of better empirical data and/or a superior conceptual apparatus.

If we go a little further with Strawson, we shall learn what in a conceptual way can be minimally established about the nature of selves or persons. Here the point of departure is the peculiar fact that in our self-ascriptions we attribute mental states (intentions, thoughts, memories, etc.) to the same entity of which we predicate physical characteristics (height, weight, size, etc.). That we do so in regard to the latter seems unproblematic since we are material bodies to which (equally identifiable) physical characteristics can be ascribed. But it is less clear how the very different mental "predicables" (experiences) can be ascribed to the same thing, and indeed the question may not unreasonably be posed, "Why are our states of consciousness ascribed to anything at all?"

Strawson's answer turns out to be indirect, indeed mediated by Hegelian-type considerations on the conditions of the possibility of self-consciousness and hence self-ascription. The key fact to be noted is that ascription logically presupposes an *empirical* identification of the entities or characteristics that are to be joined by the terms of ascription. This objectification is what allows for verifying whether the ascription is true or not. But whereas for our ascriptions of experiences to others there is in instances of uncertainty a method of verification—we simply ask them—in one's own case, the knowledge of one's own states is not, in fact cannot be, empirical and verifiable *in the same sense* (if it indeed makes *any* sense to talk about verifying our own mental states). Consequently, Strawson argues, it must be the condition of our ascribing experiences to ourselves, in the way we ordinarily and uncontroversially do as their "owners," that we should also ascribe them to others, that is, take others as just those entities of whom experience can be predicated (99). For us, the self-distancing and self-objectification required for self-ascription cannot arise in any other way; it is intimately linked to our consciousness of others as "objects" that are at once *subjects of experience,* for only then can we grasp ourselves as subjects who are *also* objects and thus subject to ascription in the ordinary sense of that term.

What finally emerges from these considerations is a most important conclusion about persons. For it must be the case that given our capacity for self-ascriptions as conditional on our ascribing experiences to others, which in turn means first recognizing them as subjects of experience, we would not be able to identify those others were they only disembodied Cartesian egos or pure possessors of nothing but states of consciousness. In short, the seemingly self-enclosing and tortuous investigation into the conditions of self-consciousness and self-ascription yields a radically antisolipsistic and antidualist concept of persons. The latter refers to "a type of entity such that *both* predicates ascribing states of consciousness *and* predicates ascribing corporeal characteristics, a physical situation, etc. are equally applicable to an individual entity of that type" (Strawson 1959, 104).

In this view, a person or self cannot be a disembodied consciousness, a Cartesian "thinking thing," nor a composite of mind or consciousness and body. Rather, *person* is an unanalyzable primitive, a "basic or fundamental particular" in relation to which other types of particulars such as a pure ego are secondary and derivative. In more concrete terms, it refers to the (apparently universal and historically unconditioned) awareness of our bodies as well as our psychological and physical individuality. For Strawson takes the concept as one which in its "fundamental character change[s] not at all . . . [belonging to] the massive central core of human thinking which has no history." Not being a product of sophisticated intellectual evolution, the concept is at once a "commonplace of the least refined thinking" as well as part of "the indispensable core of the conceptual equipment of the most sophisticated human beings" (10).

Anthropological evidence—in particular the universality of use of personal reflexive pronouns—seems to support Strawson's conceptually derived conclusions. All human societies appear to recognize that sense of human individuality that is contained in the notion of person as an embodied agent. On the other hand, and notwithstanding formal similarities in language use and structure, there are enormous variations among different cultures (or even within a culture) regarding the degree of singularity or idiosyncrasy with which experiences are organized into mental lives of persons as their own. How exactly are thoughts and feelings centered—"where," that is, is their locus of "origin" (whether as seen through explicit articulations of theory-oriented cultures like ours or as more immediately embedded in the actual practices that constitute various "indigenous psychologies" encountered by anthropologists)—all this must remain open to actual investigations that the above-mentioned similarities have all too often been used to foreclose. For example, an idea such as one that suggests that Western man has historically lived under a comparatively greater strain of anxiety will not find substantiation in conceptual analysis but in a review of specific forms of self-identification conducive to generating life with that experiential quality. To consider another example very specific to our culture, a phenomenon like romantic love is unlikely to be understood without a theoretically sophisticated psychodynamic approach that addresses the various idealizations and projections that in part constitute that phenomenon.

All of which is to say that Strawson's notion of what persons or selves are, while unquestionably valuable, is at the same time, and by virtue of its generality, no more than a skeletal one. Elsewhere (1974), and much closer to the concerns of this essay, he proposes (though not in the terms of any *explicit* concern with the self) that the notion of the person refers us primarily to a structure of emotions.[2] What Strawson has in mind is the existence of (and our natural commitment to) a "general framework of human life" (13) constituted by a constellation of "reactive attitudes" that range from nondetached responses toward others (e.g., gratitude, love, resentment) through vicarious or impersonal reactions typically linked with morality (e.g., indignation) and finally including self-conscious reactions toward oneself in relation to oneself and/or others (e.g., guilt, shame, obligation).

Significantly, all of these presuppose or pertain outright to intersubjectivity. Moreover, the network is foundational in the sense that the engagements of which these attitudes are expressive are not optional, in a practical sense, for us as human agents. To be sure, in special circumstances (e.g., stress, psychological abnormalities) we disengage ourselves from, and objectify, others because they do not possess or exhibit the range of capacities we normally associate with persons as *loci of responsibility*. And certainly, even within personal relationships, it is not unusual to oscillate between immediate response and an "explanatory" stance that neutralizes the other's particular action as one that calls for a *moral* assessment. Yet it does not seem possible, even if we rationally came to believe that determinism holds true for all facets of human existence, that we could consistently sustain an objectivizing attitude toward others. For one thing, our suspension of ordinary emotional reactions appears very context-specific, that is, independent of any possible "covering law" of determinism. For another, the entailed sense of isolation would simply be too much to bear. The costs of abandoning our ordinary affective-valuational scheme, were this at all a matter of choice, would far outweigh any gains. Stated in somewhat stronger terms (in a formulation that echoes Aristotle's grounding of his strictures on excessive rationality in a view about human nature), is it not, Strawson suggests, *useless* to consider the rationality of doing something we are constitutively (probably) unable to do? (18). As something "given with the fact of human society, [its existence] as a whole neither calls for, nor permits, an external 'rational' justification" (23). Any criticism, justification, or modification of our emotions can be accomplished only *within* the very framework they constitute.

This is an important thesis. For us, its force lies precisely in the pressing of emotions into the service of establishing personhood and subjectivity, and doing so against a powerful adversary: the combined strength of our commitment to rationality as acceptance of what is real *and* a real possibility of comprehensive determinism. For such determinism has traditionally been held up as the strongest motive for minimizing subjectivity or even rejecting it altogether. In this picture, the "self," along with its first-person intentional idiom, wind up as nothing but a confused way of speaking that awaits replacement by some scheme that will allegedly hook us up with reality in a superior, less confused manner. Correlatively, the ordinary self-involved attitudes (i.e., emotions) are seldom taken seriously as something that plays a significant role in our lives.

These considerations have moved us considerably beyond the initially outlined bare conception of the person as embodied agent, doing so moreover in a way highly favorable to the concerns here at hand. For what was of interest from the start was a notion of personhood that goes beyond the function of (merely) unifying experiences and is capable of being claimed within *moral* contexts, within which (recall) emotions were also situated in the last chapter. Still, Strawson's significant enrichment of the notion of self or person hangs in the air, as it were, not tied in any strong sense to an anthropology, that is, to an explicitly asserted *substantive* view of man. So while intuitively agreeing with him, we want to know in greater detail *why* and *how* acceptance of a thoroughgoing objectivism and a corresponding neutralization of our capacities for emotional response would lead to a genuine *self*-contradiction, that is, an existential diminishing or negation of self as self. How, in other words, what exists as a logical possibility—since it is not self-contradictory to imagine that such a situation could arise—nevertheless means conflict and disintegration when posed in terms of a concrete life. What is demanded here is simply a fuller justification that emotions are foundational to personhood.

A possible extension of understanding the issue comes with reflection on such directly self-referring emotions as shame and remorse as paradigm instantiations of the very combination of (ontological) features that make us human: reflexivity, intentionality, and mutuality. For I can be ashamed only on condition of being aware of myself, under a particular description that *I myself* find fitting as attributable to myself and at the same time carries (for me and) in public before others the meaning that this type of person is in some sense unworthy. The upshot of this is that human consciousness intends not just intellectual (i.e., representational or propositional) but also moral truth, and indeed if it were unable to *be* a moral awareness, it could not be a human one either. This explains why we feel such an eerieness (and at times even horror) in the presence of those who are incapable of shame or remorse. For we quite properly regard one who shows no remorse after a horrible act as someone who has "lost his mind," who is not exercising some key human powers—principally recognition of mutuality—and hence is not fully a person either, even if he appears "normal" by showing rational-calculative abilities. Thus it can readily be seen how our shock at an atrocity may quite easily be displaced by an even more profound unease at *the absence of mind and person* in the human being who committed it but fails to regret it or, in the extreme, even to acknowledge it. In this view, person, mind, emotion, and mutuality turn out to be inescapably symbiotic notions. Denying one puts the rest in jeopardy.

In expanding the notion of the self in this direction, the implicit contrast has been with viewing it as a structure constituted by certain basic beliefs.[3] The latter would be answers to such fundamental questions as regard the distinction of persons from other conscious agents, the relation of individual and society, the relation of the self to its possible roles, ends, and purposes, and what makes for a unified life. Like Strawson's sentiments or "reactive attitudes," these beliefs too— the questions being inescapable for beings like us—would constitute a universal and necessary network or background in the absence of which it would be doubtful that anything that *we* could call a human society existed.

Now, to a certain extent, the contrast drawn is surely forced. For having on the one hand asserted that emotions are strongly cognitive, that as intentional their objects must come under particular descriptions that thus make the involvement of "beliefs" inescapable, while on the other hand insisting that (the bodily felt) behavioral know-how is implicit in even the most abstract forms of intentionality, it should be evident that no fast and absolute distinction can be made between emotions and beliefs. Emotions vitalize beliefs, without which in turn they would be, lacking focused direction and factual premises, just plain stupid if not obnoxious. Just as love, shame, and resentment take a specific form because I understand that they do not apply to animals and would indeed change form were I to include the latter, so the foundational beliefs are sustained by specific forms of affective self-experiences. And so perhaps one could combine the two perspectives and suggest more correctly that the notion of self refers to a structure of emotions as *mediated* or *informed* by the fundamental beliefs of the sort mentioned.

But this way of formulating the issue still gives a certain priority to the emotional. Why? For one thing, this *seems* right because incipient selfhood appears in children prior to their acquisition of language and more complex conceptual skills that could address the inescapable identity-pressing questions. Arguably, the beliefs in question are not propositional in nature but immediately embedded in the "life forms" that express them. But then they are closer to the immediate self-involved experience associated with emotion, so there seems little reason at that level to introduce a distinction between *emotion* and *belief* in the first place. Still, something more substantive can be offered, I believe, in defense of the thesis that the self is at bottom an affective phenomenon.

This may yet prove a quite demanding task, though. For one thing, to the extent that modern philosophy defines subjectivity in relation to a pure reason concerned principally with epistemic norms and acquisition of knowledge, there does not seem to be much it could offer to support the perspective pursued here. But then, neither is it automatic that we can turn for clarification to the logical alternatives—the great protagonists of self as rooted in affectivity such as Rousseau or Nietzsche. The problem with the latter, I submit, is precisely the extreme degree of their deprecation and marginalization of reason. This effectively preempts ordinary "rational" experience shared with others as a source of (and perhaps constraint to) our reflections on the self, mind, emotion, reason. What can profitably be said about the "real" self when it is completely extracted from the sphere of intersubjectivity (Rousseau), when consciousness is nothing but a dissimulation of power (Nietzsche), or when it is claimed, as in the perspective of that great neo-Nietzschean "master of suspicion," Freud, that the self is *never* the self it thinks it is? Leaving aside the logical point that falsehood and dissimulation cannot serve as foundational points of any inquiry because no distinction from truth could get off the ground in the first place, are not these positions, by virtue of their dismissal or reduction of or divorce from ordinary experience, as *abstract* as those of any rationalist? (To expose and destroy the various pretenses of which it is perfectly capable neither entails, nor should require, reason's complete degradation. Why not keep it as essentially linked to affectivity but make it an expression of a more noble [though by no means infallible] drive or aspiration—for example, for progressive integration, coherence, mutuality? Surely these are just as concrete for humans as any of the more obviously self-centered drives for power or pleasure. That consciousness is not perfectly transparent to itself or that the self cannot in principle know itself completely is one thing. But it is entirely another to pass from that solid premise to a conclusion that consciousness is a lie, that the self always deceives itself, or even, less dramatically, that it can never know itself adequately. It is no small coincidence that those who subscribe to the latter views typically have *no positive conception* of intersubjectivity and community. Each reinforces and points to the other. Of course, knowing oneself is a *task*, at times arduous and with many pitfalls. But naturally it will seem all the more impossible if one misses *the* indispensable, if by no means sufficient, condition for the self to have any chance of finding and knowing itself.)

Be that as it may, and whatever they ultimately take the self to be, the practitioners of suspicion are nonetheless profoundly correct in at least one respect: the self *is* an elusive phenomenon, enigmatic for itself and others, and only indirectly accessible. And this is something shared even by those who take a more optimistic view of human nature. Thus, Paul Ricoeur, who has expended considerable efforts to elucidate the self, insists throughout that such elucidation essentially requires an interpretative or hermeneutic approach. It is not just that the self if never an object of some experience, as Hume and Kant saw; rather it is principally because the self is something that forever eludes *univocal* description.

It is also Ricoeur's *Freud and Philosophy* that approaches the self, it seems to me, in a way valuable for its balance and capacity to address the (antireductionist) points just raised. One of the central themes of this work is to come to a reflective understanding of the self after an encounter with Freud. In short, what must the self be, given the acceptance of some key propositions of Freud's doctrine, in particular the trifold "dispossession" or displacement of consciousness, object, and ego from their (exalted) status as self-evident phenomona, that is, as immediately given over to us and perfectly understood in their own terms? For clearly it will be a different self if these pillars of modern understanding of subjectivity are even in part subsumed under Freud's libidinal energetics that trade on gaps in consciousness, instincts (as underlying the standard meanings of objects), and finally a determinism that denies the self powers of full autodetermination.

For us, it is Ricoeur's conclusion about the roots of the self that proves critical. For having earlier complained that the Cartesian ego in effect stands for not much more than a ghost existence, what Freud's regressive "archaeology" of instincts reveals for Ricoeur is the primordiality of affect, effort, and desire in the constitution of selfhood, *even if* consciousness, object, ego are not what they appear to be (Ricoeur 1970, 439). The positive side of the descent into the darkness of instincts is that it "designates . . . precisely the *sum* of the Cogito" (454), reaching back into the unconscious to a substrate that cannot be (ideationally) represented: "desire as desire." In short, the core sense of self is to be found in effort and striving, at bottom an elemental urge-to-be of various drives incessantly seeking objects on which to invest their energies, and not in the cool refractory rays of perceptual awareness or abstract cognition—something affirmed, at least in Freud's work, in the seemingly necessary employment of the (hydraulic) metaphors of force, energy, and potency the deeper one probes into the depths of self (Zaner 1981, 125).

But what of the autonomy of reason neglected by the practitioners of suspicion but necessary to deflect charges of reductionism, one-sidedness, and incoherence? Ricoeur can be seen as addressing this issue by turning to Hegel's explication of the teleological thrust of self and consciousness, wherein it is the latter's later achievements that give significance to the anterior moments that led up to them. There is here a natural progression dictated by Freud's displacement of consciousness from center stage and showing that the key problem of growth and development is far less being conscious *tout court* than *becoming* aware of certain things that inhibit that development and that one would rather not admit to oneself. But "becoming" forces on the agenda a provision of its goal ("becoming what?"). By itself, backward-looking analysis would hang in the air, as it were, and so demands a teleology. At the same time it must be remembered that what for Hegel "energizes" the progressive movement of self and consciousness is not commensurable with the drives or instincts that Freud takes as underlying psychic life. It lies rather just in the fact of the mind's noncoincidence with itself and thus in its necessity to appropriate that which it is not as a condition of (a more comprehensive) understanding, that is, as a condition of its life as mind. Here, in this moment of "restlessness" intrinsic to the mind, we find the autonomy we have been demanding.

Still, this autonomy is not absolute. The movement of self generated via dialectical tensions gives only the form, as it were, of mind's life. It points to a progression of truths without, however, specifying their content. The latter must be reflectively elaborated on the basis of actual life experience, which in turn reveals that effort and desire are inescapable components of all stages of the dialectic. Nowhere is this desire more evident than in our fundamental aspiration to be *recognized by others*. It is certainly not fortuitous that the stage of recognition is metaphorically presented by Hegel as a great life-and-death struggle. For since recognition by others both integrates us as self-conscious beings and at once consolidates our status as autonomus agents, what is at stake is none other than the life of our being selves. The aspiration to be recognized is essentially the desire and effort to *be*.

Thus is Freud wedded by Ricoeur to Hegel in a presentation of the two transcendental correlates of existence that simultaneously "determine" the ground from which human selves or persons come to be and develop: instinctual drives and impulses on one hand and an orientation toward other selves on the other, with desire providing the underlying common thread joining these terms.

Nevertheless, Ricoeur's theses about the self in relation to effort and desire are necessarily "weak," for the simple reason that while his claims do indeed pertain to the foundational level of the conditions of selfhood, the foundational or transcendental question is not the one he is explicitly addressing. To do that (especially on the side of instincts and impulses) would require first a critical grounding of the Freudian self rather than buying into it and accepting it as just "a stage of reflection."

Just this line of criticism is advanced against Ricoeur by the Gestalt phenomenologist Richard Zaner, in whose judgment Ricoeur's descriptions do either of the following: suppose the truth of Freud's archaeology of the self or simply "phenomenologically 'verify' the properly philosophical content of Freudian analysis" (1981, 134). But in neither case do they examine the "transcendental conditions for the possibility of being-as-self such that to be this is likewise to be able-to-be both reflectively apprehended and neurotic" (133). In short, the too quick acceptance of psychoanalysis preempts the more radical questioning of what makes subjectivity in Fruedian archaeology of the self possible in the first place. For the need for such questioning is certainly not obviated by the focus on the abnormal; the various deceptions, feignings, and illusions that mark the neurotic self characteristically have to be *maintained,* so are in that sense as much a task (and hence a matter of desire and effort) as is the often arduous pursuit of truth (137).

Advancing from this critique of Ricoeur, it is Zaner's express aim to articulate more radically the sense in which selfhood is anchored in desire, effort, and affectivity in general. His strategy is to see what can be gained in this respect from phenomenological description (to which he is methodologically thoroughly committed) of a number of experiences that can plausibly be gathered—just because they have the potential to alter radically or even transform our lives—as an "eidetic core of being-self." Omitting the details of Zaner's argument, I shall touch on only its most salient features. Initially, the experiences of self-realization and self-awakening, to be addressed momentarily, are given the most weight.

First—and this in line with the now widely shared assumption that self-consciousness and sense of identity are coordinate and mutually implicative notions—self is generically defined as a situated reflexivity. By this is meant a self-referencing of human beings at the dual levels of mental life and the lived-body, the latter also bearing principal responsibility for the situated or perspectival character of this referencing. Self thus also exhibits an experiential "weight" or inwardness constituted by its various strata "collapsing" onto themselves as well as (presuming integration) onto one another. This also accounts for the sense in which the self is/has a "life of its own" (145-51).

Against this background there emerge a number of important descriptions pertaining to our encounter with, or the appearance of, the phenomenon of self. First, for every self, there is "that by which it is itself and is utterly alone" (151), an awareness that one is an individual self standing apart from other selves. This awareness is accessible only to oneself. It is also completely spontaneous, that is, not chosen, and as such (and as against Freud) it comes prior to any masks or screens that we may create to conceal ourselves from ourselves or from others. What is critical, however, is that joined simultaneously to this awareness of oneself as individual and separate there is an experienced urgency to express or manifest oneself explicitly and outwardly to (and for) oneself and others—a "desire for 'speech' " that has a dual aim of on the the one hand "fixing" for ourselves meaning, clarity, and order (i.e., something to "hold by") while on the other hand seeking to share our inwardenss with another self.[4] That is, "the effort to 'say' is also (and essentially) the effort to 'tell' " (155), to find some other who like us, desires to express the inwardness of his or her self to us. (Here, incidentally, we grasp the meaning of Hegel's enigmatic claim that ultimately desire is for *another* desire, that is, for *an other* who will desire vis-à-vis us what we desire vis-à-vis them, namely, to express self. For only then is authentic mutuality ensured and with it the possibility of recognition and thus self-affirmation.)

But on the negative side too, the self in this context is affected by an immediate awareness of its *relational* status and that the fundamental possibilities for meaning, coherence, and integrative confirmation that anchor it are just that—possibilities. Hence the self can just as fundamentally be experienced as an anxiety over their disappearance or withdrawal. Moreover, in the face of nonrecognition and consequent lack of empowerment, and perhaps as a measure of last resort, we may in fact snuff out and lose any need and desire for connectedness with others, as in psychosis, a process whose terminus can be seen in a severe schizophrenic's complete withdrawal from the public world. (Of course, the paradoxical, and vicious, character of this manner of "saving" oneself is that the withdrawal from the world leads to further loss of personal capacities and hence to the further diminution of precisely the self that was to be rescued by this effort.)

There are yet other affective aspects present in self-encounter. The pertinent observations are those that refer to what could be called contingent self-possession. These can be seen as underlying our awareness not of being individual and separate but unique. There is a perception that one is a self belonging solely to precisely the self one has identified oneself to be, but coupled with a sense that one's particular body, birth, personal history and destiny, and present location, are all contingent matters—that they all could have been other than what they actually are. In this progressively insistent contrasting of the self from "everything else," the affective component can be seen as comprising two aspects: (1) our wonder or amazement at being a particular self and (2) arising out of the realization of the contingency of our circumstances, a sense of ourselves as *loci of agency*. The self turns out to be, as it were, an event-being "whereby what is possible is able to be actualized" (163) and the flip side of the fact that nothing actual could be grasped as actual without simultaneously being apprehended as one among other possibilities (179). But this latter sense is also very much of a piece with what is necessary for us to come in contact with other reflexive presences (i.e., other selves), namely, a minimal awareness of "other possible" ways of being aware, since without this moment of otherness (of another autonomous agent), we could not talk of recognition and mutuality but only of a (solipsistic) duplication of the self via identical reflection of itself in another.

The capacity to experience one's own as well as another's existence as essentially (open ended) realms of possibility thus appears as perhaps *the* critical aspect of selfhood. But to experience oneself in this special manner presupposes in turn that the (correlate) world we inhabit and the situations we encounter can be so experienced as well, that is, experienced as amenable to alternation and alternatives rather than something that wholly claims or determines us. It is here, in particular through observing various physiologically grounded pathologies and the self's *effort* to compensate for or overcome them and thus attain equilibrium, that we can come to appreciate the integral role played by a normally functioning body in the establishment of selfhood.

What naturally comes first to mind are instances of impaired mobility through loss of limb or paralysis, the *anger, frustration,* and indeed (maybe often even in the first place) *shame*[5] due to loss of independence and personal powers of choice, decision, self-direction, and the anxieties incurred when faced with quantitatively greater number of (formerly simple but now) overwhelming tasks such as climbing stairs. Further along the spectrum of pathology, analogous observations obtain in Kurt Goldstein's work with brain-injured patients whose loss of capacity for abstraction manifested itself in greater passivity, compulsion, rigidity of behavior, and correspondingly severe anxieties when success in performing a task demanded a measure of distancing themselves from the immediate situation (Zaner 1981, 174). But even such slight "failures" as a common cold, as most of us know all too well, can dramatically reveal the restriction of our possibilities. Though in varying degrees, in all of these instances the underlying common factor is a diminution of desire in its generic sense (i.e., as sentience for goals that inheres in the present as a potentiality), an inability to "realize" or think of what is possible due to being locked into the immediacy of the actual (176). We glimpse here at once the sense of how much the world can be an obstacle and consequently how much normal existence is a matter of effort that is invisible and taken for granted precisely because a healthy, well-functioning body feels effortless.

Whether in relation thus to the properly intersubjective realms or to our well-functioning embodiment that is their condition, the self comes through experientially as a form of a balanced *tension* centered on a "possibilizing" whose disturbance (and our immediate attention to, and concern for, such) in turn highlights the self's roots in desire and effort. Another way to express this grounding in affectivity is to say that the self is essentially *actional*.

Recalling now the original definition of emotions as modalities of mind that thematize our *engagement* in the world (see Chapter 1) should obviate, I think, any need to justify extensively why I have engaged in showing how this is so—why, that is, starting from the rather abstract Strawson-backed conceptual argument for "selves," I have chosen progressively to concretize the self in just this manner. "Emotion" and "self" turn out to be coordinate notions, and considerations of the kind advanced here are presupposed, it seems to me, in any viable discussion of either emotion or selfhood. To consider but one example, perhaps the most significant (and profitable) of recent theorizing about the self, I have in mind those inspired by the narrativist approach wherein the self is neither a static thing nor a substance but a "configuring of personal events into a historical unity" (Polkinghorne 1988, 150), with narrative seen as the principle whereby this unity is effected. But does not this approach in turn take as given effort and aspiration to coherence and integration? By itself, narrative can do very little; it needs to be "enfleshed" and tied to motivation, like *a fortiori* any conception of the "self of emotions."

But there is a yet more radical level, one that goes beyond the details furnished by failed embodiment, at which the actional sense can be seen as foundational to selfhood and as such, justifying considering the self as a structure of emotions. I want to appeal here to a tradition of "voluntative realism"—of which, among others, including

Schopenhauer, Schelling, and Bergson, Scheler was a systematic proponent. In brief, this position argues that the *reality* of entities (as distinguished from their meaning) is not given through the mind—as it is, for example, for such more "intellectualist" approaches as that of Husserl, who takes the "realness" of the content of something as given in "thetic" or "positional" consciousness—but through the factor of *resistance* that a live being experiences in pressing against that which it is not (Frings 1978, 146–47). But simultaneously, only through this resistance is the animated being informed of its *own* existence; it can exist "for" and "to" itself and develop a sense of self-reference, that is, *be* an "inwardness," only through a *live relatedness* to what is on its "outside."

We thus arrive at a comprehension of the actional sense at its most basic. Vital powers and motility turn out to be *the* condition without which, Descartes notwithstanding, none of us could be certain of his or her existence.[6] And to the extent that *any* inwardness needs entities beyond the boundaries of the organism in order to develop at all, to that extent our own selfhood as marked by a reflexively attained interiority is analogously subject to contingency and dependence, and hence to a potential anxiety of a rather fundamental kind.

Does not this push things a little too far, though? I mean, can the proposition that we are essentially a structure of emotions be supported by an appeal to this level of existence? Surely, the objection may run, the actional sense within emotion as a linguistically informed intentional experience with representational content is eons away from a (brute) primordial urge to movement as described by the metaphysics of the life-drive, whose "inwardness" and "anxieties" in turn are at best metaphorical constructs that refer at most to an organic density the opaque character of which knows nothing of "spirit." It would of course be ludicrous to deny their difference, reducing the developed to the primitive and collapsing millennia of evolution. The gap between the two levels is enormous. And yet, I want to suggest that one can plausibly press for a meaningful continuity from one to the other. For just as I earlier insisted that behavioral know-how is an integral component of intentionality even when approached more or less solely from the side of its representational function (Chapter 2), so too, and from the opposite direction, what voluntative realism most radically suggests is that intentionality (construed now in its generic sense as a property of a thing's relatedness to what is beyond it) is already a feature of the biological. Contemporarily, it belongs to the genius of Merleau-Ponty to have recognized this and to have attempted (especially in his principal works, *The Structure of Behavior* and *The Phenomenology of Perception*) through a dialectical inter-play of *logos* and *bios* a concrete filling out of what intuitively seem in our dualistic inspirations unbridgeable gaps between the two poles sketched out. (The descriptions of psychological symbiosis [see Chapter 4], wherein the learning of an emotion was seen as prototypically involving a combination of the infant's motor and perceptual skills *and* the caregiver's imparting intentions, headed, much more modestly, in the same direction.) It hardly needs stating that this "gap filling" is an enterprise of enormous proportions.

In addressing the self thus far, I have aimed to do so in the broadest possible way, seeing how that in turn can furnish plausible support for conceiving subjectivity as governed principally by emotion. But what about the "secondary structure," that is, the myriad ways what I have attempted to clarify at a transcendental or foundational level becomes differentially construed in an almost infinite variety of historical and cultural settings formed into specific behavior-informing understandings of what selves and their capacities are? Of necessity, I will be very brief here, because I have given concrete examples of how self-understanding impacts the *experiencing* of emotions (see Chapter 4) and because my account here has already sprawled beyond its intended (quantitative) limits.

First—and in line with what to my knowledge is the best argument to the effect, namely Harré's (1984, chap. 4)—I take it that the acquisition of specific notions of selfhood occurs concretely via institutionalized conducts mediated by speech, or what has popularly come to be known since Wittgenstein as "language games." From this base I think we can leave it to the hermeneutically oriented social scientists (i.e., those that begin with self-understanding as the primary datum in explanation of behavior) to come up with adequate explanations of why particular peoples, speaking particular languages, forming specific polities, inheriting unique traditions and economic circumstances, "have" the selves they think themselves to be (e.g., English, more than Eskimo, appears to induce thought about the self as a substance). Michelle Rosaldo, an anthropologist, provides one excellent example of such work, especially since (significantly for the perspective pursued here) she treats culture as "organized views of possibility and sense" (1984, 140) and takes these, as we would, to be critical for the acquisition of selfhood. Her notion of self is clearly strongly "actional."

Looking back to the desire for recognition as one constitutive moment of selfhood, one aspect that ought as a matter of methodological assumption to figure centrally in all research on self and emotions is self-esteem,[7] especially if the people under consideration belong to a strongly hierarchized culture and even more so if individualism is a constitutive feature of that culture's ethos. (Indeed, there is no reason why "self-esteem" should not plausibly become an authentic object of investigations for any "sociology of emotions.")

Which brings me finally to *our,* Western self. For surely there is such a phenomenon, a "peculiar variant" (Berger 1985) of what humans can be that exists both as an idea and a deeply institutionalized way of experiencing. I am referring to the "autonomous individual," the "possessor" of his or her (alienable) experiences, whose roots can be traced back to the Hellenic and Israelite traditions but who, helped along by Christianity and the latter's Renaissance and Reformation revolutions, becomes supreme with (and defining of) modernity. A further entrenchment occurs with romanticism and the novel of first-person sensibility (Rorty 1976, 11), no doubt also greatly aided by the transformations and dislocations brought on by developing capitalism's market economies and commodity production. Contemporarily, again through our moral-religious customs, legal frameworks, economic relations, and cultural metaphors, we socialize deep intuitions about a private, individual, autonomous self that takes itself as unique in the traits beyond those it has in common with even the closest others. And we begin early, advising our children to figure things out for themselves, allowing a wide range of choosing in their lives, affording them plenty of privacy, and sending them into solitude to "think things over" when they have committed mischief.

No doubt, "relentless reason" and "relentless conscience" (to borrow from Berger), as in Descartes, Rousseau, and the individualist ethos in general, have made possible innumerable new articulations that in turn opened on vast enrichment of the self and its emotional dimensions. Some emotions, like romantic love, indeed appear limited (as a widespread phenomenon) to the individualist West. And would not life be dull without it? At the same time, it must be admitted that our "centered" model of experience is not a dispensable option in *our* psychology but a quasi-permanent salience required to realize those psychological attributes that within our moral order will enable and entitle us to be recognized as persons by others, that is, to be selves. Stated the other way around, if the moral order is premised on, say, responsibility, rational calculation, and choice as locused in the individual human being, selfhood will develop as the acquisition of these capacities.

But while reflecting on such gains and necessities of being a Western self, we ought not lose sight of potential heavy costs of excessive autonomy. As was shown, meaningful intimacy as a response to desire for recognition is critical for personal integration and emergence of full selfhood. Thus, certain romantic pretensions aside, only in and through genuine community can an authentically individual self come to the fore and flourish. Conversely, it is loneliness and separation—considered now by some as having reached epidemic proportions in North America—that lead to the impoverishment of selfhood and, as evidenced by the crass subjectivist clamor for the pursuit and expression of "feelings," to the standardization of emotional life. For on a closer look, it turns out that all those insistent on pursuing "their own thing" within a tightly guarded private sphere (as an expression of putatively idiosyncratic feelings) are mostly doing the *same* things, and often doing them in a rather anxious and frantic manner. Then too, it must be noted that these experiential qualities reflect nothing but a concerted effort on our part to (re)vitalize ourselves, to resuscitate our increasingly flat emotional lives.

No doubt there are other factors with powerful potential to join and contribute to an increasingly passionless, disengaged existence. Being a relational phenomenon, existing as a self is a fragile business at the best of times. Yet as a generality, it cannot be missed that if anything characterizes modernity, it is its constant changing of the locus of belonging, its lack of integrating stability at the level of objects and now increasingly the level of persons. Thus the "self industry"—so much talk and print about how to find, help, and manage ourselves as we try to negotiate current turbulences (here instrumentalism vis-à-vis self joins that effected toward the world), with those unable to cope condemned to a life of what Lasch (1984) has so aptly called the "minimal self."

But enough of this negative tone. There are already too many naysayers among us, and I have neither the desire nor any specific reasons to seize exclusively upon a diminishing potential for mutuality in relation to emotions and the prospects of our selves. Nor has it been my intention to become unduly pessimistic in a larger sense. I recognize that one possible interpretation of what is implied in the immediately preceding considerations is that the "feeling self" is all too easily a victim of contingencies that lie beyond its power of influence. In the next chapter, I shall therefore attempt to argue the contrary by delineating a positive sense in which we are responsible for our emotions.

6
EMOTIONS AND RESPONSIBILITY

It is against the background of an unqualified acceptance of determinism in the phenomenal order on the one hand and refusing to ground the postulates of our practical life in any naturalistic psychology on the other that Kant's insistence that we are autonomous and responsible agents acquires so much force. Simply put, Kant saw how profoundly it matters to us that we assume (and demand) responsibility, since this reflects our potential as "active and self-aware beings with perspectives on what we do and with a contributing and creative role to play in what we become" (Schoeman 1987, 1). Indeed, to make concessions in the (inter)personal realm to factors we think beyond our control inevitably attenuates our sense of self; it leaves us, as it were, in a "diminished position in the great chain of being" (2).

Ironically, the philosopher who could arguably be regarded as the most critical advocate of autonomy and responsibility, especially if one considers his influence on subsequent existentialist thought on the subject, also did much to dissuade us from thinking about emotions in relation to these dimensions of personhood. This fact was ensured by Kant's vigorous denial that emotions can play any *positive* role in moral agency—his judgment being that they possess features inimical to both full autonomy and universalization. But if emotions are critical to selfhood and identity, it is vital that we bring them within the ambit of "responsibility." Indeed, because emotions motivate behavior and the framing of (motivating) intentions is part of any act, the issue seems unavoidable.

To be sure, Kant's position (and what it implies) is fairly standard. The attempt to bring together "emotions" and "responsibility" is typically seen as nothing less than a symptom of a serious category mistake. And although in our daily lives we may customarily reproach others and ourselves for having inappropriate or even unjustified emotions,[1] this practice, usually and for most, cannot bear the weight of its own scrutiny.[2] Anxious in the face of the progressive disappearance of an objective framework for our actions, we develop a defensiveness that largely overrides the emancipatory potential of our increased insights into the causes of our psychological states and behavior. That very anxiety and defensiveness are also what keep us focused on the seedy side of our emotional life, prompting us to select the most disruptive passions as paradigms of emotionality and to insist that the latter's potential for unhinging reason and volition is its principal functional feature. To be sure, there are on the other side many contemporary romantics willing to exalt emotions as superior modalities of the mind. But critically they share with the former group the important judgment about the impossibility (or even desirability) of a more integrated picture of personhood.

In effect, we hardly put our best foot forward. We may timidly assert that we are at best responsible for the *expressions* (and to a lesser extent signs and symptoms, if there are any) of various emotions but not for *having* these emotions themselves. Here the operative assumption is that it is only the former, as intent-backed "behavior," that can reasonably be said to be under our control. The strictly experiential part of an emotion is standardly taken to come over us pretty much like the weather; whatever it is, it certainly is not something we ourselves initiate and hence can be held accountable for. The argument for this is generally thought to be clinched by the passivity conveyed in pervasively used expressions that have us "falling in love," "overcome by anger," "struck by jealousy," and so on.

As I pointed out in Chapter 1, the philosophical roots of this picture can be traced back to Plato's tripartite division of the human soul and his localization of psychological functions in specific areas of the human organism. I also mentioned the substantive contribution of extrascientific concerns in regard to his decisions. Thus thought, considered by Plato a form of self-motion, was naturally placed in the head because the latter, as circular, possessed (in line with the symbolism of the broader cosmological framework) the property definitive of self-sustenance. By default, then, human emotions were rendered both passive and bodily. The fact of obsessive and/or wandering thoughts apparently did not carry appreciably sufficient force for Plato to reconsider this division.

Still, and in spite of their mythical inspiration, because these views are embedded in our culture to the point of being self-evident or unreflectively taken for granted, it might be tempting to try to prop them up with what passes for relevant research. For example, today we know from neurophysiology that because the more strictly cerebral functions (e.g., computation, logical reasoning) involve predominantly extremely fast electrophysical modulation of neurotransmitters, they are experienced as under our immediate control, whereas the emotional circuitry, grounded in the glandular-hormonal processes relying on less quick chemical transformations, is considerably more cumbersome and that much slower to react to whatever willful initiatives we may take to alter it. The latter system will also tend to engage much more the entire organism.

But the critical point to be noted here is that the "supporting" empirical features *follow* a conceptual decision about what is to count as an emotional state in the first place, where the principles of distinction are "political" in the sense that they are within certain admittedly rather broad and vague limits subject to intra- and intersubjective interpretation and negotiation. However "intuitive" such principles may seem, their basis is not some immutable objective datum independent of mutually shared understandings of those who apprehend it. (And should we have chosen to investigate the physiology of a different mental state, our brain scans would have shown a different mix of "fast" and "slow" circuitry.)

What in this instance neurology thus furnishes is no more than a *causal* explanation of the phenomenal feature of passivity—especially in those experiences where the standardly "cognitive" factors (i.e., perceptions, inferences, beliefs, judgments) are negligible or absent—but not any *reasons* why experience itself ought to be divided along the active-passive axis in any specific manner. We can thus also understand why, so long as we focus exclusively on those emotions with the least cognitive content, we shall deny ourselves the experiential basis empowering us to challenge the alleged passivity of emotions. (It hardly needs saying, I think, that with such a focus we would also have little by way of an emotional life worth talking about.) But the choice of focus is still largely an extrascientific matter, and pending complete conceptual replacement (rather than just modification) of our ordinary ways of thinking about ourselves by the abstract language of science, the latter cannot but lag behind the former. Any notion, then, that Plato and the tradition could thus be vindicated (or challenged) by modern medical research is misconceived. Nonetheless, it puts in clear relief the sense in which he stands accused of being insufficiently sensitive to empirical knowledge as something afforded *within* ordinary experience itself. Clearly, a more inclusive and balanced interpretation of emotions could have been achieved had it not been crowded out by an excessively intellectualistic notion of personhood that was concurrently at best tenously linked to its immediate natural and social context.

Be all that as it may, in broaching the issues related to responsibility, it is, as with so many other philosophical problems, profitable to begin with Aristotle's reflections on the subject. In book 3 of the *Ethics,* and proceeding from the critical assumption that voluntariness is to mark the domain of the responsible, the discussion begins with the distinction between involuntary and free action. To the former category belong acts performed either under compulsion or out of ignorance; voluntary action, on the other hand, is simply action where these conditions do not obtain. Compulsion in turn is specified, initially at least, in terms of the location of an action's determining factors (its efficient causes). Thus an involuntary or compelled action is one whose cause resides outside the agent (e.g., when I am tossed around by wind), and a voluntary act is marked by the fact that its starting points lie solely within us.

Now, Aristotle is surely correct that the delineation of what the agent contributed to any outcome is critical for assessing and attributing responsibility for it. But what at first approximation seems an eminently commonsensical way to establish this contribution soon breaks down under a barrage of counterexamples or cases that must be assessed but fall beyond the scope of the procedure—especially that Aristotle understands the outside-within distinction primarily in a spatial sense. For instance, if we take our beliefs to play a causal role in action, it would be inadmissable that they be purely internally generated since it is precisely their appropriate connectedness to the world that is criterial for our being declared sane, hence responsible in the first place (Schoeman 1987, 2). Another set of problems is made salient by neurosis-grounded obsessions and compulsions, structures of thought and behaviour whose very rigidity inclines us to view them as (determining) "mechanisms" but that strictly speaking, lie solely within us and so should not be considered as factors of constraint. Perhaps the day can be saved by an existentially oriented psychiatrist who will insist that neurotics are not just passive victims but also more or less active contributors to their own suffering. But even conceding this point, we clearly must allow, as our legal doctrines do, for instances of some internal incapacitations that place the agent beyond any claim of accountability. Just as there are movements originating within our bodies that are not "up to us" (e.g., spasms), there should be no presumption against this holding (to at least some degree) in the psychological realm as well (Frankfurt 1976).

Not surprisingly, then, tracing the causal chain to its origin in the agent to mark voluntariness is far from the whole story in Aristotle. For although not privy to the insights of contemporary psychoanalysis and existential psychologies, he is sufficiently aware of the many cases where an action cannot be *unambiguously,* or at least unproblematically, judged as either voluntary or involuntary, and thus the initially criterial outside-within distinction fades into the background. What comes to prominence instead is examples focusing on the nature of the *relationship* that obtains between a particular outcome and the agent, independently of the issue of where the immediate or efficient cause of the former lies. And the assessment of that relationship as proper or incorrect is afforded by what *social* practice suggests as the conditions under which *normal* inferences about an individual's character can be made (Schoeman 1987, 3). Thus, while it remains my option to do something or not to do it under the threat of death, and in that sense whatever I eventually do is free, overall the action cannot be said to be voluntary and I accountable for it. Though we may find it commendable when a person manages to resist such a threat, to insist unequivocally on accountability would just be unreasonable in view of how drastically the conditions of ordinary life (and hence a chance for a proper relationship of agent to act) have been altered.

What these considerations at once reveal is the inclusion of a temporal dimension as pertinent to accountability, and this is something that in turn informs Aristotle's thinking on how we can be said to be responsible for what we are (*Ethics,* bk. 3, chap. 5). Though much of the latter, in negative and positive aspects, is consequent of seemingly intractable habits, the *formation* of habits in general is something that in principle is at least in part amenable to our intervention. Again, social knowledge of causal histories and developmental dynamics of our dispositions provides the terms on which imputation of responsibility for what we have become can be made. Thus, to the extent that it is commonly known what sorts of actions lead one to being overweight (and barring special circumstances that somehow prevent me from having access to this knowledge), I am surely responsible for being fat, even if I experience my present appetite as uncontrollable.

This is essentially the picture that obtains for Aristotle when it comes to emotions. In line with his general (metaphysical) theory of potentiality, which accepts the existence of passive and active powers (Kosman 1980, 106), Aristotle is quite willing, but at once untroubled, to view emotions as passions (i.e., something that we undergo or "suffer"). For although he contends our being subject to fear or anger is not deliberately and immediately chosen, these "passive potentialities"—in line now with the integrationist picture advanced in his psychology—are nonetheless features that are *internal* and not external to our nature. They are human *powers* to be affected in certain ways not altogether different from the way perception and reason can be acted upon by the sensible and intelligible forms of objects in the world (107). And if it can be shown in turn that we are responsible for character as the dispositional source of those experiences, this consideration will override the restrictions on responsibility imposed by looking at emotions principally as if they were discrete, context-free particulars unrelated to the rest of our being but nevertheless somehow influence us. Clearly, and critically, for Aristotle, choice is a concept that at best only marginally governs individual actions divorced from the framework of goals and habits (114). It is the latter—and precisely because it is a product of sustained effort and practice—to which the notions of choice and responsibility are more properly applicable. On this picture, to the extent that certain voluntary practices end up disposing us to feel in particular ways, there is nothing incongruent in suggesting that the emergent emotions themselves were chosen.

Notwithstanding this progressively "existentialist" direction of Aristotle's thought, the bulk of his considerations pertain to what might be called retrospective responsibility, one that accrues to the agent in virtue of his or her voluntary engagements in *past* activities known at the time to be formative for certain subsequent outcomes. Within this (predominant) sense we can of course accommodate numerous instances in which experiencing an emotion is under our control far more immediately than striving to develop a long-term disposition for it, though the "product" of such efforts will typically be episodic and not self-sustaining. I have in mind here "working" ourselves into anger, "psyching" ourselves up, "controlling" our enthusiasm—willful processes wherein we end up with what experientially are felt as genuine, objectively grounded emotions (even if the primary focus was on their strictly expressive aspects). Then too, there are the numerous ways of controlling emotions by acting on their known physiological and psychological *causes*—for example, getting more sleep, drinking less coffee, avoiding heights, avoiding someone we know irritates us. And if certain assessments in an emotion (and hence its existence) are predicated upon an easily ascertainable empirical belief (e.g., did Ricky break the bicycle or not?), then we are most certainly at fault for having and/or sustaining that emotion where the belief is false. Nothing prevents us from getting the facts straight.

Still, this sense of responsibility, one premised mainly on *controlling* antecedents, inevitably runs up against limits. Certainly it shows the falsehood of blanket statements to the effect that we *never* have any control of *any* emotion (Sankowski 1977, 834) while also providing us with a strong sense of their *contingency* (i.e., it is not inevitable that we currently experience just this emotion, or of that quality, as opposed to another). It is also enormously helpful in overcoming the pernicious tendency to atomize our experience by looking at mental life in isolated time slices. Such neutralization of our historicity blocks out any sense of self-directedness and choice for anything less than immediate intentions to act. Still, even granting that the scope of self-intervention goes far beyond what we generally assume, we cannot be aware of all the pertinent causalities of which many may contain strong (perhaps even determining) dispositions whose formation extends considerably into our past, is in large measure embedded in (extraindividual) socialization processes, and so could hardly have been chosen in the requisite sense.[3] On the retrospective view, we should not be held responsible for the ensuing emotions; there seems no way to insert an element of activity "into" them.

But perhaps this is to concede too easily the validity and force of the traditional active-passive distinction in our lives. After all, if an action issuing from a strong emotion has had significant consequences for others, *should* it be claimed that no one is responsible for it just because it is hard to specify the intentional element in the emotion's formation? One thing is certain: it would certainly not be a very robust notion of responsibility that allowed for a too easy detachment of intentions framing an act from the acting agent.

Published originally in 1939, Sartre's *The Emotions: Outline of a Theory* is a work whose size belies its importance for theorizing about emotions. In it Sartre radically departs from the traditional model of emotions as foreign intruders of rationality. The break is essentially accomplished through the incorporation of Husserlian phenomenology within the broader existentialist frameworks of Kierkegaard and Heidegger.

The adoption of the phenomenological method (and its first-person or "internalist" standpoint) as appropriate for studying emotions follows directly from their ontological relocation. Against the "peripheric" accounts of emotion as preferred by the psychologies then in vogue (e.g., James's view of emotion as a proprioceptive state that epihenomenally manifests itself in consciousness), Sartre insists that emotions are intentional *acts* (in Husserl's sense), that is, structures *of* consciousness. This being sent "back to consciousness" (Sartre 1948, 40), he remarks, is a conclusion that flows naturally when one surveys the failures of the successive theories that putatively improved on the Jamesian position. In particular, once we admit a certain "transformation of form" of objects (i.e., their being imbued with new and different qualities) in emotion as the latter's cardinal phenomenological feature, consciousness is necessarily presupposed because it "alone, by its synthetic activity, can brake and reconstitute forms ceaselessly" (40). Moreover, the strong link with the subjective factors involved is also necessary (to account for emotions) because no specification of evoking context will explain why a *particular* emotional reaction occurred and not another. In Sartre's view, then, emotions are nothing less than specific ways of apprehending the world; they are *consciousness-organized* modes of human existence. But this move at once proves critical for denying that they are in any way *accidental.* For to suggest that emotions are just states that somehow befall us would be tantamount to claiming that consciousness itself, in its signifying processes, is purposeless, hence a return to the already discredited epiphenomenalism.

The fundamental emphasis on consciousness allows for some initial general observations. On the assumption of the transparency of consciousness, and as against Freud, there are for Sartre no unconscious purposes and consequently no unconscious emotions—since that would imply an inexplicable disjunction in the mind, making self-awareness in turn impossible (46). Grafting the Heideggerian theme of the need to assume responsibility for ourselves to a conception of consciousness as spontaneous activity, radical choice and freedom, all emotions become by definition voluntary self-identifications and world-interpretations. They do not just befall us, we choose them. Even if they are typically unreflective (i.e., not products of deliberation), their context is one of *action.*

This is as radical a solution as one may imagine to the challenges posed for accountability for emotions by their alleged passivity. Indeed there is a temptation to dismiss Sartre for arbitrarily doing away with the standard conceptual distinction between "actions" and "passions," one whose force and pervasiveness, it stands to reason, must point to real phenomena informing it. But Sartre does not deny the distinction. Rather, his point is that the *criteria* that have been used to mark it are themselves misguided and in need of conceptual relocation. Thus actions and passions do not differ because the former are chosen and the latter are not but because they are different *types* of choice itself (Bernstein 1971, 296). And choice, of course, serves as the unifying principle and defining phenomenon because it captures the independence (and hence freedom) of the intentional order of consciousness (as *no-thingness*) from the causal-deterministic one. Consciousness, choice, freedom, intentionality—all of these, as is well known, are interchangeable for Sartre. Thus viewing emotions as structures of consciousness simultaneously endows them with all the other predicates pertinent to consciousness itself.

This causality-obviating extreme voluntarism has come in for severe criticisms too frequent to need restating here. We may appreciate that this ontology of consciousness and emotions is embedded in a decidedly larger moral concern to establish human freedom and responsibility in a *categorial* sense (i.e., as a noncontingent constitutive human feature). But even granting the understandable existentialist reluctance to give too definite a content to "human nature" for fear of prejudging our (specifically human) powers of self-formation, Sartre's expansion of freedom and responsibility seems just too broad and unqualified, too aprioristic in fact, to be helpful in everyday contexts. But this judgment can be fully substantiated only if we examine a little further the experiential background that informs Sartre's view of emotions. For after all, it is precisely Sartre's claim that his view is based on real phenomena.

First, when we inquire into the specific function, the overriding or basic purpose of emotions-as-choices, the latter turns out to be none too edifying. Briefly, emotions allow us to cope with our impotence in the face of an obdurate and difficult world. Finding that we cannot effectively change a given situation in the sense of intervening in the real factors that lead to our frustration, it is the direction of consciousness, our intentions and behavior, that we proceed to alter. The transformation thus effected is purely within our subjectivity; the real, objective world becomes bearable because we take a radically different stance toward it. As Sartre puts it, the essence of an emotion is to "change (our) relations with the world in order that the world may change its qualities" (Sartre 1948, 61). So we "change our mind" and decide that the desired grapes we cannot reach are too sour anyway. Of course, we have done nothing to alter them, but this is now irrelevant since the effectiveness of our activity lies elsewhere, in how well it has managed to overcome our disappointment and impotence. Herein lies the meaning of that much misunderstood sense in which Sartre calls emotions "magical transformations" of the world: suddenly we believe the world to be different and suitable to us.

It is clear that this account of the aim of emotions is a variant of a more pervasive theme in Sartre, namely, that of Hegel's "Unhappy Consciousness" unable to face its own contingency on (and thus alienation from) its objects. For what it comes down to is that emotions are structures of consciousness designed to overcome this basic deficit (or at the very least to obscure its recognition), so that Sartre is forced to assume on his own premises that they are all forms of bad faith or self-deception. To put it more starkly, the condition of authenticity is to be *without* emotions.

But this is an absurd conclusion, one that generates strong ambivalence about the Sartrean picture. On the one hand, there is a genuine contribution in the insistence that emotions are structures through and in which we *live—acts* of, and not *episodes* in, consciousness. On the other hand, the contribution is tainted because, as Solomon (1981) points out, the idea of emotions as compensations for our impotence returns us to the traditional prejudice that they are inferior, irrational, and degrading modes of being.

The critical point to note here is that Sartre's examples typically highlight those situations in which we want to *withdraw* from the world and for that very reason cannot be taken as a basis for a universalization about the essence and function of *all* emotions. On the contrary, the ubiquity of emotions is such that they motivate and sustain *all* our actions and commitments, sincere and insincere, including precisely Sartre's project of describing the emotions in the terms that he does. This cannot be discounted. Having postulated "a sharp disjunction between a nonemotional instrumental field of reality and an emotional noninstrumental (magical) field of unreality (Fell 1965, 123), it is the latter within which Sartre is by definition compelled to account completely for emotions. It is notable, however, that Heidegger—from whom Sartre directly appropriates both the notion of an instrumental life-world as a primordial sphere of existence and emotion as a mode of being-in-the-world (i.e., an existential structure)—never maintained such an antithesis, seeing mood, on the contrary, as pervasive (Fell 1965, 129). This Cartesian diremption is clearly illegitimate. In the end, if the plausibility of the interesting emotion-as-choice thesis can be demonstrated and bought only on condition of putting emotions nowhere but in the world of the imaginary, it threatens Sartre's picture with being irrelevant.

No doubt there are many who would relish—insincerely, I think—just such a prospect. But there has hardly been anyone as forceful as Sartre in calling us to accountability for ourselves, and for that reason alone he deserves our attention, especially in view of how facile and pervasive is the use of emotions as excuses or mitigating factors for inexcusable actions. What we need, then, is to maintain the spirit of Sartre's strong responsibilism without, however, being taken in by his theoretical failures, in particular the failure to show how emotions are activities in a sense other than the Pickwickian one he provides. Also, Sartre's insistence that emotions are acts of consciousness is immensely valuable and correct; it intimates, as will be seen, a viable sense of responsibility for emotions even if Sartre himself misses it.

First, though, something of a fresh start. For it may appear that we have not come very far with either of the two main pictures so far presented. Yet what may be partly misconstrued is the nature of the task to be accomplished in support of attributions of responsibility. Must it necessarily hang on the "activation" of emotions in the sense of showing how we willfully (if not deliberately) stand at the point of their initiation? This clearly is what motivates both the retrospective view and Sartre's position that the conventional distinction between actions and passions is conceptually mislocated and his consequent "legislation" that emotions are actions.

The first counsel is not to endow the distinction, wherever it is conceptually placed, with as much force as it traditionally has held. There appear to be experiential grounds for a less polarized position over and above any that have been advanced within the two perspectives so far examined. For example, Robert Gordon has recently argued that the concession that emotions are passive (in the sense in which this is conventionally accepted and grammatically underscored) does not mean that they are altogether involuntary or states with respect to which we are passive (Gordon 1986, 372). Making a useful analogy— based on the assumption that the shared passive voice in such locutions as "I am intoxicated" and "I am embarrassed" may be a hint of a common "metaphysical" passivity—he suggests that just as *at moderate dosage levels* certain psychoactive substances (e.g., alcohol, marijuana) will intoxicate a person only if she wants or actively "assents" to be (or believes that she is) intoxicated, so whether one is going to be embarrassed or not may in certain instances be a matter of a "decision" to be, or a belief about actually being, embarrassed (378).

Although Gordon's view of emotion is not the one defended here—he seems to take it principally as a feeling consequent of certain cognitions—I believe he makes a valid point that in normal (i.e., nonextreme) circumstances emotions incorporate a certain degree of reflexivity that allows for second-order judgments-decisions about them, which judgments-decisions will in turn be determinant of the qualities of the experience if not whether one will sustain it in the first place (as in "I'll be darned if I let this 'get to me'"). This suggests at the very least the falsehood of attempts to substantiate emotional passivity on grammatical grounds. "Grammatical passivity" appears compatible with our having a "*wide range of active roles* in controlling our states" (379). The passivity of emotion is not always, or even typically, like being overcome by an illness but rather, as in perception[4] (where even though things "come at us," we may have nonarbitrary reasons to deny the actuality of what is, or will be, perceived), we may find good reasons to deny "living through" a particular emotion ostensibly attributable for the occasion.

From the other side, the analysis of action, we discover the naiveté of thinking that actions straightforwardly follow (their causing) intentions or that they are always a result of conscious deliberation, a product of a chain of practical reasoning. It certainly is the essence of actions (and the condition of their identification) to be animated by an intention. But as Adam Morton suggests, in countering a "simplistic view of responsibility and a Cartesian picture of the will," there is no simple congruence between the content of intentions and the nature of the achieved result, not even for some "natural" class of "basic" actions (1980, 131). Typically, our paradigm examples of voluntary intentional actions, the ones that in contrast give the greatest force to the alleged passivity of emotions, restrict themselves to simple planned physical movements consequent of some desire: "I want some fresh air"; "I walk over and open the window"; "I was free to decide and do otherwise." But most of our actions are temporally extended, incorporating spontaneous adjustments and *reactions* to the environment and assimilations of information (as in a conversation), where the unfolding "subcomponents" reflect much less the initiating plans and where indeed, in an "obvious inversion" of what we take to be the right or standard causal order, the point of the action frequently reveals itself "after the fact" of performing it (132). For any analysis of action, then, we should—as indeed it seems we must, save for the most superficial cases—distinguish between (deliberate) *prior* intentions and (spontaneous) *intentions-in-action* (Searle 1984, 65)[5] and also admit that the latter significantly structure actions.

But this admission at once opens on the numerous possibilities of ambiguity and ambivalence, that is, the ways our actions are consequences of mixed and conflicting reasons and motives. In Annette Baier's (1985, chap. 7) felicitous description, there are many shadows that can fall between reasons, intentions, and actions. Which is to say that there is much in the content of actions that is not within our explicit purview and (at least immediately) up to us, and hence is, per convention, "passive." The mind being, against Descartes, an intrinsically plural thing and not merely self-present thought, the infrastructure of actions will contain elements that are simply too deep and/or too general for direct intervention.[6] While not clearly intentional-deliberate, surely such elements cannot on the other hand be pigeonholed as nonintentional slips or actions from ignorance. But where else, on the standard view, should we put them? As in most other either-or disjunctions, this one too fails to address the complexities of experience and suggests an absurd conclusion that, it would logically follow, puts in question our notion of voluntary and autonomous action altogether.

The point of these elaborations on the "impurity" of actions and passions is not to deny the distinction between the former and the latter but to fine-grain it, to make us realize that it generally draws its force from simplistic and polarized thinking that takes extremes to be the standard cases and consequently to reject the overriding role it plays in settling our attributions of responsibility for emotions.

But the distinction can be suspect on still other grounds and from a somewhat different vantage point. For precisely to the extent that it is used to settle the issue of responsibility, it begs the question of whether it is *rational* to frame that issue in just this way. On the face of things, the enterprise seems noble—the principal motivation behind arguing that we somehow choose our emotions being to obviate the deleterious irresponsibleness of invoking them as states that interfere with agency. The strength of the impulse to disown inexcusable actions cannot be underestimated, and we ought to resist it by any possible means.

Still, and notwithstanding the validity of its inspiration, this effort must be importantly qualified. For it is a critical assumption of some of our most important human attitudes, in particular those that sustain our sense of community, that we are precisely *vulnerable* emotionally in ways we cannot fully control (Sabini and Silver 1987). We could not experience such emotions as sympathy and moral caring were the pain and sense of loss of grieving persons their willfully chosen states. To think so would be a height of intellectualistic self-deception that in denying our conditions of fragility and contingency, actually falsified human reality itself. And we may also value a measure of passivity in emotions for the guarantees it offers regarding our sincerity, deception being far easier with words than with face, tone of voice, or hands (Baier 1987).

How, then, can we frame the issue of responsibility for emotions doing justice to the diversity of considerations pertinent to it? Where to draw the strategic lines given the fact that much of our emotional life is under our control but some (and to the good) is not? How do we factor in the important notion of retrospective responsibility but accept that unable to completely eradicate escapism, it does not do the whole job? What about Sartre's critical insistence on unconditional responsibility, however distorted and one-sided his view of emotions? What of the fact that we routinely credit or discredit people for their emotions without prior consideration whether these were a matter of will and choice?[7]

In the attempt to cut across these questions without a priori excluding any of them, I believe some inroads can be made by drawing on Charles Taylor's (1976) delineation of responsibility, which is bound up with our conception of a person or self. Taylor's first move is to adopt a notion introduced by Harry Frankfurt (1971), namely, that what distinguishes us from other animals is a "capacity for reflective self-evaluation . . . manifest in the formation of second-order desires" (Taylor 1976, 281). On this view, a person is not just a subject of desires, choices, or even deliberation. Rather, the peculiarly human capacity for second-order desires implies that as persons, we want certain first-order desires to be the ones that motivate our actions. In short, a person is a subject capable of posing the question, "Am I the kind of being I ought to be, or really want to be?" The question has a familiar Heideggerian ring to it. Humans are just those beings whose existence inescapably entails an evaluative questioning about what sort of being they are going to realize. And to the extent that we can shape ourselves on this evaluation, this becoming is "up to us," a responsibility in our hands.

Because the content and mode of the evaluative process is left somewhat underdetermined in Frankfurt's formulation, Taylor makes a further and very helpful distinction between two senses in which one could be said to be evaluating one's desires. On the one hand, we can examine the latter (and the actions they motivate) simply on the basis of convenience or how to make the different desires compatible or compossible. The important point about this sort of evaluation is that desires and actions are viewed both as members of the same order and contingently, that is, in relation to an assumed value *extrinsic* to them (e.g., the maximization of satisfaction, avoidance of pain, etc.). This vision of evaluation as primarily a calculative process is the essence of utilitarianism and can be seen in turn as part of the broader instrumentalism pervading modern thought. Taylor proposes to call it "weak" evaluation. The essence of "strong" evaluation on the other hand is to apply to our desires and actions qualitative distinctions of worth—to see them as virtuous or vicious, noble or base, profound or superficial—whereby these distinctions are judged to reflect and sustain qualitatively different modes of life—for example, fragmented or integrated, alienated or free, saintly or merely human (282). On this view, the self is not just a bearer of preferences to which it strategically relates but is actually constituted by such judgments.

What strong evaluation in turn presupposes, and what is missing from its weak version, is the deployment of a language capable of contrastive characterization. To reflect thus upon our desires is not just to step back from the immediacy of the present situation in order to calculate consequences or assess which one "feels" better. It means, rather, to articulate and bring into focus something that is initially diffuse and imprecise, yet of great significance to us because it informs the kind of life we lead. Thus, another way to get at the contrast between weak and strong evaluation is to see that the objects of strong evaluation are never fully independent, that as consequent to strong evaluation they are indeed constituted by this process in a way the objects of weak evaluation never are.

Just here, it seems to me, is a valuable point of entry for a notion of responsibility for emotions. To articulate a desire or an emotion is to alter it, thereby also altering our stance toward it.[8] What a given emotion means to us is in large measure contingent on how we interpret it through our articulations, how we frame it in the language of contrastive evaluation. But the important point to be made here about strong evaluation is that its articulations can be more or less adequate, more or less true to life, providing us with greater clarity about ourselves or leading to self-delusion. And this applies both quantitatively and qualitatively. On the one hand, our sense of what is truly important, worthy, or more integrated appears always to escape full and satisfactory articulation, its topic seemingly inexhaustible. On the other hand, the topic is our very core, so that there is much room for distortion, blindness, and insensitivity. This means that we cannot absolutize our articulations, that indeed they all must be held as in principle revisable or under an injunction always to look again to see whether we have them right. In short, the very nature of strong evaluation presupposes that there is always a continuous *re*evaluation (296).

This, then, is the sense on behalf of which I believe it is reasonable to propose that we are responsible for our emotions—not in the sense that we choose them (in some cases we do, but there are too many counterexamples to absolutize this position) but in the sense that as agents capable of strong evaluation, we are radically responsible for assessing the adequacy of their formulations, the standards that guide this assessment, as well as the standards that guide these standards, and so on. Even if they are usually experienced as something that spontaneously "comes upon us," we are responsible for our emotions because the capacity to entertain them in their depth provides us with alternative stances through which they can be lived.

Here the emphasis on choice, especially of the ex nihilo Sartrean variety, is replaced by stressing how much the process of self-interpretation and self-understanding is also a *self-(trans)formative* process.

Choosing, in this context, is not thereby denied, only displaced.[9] The choice pertains not to the emotion per se, but to the degree to which each of us wishes to reflect on it and ground it in descriptions whose appropriateness is premised on the fact that the reflection is motivated by progressively less superficial aspects of personhood. And it is this fundamental capacity to inform and thereby shape our emotions by those deeper aspects of ourselves on which capacity as a basis, in turn, any viable categorial notion of responsibility for emotions can be maintained. (We are responsible because emotions are the sorts of things vis-à-vis, and "on behalf" of which, one can—via reflection and articulation—*respond* with *norms* that bear on them. Which is another way of saying that we are responsible for emotions precisely because they are significantly constituted by those features that make us interlocutors or respondents, hence answerable, in the first place. Whatever choices we may effect are based on this fundamental fact.)

There is much that recommends itself in this position, which Susan Wolf has dubbed the "deep-self" view. In particular, it gives us a handle on many instances of diminished capacities for accountability. For such cases as brainwashing, kleptomania, or posthypnotic suggestion, responsibility is not demanded just because the victims are alienated from their motivations and actions. The drastic suppression of the connection between their will and their second-order (deep-self) desires rightly makes these instances paradigms of psychological determinism; the ensuing states or actions are not governed by anything deeper in the agent (Wolf 1987, 50).

But as promising, valuable, and reasonable as the Frankfurt-Taylor approach appears to be, it cannot do the whole job, running up against two significant objections. First, if the principle of responsibility for any emotion, desire, or act is established by virtue of their occurring under the influence of a supervening higher-order aspect of personality, the question naturally arises, "What makes us responsible for the latter?" Admittedly, the second-order desires stand to be informed by third-order ones, these by fourth-order ones, and so on. Yet even granting a vast extension of the psychological limits to which this process can be carried out, we shall inevitably have to ask what governs the deepest self and on pain of courting infinite regress, logically answer that this self must ultimately be governed by something outside it (Wolf 1987, 52). But then, without further qualification, it appears that in an important respect both the compulsive and the normal person are on equal footing; both possess basic features of themselves unaccountable for by looking for anything deeper in the agents themselves (Schoeman 1987, 11).

Second, the "deep-self" view discounts the possibility of deviant yet self-directed development. Wolf constructs a hypothetical but plausible scenario in which because of upbringing, education, and acceptance of a loved (but evil and sadistic) parent as a role model, an individual willfully chooses to be the sort of person her parent is. She acts according to her own desires (i.e., without coercion), and moreover those desires are precisely the desires the person wants to have; they express the deep self, the self the person most wishes to be. But the evil nature of the actions performed by such an individual make the claim that she is a fully responsible agent counterintuitive. We are more inclined to think that she was just not in a position to develop otherwise and that indeed, however coherent and rational from her (i.e., internal) point of view her picture of the world appears, from a broader (external) perspective we must judge her insane. Accordingly, for Wolf, it is the condition of responsibility that agents in their core aspects be sane, that is, that they "recognize and appreciate the world for what it is" (Wolf 1987, 58).

Now, I think that the first of the above objections gets some of its force from neglecting the human capacity for *decision* as a requirement of our integration. That is, if I am to avoid becoming paralyzed by the endless inquiry into the foundations of my core aspects, at some point I must neccessarily assert that they are *mine* and that I am their ground, even if this assertion is surrounded by a halo of open-endedness and provisionalism. (Decision in this sense is not optional for a self; it seems in fact, as the existentialists have taught us, a necessary condition for the constitution of self-identity.) As for the second objection, the reflective "self-formationist" could argue against it that humans are in principle ordered to truth and development rather than falsity and involution. In John McGraw's formulation, "unless the self of and by itself can decide between what is true self and false self, another self as referee would have to be invoked to decide between the true and false selves" (1986, 228). But this would require another self to judge the truth or falsehood of the referee, and so on infinitely.[10]

Nevertheless, such potential counterarguments—the second in particular—to Wolf's objections are not, it seems to me, decisive. They would miss the point of her insistence on sanity as a condition of responsibility for what one is and does. For although she does not treat it as such, I take the force of that insistence as a general demand that any *nonvacuous* view of responsibility for character must be concretely embedded in a psychological theory of motivation and a developmental-normative view of human nature.[11]

To be sure, deep reflection is a process that usually gets the self on a more truthful course, and for those of its states that are more obstinate in yielding their grounding reasons we can enlist the aid of a fellow person. We certainly ought to demand of ourselves and others to be responsible for our characters because we ordinarily *can* be and because much good can come of setting higher standards for ourselves, even if they at times appear abstract. At the same time, for the injunction of responsibility for self to be neither dogmatic nor highhandedly moralistic, it is incumbent on us first to understand the real social and psychological conditions that make such responsibility an experiential reality. Any genuine self-understanding, one that ensues in the person's taking greater responsibility for her acts and states, cannot have merely intellectual presuppositions.

In a way, this is where all the difficult work begins in considering responsibility for emotions. For even if we insist that such responsibility is moral—the capacity for strong evaluation being a shared and defining feature of all whom we call persons—it must be imputed differentially; that all possess the relevant capacity does not entail that all share equally in it. Thus we normally believe that the ability of children to reflect, assess, and act on their emotions is less than that of adults.[12] Beyond such obvious distinctions, however, we need to fine-grain our attributions regarding that critical presupposition of responsibility, namely, autonomy. The basic fact seems to be that the sense of possibility of *alternative* courses of action is built into the simplest of everyday actions; the sense that I am making something happen incorporates in it the sense that I could be doing something else (Searle 1984, 95). But there is a world of experiential difference between this sort of (trivial) "actor" autonomy as freedom of exercise that can be predicated of any being with consciousness and the autonomy true of the higher stages of human development wherein one identifies one's whole being with a reflectively elaborated ethical vision of life. In the latter case, autonomy does not reveal itself in an instantaneous flash of the will but paradoxically as a sort of personal *destiny,* as in the medieval notion of eminent neccessity expressive of the confluence of what must be with what is and what ought to be (McGraw 1986, 228). Likewise, when Sartre declares that each of us is *condemned* to choose and be free, he is far closer to describing the rather rare highly integrated individual whose ethical commitment to assume unconditionally all his acts *as his own* is precisely what allows the claim to resonate within that individual's experience and not be a mere abstraction. And it is of such "driven" persons (and not of a consciousness as emptiness) that it is descriptively most accurate to say that they have chosen, and are responsible for, their emotions. Such individuals seem to have the most "access" to their emotions because it is a *reflectively* held, hence accessible moral ideal that provides the reasons for all personal states. Experientially, they possess the greatest certitude about their emotions as authentically their very own because they have taken much effort and care in informing them with more than just a superficial understanding of circumstances and context as well as insight into the entire fabric of their desires, plans, hopes, and so on.

As for the social conditions of responsibility for emotions, because much on the picture I have sketched depends on whether and how we are using our reflective powers, a critical factor will be the value assigned to reflection in a given culture. Perhaps against our intuitions, "metacognitive" activity (i.e., self-monitoring and self-correction) is, as Jerome Bruner tells us, an unevenly distributed and culturally variable *skill.* From its rudimentary beginnings, currently estimated at about eighteen months of life, "how much and in what form it develops will depend upon the demands of the culture in which one lives—represented by particular others and by some notion of the 'generalized other' one forms" (Bruner 1986, 67). Our liberty to change our minds is not, again counterintuitively, a strictly private matter; it depends on and cannot be divorced from membership in a community that trains us in the conventions of criticism, affirmation, and second-thinking (Baier 1985, chap. 4).

Relatedly, and minimally, the prevailing ideology of emotions must be such as to consider them worthwhile objects of reflection; mere sensations or self-enclosed, nonintentional "feels" will not (justifiably) draw extended attention. But we must also remember that as an assumption of self-forming, the personal autonomy that we take so much for granted is a "violatable social gift, the product of what *others* are willing to respect and protect us from . . . the product of the rights and privileges we are granted by others in numerous 'territories of the self'" (Schweder and LeVine 1984, 194). There is, as Peter Berger (1985) argues, a "social map of freedom" because individual autonomy, as we conceive it, is very much a social and historical construction with an institutional matrix, with collectivism being much more the "common human pattern." To furnish but one example: in cultures espousing "moralities of conation" (e.g., Muslims), the notion of freedom as deciding for oneself what is desirable or proper, the correct way to be, is quite foreign. The right path in life is determined by Deity in advance, and freedom relates strictly to the personal power of being able or not to follow that path (Harré 1984, 243).

In a similar vein, we will less readily ask persons to respond for their not having certain other-oriented emotions (e.g., collective guilt) if they live in highly individualistic and atomized cultures. Members of the latter simply lack the requisite experiential grounds for such emotions. We may also find it increasingly difficult to impute responsibility generally for the self in a society (like ours) that has progressively suppressed the use of character terms in favor of clinical-scientific descriptions. (The issue here is more complex than can be stated just in terms of science's allegedly imperial encroachment on the life-world. For part of what science does is to deepen our sense of dependence and contingency, which sense in turn grounds our interest to put some *restrictions* on personal responsibility. Lest we become too zealous and hard-nosed about responsibility for oneself, it is useful to remember that any harshly uncompromising view will restrict our own scope of action as well. In certain contexts some diminishing of the degree of responsibility for what is done, felt, and desired, functions precisely to secure that scope [Dworkin 1987].) And finally, when we have gathered all the cognitive and motivational factors in our environments we think pertinent to assessments of responsibility for character, we must remind ourselves that in human development there are no algorithms. As Ferdinand Schoeman (1987, 6) reminds us, some who succeed in changing themselves have less going for them in terms of the factors we think promote success than others who fail.

Perhaps I have strayed too far from the standard and core preoccupation of sifting whether emotions are actions or we are their victims. But these broad considerations, I want to insist in light of that obviously restrictive focus, are legitimate and inevitable items on the agenda of any viable discussion of responsibility for emotions. If nothing else, I hope to have at least succeeded in conveying some of the complexities of this issue. In any event, our insight into it should be furthered in the examination of another (related) topic that must be addressed, it seems to me, in any sustained reflection on emotions. That topic is self-deception, and it is the subject of the penultimate chapter of this essay.

7
SELF-DECEPTION

Although the overall thrust of this essay is to argue against the all too facile acceptance of emotions as states that intrinsically subvert the stability and coherence furnished by the intellect, it is nevertheless vital to admit the large grain of truth contained in the received view: whenever our motivations are confused, our vision clouded, or the ends we seek undermined, the emotions are all too frequently and pervasively implicated. Indeed, as Nietzsche (1956) and Scheler (1972) have argued in their writings on *ressentiment,* emotions can contribute to the subversion of an entire (value) worldview, the falsification extending beyond individuals to a whole culture or subculture.

To address and explore the issue of self-deception—understood here generically as a failure to be honest in and about one's emotions —thus becomes an important requirement of any systematic treatment of emotions. This requirement should concern us all the more in view of the last chapter's emphasis on reflection and articulation as the principal means of attaining responsibility for them. For to the extent that self-deception is precisely the antithesis that blocks self-understanding, it at once puts in jeopardy the claims that were made in defense of such responsibility. Additionally, it challenges the "purity of commitment" (Martin 1986, 1) to the values of reason, truth, and truthfulness whose exaltation and institutionalizing is arguably the defining characteristic of modern scientific cultures. Who among us does not wish to think of himself as impartial, sincere, and honest? In context, it follows that self-deception, at least implicitly, incorporates a significant moral dimension.

"There is nothing easier for me to know than my own mind,"

Descartes tells us in the second of his *Meditations,* a claim that in its ambiguity neatly captures the two cardinal features that have defined the philosophical and psychological tradition he initiated: the certitude of primacy of knowing *that* each of us is a thinking being and has a mind on the one hand, the incorrigibility of the knowledge of the *content* of that mind on the other. Of course, the two things need not be related, and we can see in Descartes himself that the foundational "clear and distinct ideas" are not the initial givens of consciousness but something he arrives at only with considerable effort and an ascetic procedure. But elsewhere, in *The Passions of the Soul,* he is quite clear about the basis for maintaining incorrigibility with respect to the various *cogitata;* the latter turns strictly on the immediacy with which they are experienced. Accordingly, and addressing himself explicitly to emotions, Descartes suggests that they are "so close and so entirely within our soul" that we cannot possibly experience them in any other manner than that which reveals their true nature (Descartes 1911, 343).

The enormously influential Cartesian tradition has of course not gone uncontested. Prior to this century, we have Nietzsche, who (following Schopenhauer) extends perhaps the most vigorous challenge to the accepted status of consciousness as primary, arguing in effect that the latter is nothing but a means of deceit and dissimulation. But it is not until Freud, whose views receive far greater hearing because they come under the favored auspices of science, that the Cartesian picture of the mind is decisively and irrevocably altered for us. Making an analogy between our awareness of external reality and consciousness of our experiences—just indeed where Descartes insists on a contrast—Freud suggests that "like the physical, the psychical is not necessarily in reality what it appears to be" (Freud 1957, 176).

Admittedly, Freud's conclusions about the mind were significantly influenced by his contact with *abnormal* psychological phenomena, which in turn both confirmed and fueled his view of humans as inherently acquisitive, hence conflicted and dissimulating beings. (We are conflicted because the individualistic gratification sought by instinctual drives has to be constrained by the interpersonal and intrapsychic requirements pertinent to sociality; it follows as a corollary that some of these requirements may be overriding to the point of necessitating the exclusion from awareness of impulses that contradict them.) But we need not be committed to this (or any other) particular picture of human nature to assert that our mental states can be other than what they seem. Rather, and taking a cue from our earlier discussion (Chapter 3), this can be stated as a matter of principle. To recall, on the assumption that there are no mind-states that are not simultaneously grounded in brain-states, introspection is just as dependent on and conditioned by the physiological apparatus of our bodies, and hence potentially as subject to deception, as the perception of the "outer" world.

The further argument to the effect that expression is essential to experience provides additional force against viewing the mind as something perfectly transparent and coincidental with its states. Just as my observable behavioral tendencies and further articulation can be far from adequate (or even false) with respect to how things really are with me, so in the opposite direction the "objective" intention embedded in any explicit expression may bear only an apparent relationship to the causally efficacious motivation of that expression. Sometimes, as in an emotion we have "worked ourselves" into, the pertinent intention (i.e., one licensing the attribution of a genuine experience) arrives late, induced by and following the pretense. Certainly, the standard and typical case is one of "correspondence" of what one means, what ensues in action and expression and embodies the intention, and what one self-reflectively apprehends of both. But clearly the immediacy needed to link introspection (or privileged access) and incorrigibility conceptually with regard to our mental states is just not there.

Moreover, we must take note of the fact that the complexity of many mental states, emotions signally among them, requires for their proper differentiation and identification knowing the "causal histories" of various meanings that have led to these states' being directed at their (current) object (Rorty 1980, 120–21). But not only does this acquaintance go well beyond that particular object's immediate specification; the common or general terms of understanding employed in it inevitably run up against the idiosyncratic component—that is, the differential sensitivity thresholds and situational peculiarities—inherent in our learning of emotions in infancy. (One could say that [mere] specification of the intentional object of an emotion often thus offers no more than a clue to, and is but a starting point for a "deep" interpretation of, what the emotion "really" is. The same point is captured by Bernard Williams's suggestion that there are "few, if any, *highly general* connexions between the emotions and moral language" [1973, 208] and Solomon's observation that recognition of an emotion is a matter of providing a "constitutive hypothesis" that accounts for the specific way we find ourselves in the world [1976, 410].) Finally, recent experimental research in social and cognitive psychology —certain variables such as novelty, intensity, and duration of stimulus, as well as expectations of the perceiver appearing critical for what is "edited" or selected for consciousness—has unearthed a vast new range of self-caused failures in both perception and introspection, thereby providing for a much broader conception of self-deceptive strategies (see Wilson 1985).[1]

It is frequently remarked that self-deception is a paradoxical notion, and this notwithstanding wide agreement and centuries-long acknowledgment in literature of some phenomenon taken to be its actual term of reference. The paradox arises because on the standard understanding of "deception," we assume the existence of (at least) two parties—one deceiving, the other being deceived; the former in possession of knowledge, the latter ignorant of it—in order for deception to obtain.

However, when we take this (interpersonal) model and apply it intrapersonally (i.e., think of it as a lie to oneself), a host of apparent absurdities emerge. For to sustain the formal conditions of deception, we are forced to claim both knowing something and simultaneously being ignorant of it, this being a logically contradictory condition. Moreover, as it is implicit in the notion of deception that the misleading in question is willful or intentional, there arises the problem of its psychological feasibility. That is, the act of persuading oneself intentionally to believe what one at the same time (allegedly) knows to be false demands the conscious use of one's apprehension of the truth in the very attempt to make oneself ignorant or believing falsely. It seems improbable that this grasp of the truth would not from the start undermine the effort to be deceived unless, we are inclined to think, the person was completely irrational. Such persons, however, we would sooner call mad than self-deceived.

Without delving into the vast literature that has arisen in response to the above-outlined problematic, it will suffice to indicate the principal alternative strategies employed in addressing it. One (radical) possibility, the starting point of which is strict adherence to the logical meaning of terms, is to deny that self-deception in any literal sense exists. Consequently, for this position the (incoherent) expression *self-deception* is a misdescription of the actual state of affairs, or more generously, at best a metaphor for such phenomena as wishful thinking, nonwillful bias, or deceiving others (Martin 1985, 17–18). But although the virtue of this approach lies in the avoidance of various puzzles pertaining to psychological unity that literal self-deception brings on the agenda (i.e., the apparent necessity to posit such "occult entities" as the unconscious in order to dispel the paradox of knowing and not knowing, willing and being victim, etc.), it fails to offer a credible explanation for our pervasive (yet on its own premises self-deceived) use of, and hence belief in, "self-deception" (Szabados 1985, 144–45). Moreover, as Szabados shows, notwithstanding the difficulty of defining self-deception, there are good grounds for distinguishing it from other "kin" phenomena and consequently for resisting the assimilationist tactic. In short, rather than explaining self-deception, the latter move seems to explain it away.

Freud, as is well known, addressed the paradox of lying to oneself in quite different terms, positing the existence of intrapsychic "censoring" mechanisms that keep intolerable, anxiety-provoking wishes, desires, and beliefs from reaching explicit consciousness. Thus, although such mental states are on his view more or less continuously operant and manifested in our verbal expressions and behavior, we deny having them because we have only an *unconscious* knowledge of them. (This attribute explains at once the rigid or determined character of the ensuing actions. The actions motivated by unconscious states simply do not have the flexibility of those whose intention is open to scrutiny and alteration as the action unfolds. In any event, it is the bifurcation of consciousness that resolves any ostensible contradictions.)

It did not appear plausible, most famously to Sartre, whom few have matched in the intensity of their criticisms of Freud, that this is at all a viable solution. For if consciousness exists precisely (and only) through its transcending function of having objects, Freud's cutting it off from some of them means cutting it off from itself. This is contradictory, thus theoretically unsustainable. Were there not in fact an a priori unity of intention and the object intended, self-awareness would be nothing but a chimera and not (as it is in Descartes) the simultaneous certitude of one's existence. More unacceptable still, Sartre argues, is that in proposing that our failures to admit to certain emotions, desires, and beliefs are consequent of psychic *mechanisms* to which we apparently fall victim, Freud licences the excuse that our deceptions are not of our own doing and thereby radically undermines responsible human agency. And this abandoning of oneself to the deterministic forces of causality is of course but another, indeed the worst, form of self-deception (Sartre 1966, pt. 1, chap. 2).

To be sure, there is much rhetorical overkill in Sartre's argument against Freud, as in his summary characterization that Freud substitutes for self-deception the notion of "a lie without a liar" (Sartre 1962, 163). (It seems to me, on the contrary, that however obscured by scientific motives, Freud's analysis was precisely an attempt to have the person admit the delusions as the *fusion* of lie and the one responsible for it.) Still, Sartre brings to our attention what hampers Freud's thinking about our deceiving ourselves—a failure to grasp and emphasize the deeper sense of self-knowledge as responsibility of the self for the self in terms of choice.[2] It is just for this reason that, correspondingly, Freud's view of the motivation behind self-deception discounts the complicity of the agent and so is vastly underdeveloped concerning the origin and range of this motivation as well as the content of actual consequent deceptions.

But Sartre's positive thesis is also open to question. Certainly it heads in the right direction; in moving away from treating self-deception as primarily an epistemological challenge, there is significant gain in concretizing the problems posed by it, and the lucid argument against a mechanistic unconscious eliminates one extremely appealing but morally precarious (regarding consequences) solution to it. At the same time, Sartre's voluntaristic approach discounts nonculpable ignorance and dubiously assumes for all a rather extraordinary degree of psychological perspicuity and mental transparency. Whatever cognitive and moral paradoxes the notion of self-deception presents are dissolved via a thoroughgoing and comprehensive knowledge of our intentions. Indeed, in Sartre's radical reformulation, it must be the premise of any attempt to hide an aspect of our being that we are somehow familiar with it (Sartre 1966, 83). Any "not knowing" about self becomes in effect a prereflective pretense that each of us (a priori) has the capacity to recognize. On this basis, Sartre draws a not very generous conclusion about self-deceivers: they are cowards fleeing a painful reality and are to be unqualifiedly condemned. In its uncompromising tone, this stance is surely too extreme.

Before going on to consider yet another approach, one that brokers between Freud and Sartre, it will be useful to insert a number of clarifying points with a view toward dispelling self-deception's paradoxical character. First, it should be recognized that self-deception will arise as a difficult *epistemological* challenge most naturally (and especially) for those who consider all mental acts attitudes to *propositions.* It is they who are in consequence forced to square (the simultaneous existence of) explicitly held contradictory beliefs—not a small feat by any means. For reasons given earlier (Chapter 2), this picture of mind is to be rejected, being especially inadequate when dealing with emotions and additionally forcing us to deny the normality of certain other phenomena that common sense takes for granted: for instance, ambivalence, or being moved by fictions wherein the experienced emotions have as their "cognitive core" imaginative attention rather than veridical belief (McCormick 1985). Not only are the objects of our emotions far more complex—the bare proposition can hardly contain (or even connote) all the psychological qualities of the "object"—but our minds are not some monolithic things incapable of multiaspectual apprehensions of reality. On the contrary, it can be argued equally well that explicit thought and unified mind are, while not an exception, certainly an accomplishment. While we are, after Descartes, strongly inclined to think of mind as simple and indivisible, the lability of emotion in an infant—at one moment giggling with joy over a tickle, at another raging because its movement is constrained by the arms of a parent—suggests that psychic *plurality* ought to be considered more reflective of our basic initial psychological condition (Koch 1987a, 266).

The second clarification concerns the duality of the sense in which a state or event can be qualified as having been brought about willfully or intentionally. The latter terms obviously do not apply to deterministic processes (e.g., digestion) and accidents (i.e., things that just happen to us, as when we trip over an unnoticed stone while walking). These sorts of events also provide the contrast that gives force to the primary commonsensical understanding of willful action as something deliberate, that is, a consequence of explicit thought and weighing (or at least awareness) of alternatives. The effect of this contrast, which critically focuses on there being a direct "fit" or relationship of adequacy between intentions and behaviour, denies the attribution *willful* to actions where explicit intentions are absent.

But this restriction is unwarranted. The movement of my limbs as I take a stroll is certainly willful and motivated, but hardly deliberate in the sense of being animated at every instant by conscious intentions: now to move this leg, now to move the other, the aspect of willfulness being supplied by the overall project (of taking the stroll) within which its specific subcomponents are embedded. Reminding ourselves now that being authentically in a particular mental state entails, among other things, having dispositions to behave or act in specific ways (whose animating intentions in turn we typically do not, and need not, consciously entertain), a certain *systematicity of behavior* is precisely what legitimately licences our thinking that behavior willful and intentional. This holds even when it is denied as such by the agent herself, or in more extreme cases denied outright as belonging at all to the agent. Using a metaphor, we can say that the motivation "seeps through" such systematic behavior or that the latter is a "symptom" of the former. In any event (and abstracting from psychopathological cases), the behavioral systematicity in question seems conceptually inexplicable in any other way unless (given how vast a range unexplicitly motivated actions comprise) we are prepared to accept a drastically reduced sense of personal responsibility.

To sum up, then, in place of having just one distinction, we must have two. Determined and accidental personal states are to be contrasted with intentional-as-deliberate acts on the one hand and states where the criteria of explicit thought and execution do not obtain but which nevertheless deserve the attribution *willful* on the other. As with the first "epistemological" point, the recognition of an enlarged sense of willfulness would go a long way toward eliminating some of the apparently puzzling aspects of self-deception.

The third clarification highlights the perils of making definitive ontological pronouncements regarding self-deception solely on the basis of following the logical meaning of the terms involved. In effect this is just a too rigid application of the interpersonal picture of deception to the individual self. There is no reason to declare a priori that the central cases of self-deception are only those that parallel the epistemology of interpersonal perception. As Mike Martin suggests in making a very insightful comparison with some other self-referential expressions such as *self-taught* or *self-educated,* were this position methodologically consistently adhered to, the latter also would lose their intelligibility by dissolving in a paradox of simultaneous knowledge and ignorance (1986, 20). In thinking about self-teaching, it is instructive to examine teaching others since *both* engage purposeful acts aiming at acquiring new knowledge and skills. But clearly the interpersonal model does not provide an accurate description of what it literally means to teach oneself. The latter remains an autonomous phenomenon demanding a more sophisticated conceptual understanding that would take into account in particular all the tacit processes involved when we come to know anything by our own efforts. Just as this holds for self-teaching, then, self-deception can be shown to be analogous to its interpersonal counterpart in some but not all ways (20); but this should not lead to discounting it as an intelligible notion.

Now, this gloss of a comparison between deceiving oneself and self-teaching is useful in a further important way. For it enables us to abandon the snapshot approach induced by thinking about self-deception as a problem of simultaneous knowing and ignorance in favor of considering it more as a process, or more existentially, as a personal *activity* whose concern is the self.

In what is now widely acknowledged as a seminal account of self-deception, Herbert Fingarette (1969) reoriented the discussion in just this way. In essence, he proposed to de-emphasize the *cognition-*

perception vocabulary of "knowledge" and "belief" and the entrenched modeling of these on analogy to (passive) vision (34-37) and to re-describe the phenomenon in language of action, volition, and per-sonal identity—where the latter, in line with existentialism, refers not to any objective features that distinguish individuals from each other but rather to our subjective sense of who we are (our self-image). (That sense in turn, to the extent that it is a product of what we *choose* and *commit* ourselves to treat as aspects of ourselves, is, critically, of our own authorship.) Using *engagement* now as a cover term for the multitude of modes in which we are implicated in the world (i.e., ac-tions, beliefs, emotions, purposes, desires, perceptions, etc.), this al-ternative picture sees self-deception as a person's *refusal* to avow as part of his identity engagements that person nevertheless pursues.

Typically, the refusal takes the form of not being willing to focus on and articulate explicitly, and hence to become fully conscious of, what one is engaged in. (Fingarette's views on consciousnes, articula-tion, and experience are indeed very much in line with the expressi-vist picture of mind argued for earlier in this essay.) This is so because such a "spelling out" risks the painful awareness of that engagement as inconsistent with, or even contradictory to, the avowed cluster of values that constitutes our identity. That identity, as we have already seen, is never a matter of mere "beliefs" that (as beliefs) we can adopt hypothetically and then adjust or discard with impunity if the evi-dence does not support them. Rather, deceiving ourselves about as-pects of identity concerns nothing less than psychological integrity. We suspend the exercise of some basic skills of rationality because we lack the courage to endure an even partial self-disintegration and be-cause we have little strength for the effort to make emotional and atti-tudinal adjustments required by honestly facing undesirable realities. Above all, we resist the *moral* claim made against us and proved valid if some of the tacit knowledge about ourselves was explicated.

Following Martin (1977), it is worthwhile to note how this ac-count profitably mediates the seemingly intractable opposition be-tween Sartre's uncompromising indictment of self-deceivers as gutless cheats and Freud's far less judgmental medical approach to them as victims of deterministic mechanisms. On Fingarette's view, Sartre is basically correct about the initial move *into* self-deception; in light of a standard of perfect courage and honesty that a highly developed in-dividual (e.g., Socrates) exhibits in facing painful realities, the ge-neric motive for the denial, avoidance, or distortion of the evidence afforded by one's engagements is always a lack of courage. (Freud also acknowledged this fact with a more neutral description of "the ego's . . . incapacity to bear anxiety [Fingarette 1969, 139].) On the other hand, to the extent that inarticulation and disavowal of certain engagements diminishes personal agency as a capacity to respond for and act on them—principally in neutralizing the power of reflection that can be exerted on immediate intentions, subsequently in the diminished regard for standards of rationality that habitual failure to reflect properly inevitably fosters—it gives rise to precisely the elements of compulsiveness that captured Freud's attention. Thus, another way to assess Freud's contribution to our understanding of self-deception is to say that he was correct regarding the latter's *consequences* (Martin 1977, 277–78).

With regard to the specific patterns of how we may deceive ourselves, it should be first mentioned that no comprehensive enumeration of such patterns appears to be possible. The sheer complexity of our engagements and motivations behind them makes for an enormous variety of ways we can deceive ourselves and precludes at the same time the elaboration of some set of necessary and sufficient conditions that would cover all instances of deception. Even granting a number of acceptable criteria for applying the expression *self-deception* to central or paradigmatic cases (see Martin 1986, 16–18), there are no rigid boundaries for such application—self-deception appearing to be a true resembling family of phenomena and not any natural kind identifiable via the traditional isolation of genus and difference. It may indeed be, as Jennifer Radden (1984) has urged, that an adequate understanding of self-deception cannot be attained by means of the generalizing approach favored by philosophers and must instead be sought through the particularity afforded by literature.

Second, there is a wide variety of perspectives that can inform sorting out particular patterns of deception (Martin 1986, 7). Thus Sartre works out of what he considers fundamental phenomenological distinctions concerning human consciousness and freedom,[3] and Freud's identifications of patterns of deceiving ourselves are made according to the types of psychological defenses he came across in his clinical work. Ethicists, on the other hand, are likely to consider self-deception as a perversion of some objectively ordered moral norms. Some, for example, Scheler (1972) in his studies of *ressentiment,* may employ a combination of intrapersonal dynamics along with a sociological approach to see this perversion in a broader historical and cultural framework. All these perspectives lead to some insight into the phenomenon of self-deception. Moreover, typically a strategy of deceiving oneself is multifaceted, employing (an overlapping) variety of means and shifts of focus to attain its objective. No one perspective should thus be taken as the definitive approach; likewise, none should be excluded.

The above strictures notwithstanding, and acknowledging fully that this is no more than scratching the surface, it is possible to indicate several prevalent "garden-variety" ways of being dishonest with ourselves. Here too we owe much to the initial psychoanalytical elaboration of the so-called defense mechanisms, the awareness of which, even under their technical terms, has by now become the property of commonsense intuitions. More recently, and in line with Fingarette's reorientation of the problem of self-deception as an issue concerning self-identity, Solomon (1976, chap. 13) has offered an "existentialist" reinterpretation of these "mechanisms" that drops Freud's hydraulics while avoiding the heavy-handedness of Sartrean responsibilism. In the latter picture, Freudian "repression" becomes a cover term for our *refusals* to acknowledge some truth about our emotions—most often either a truth pertaining to an emotion's existence (i.e., whether we "have" a particular emotion and are acting from it) or, admitting to an emotion, a truth that concerns its actual target (i.e., to what or whom it is "really" directed and, relatedly, for what reasons). Given the constitutive role of the (emotional) object for the experience itself, usually we effect these refusals by focusing our attention away from those features of the object that are relevant to (would be definitive of) the emotion in question in favor of being absorbed by something that will preserve the psychological status quo. This type of spontaneous yet willful distraction often reveals itself in shifting contexts of meaning (e.g., passing to generalities to avoid the troublesome particular or fixating on the particular just when it is its being part of a broader picture that counts). And we are all too familiar with the more radical move of complete forgetfulness contained in sudden proposals to switch the subject of a conversation ("Let's talk about something else") or in passing to happier thoughts in the privacy of one's mind. The overall aim of these maneuvers is clear: to avoid appropriate inquiries that one senses may uncover information that would be psychologically too costly to acknowledge fully. But distraction can be effected on the subjective side as well, affecting our powers of discernment, as when we dismiss in our experience particular sensitivities that at the extreme we may even attempt to neutralize through alcohol or other chemical means (Solomon 1976, 406).

Sometimes, however, distraction will be insufficient as a strategy of avoiding the truth about an emotion, and more will be required than mere neglect of the relevant facts. Perhaps the latter are such that they cannot be ignored, are just too obvious; we might then resort to the more drastic measure of denying them by offering a redescription of what is actually encountered (407). Again, such reinterpretation can be used on the objective or the subjective poles of experiencing. On the one hand, a redescribed object can serve to convince oneself and others that one cannot be experiencing the emotion one is suspected of; on the other, what one understands one's feelings to be may be used as the basis for arguing that the ostensible object of an emotion cannot be its actual target.

An important species of emotional deception that constitutes the more extreme possibilities offered by interpreting objects in a particular light is captured under the notion of *projection*. The range of phenomena fitting this rubric is rather large, this being partly determined by whether the projective move is a spontaneous response to an immediate threat to our self-image or part of a more elaborate long-term strategy of compensation for some basic personal deficiency that permeates every facet of a person's life. Here too, clinical practice furnishes the paradigm instances of this form of deception, the technical term *transference* indicating a process wherein the patient imbues the therapist with the qualities of someone significant in the past and with whom the patient was emotionally deeply involved.

But projection in the relevant sense discussed here is a phenomenon far too extensive to be classified strictly as pathological. As the psychoanalyst Theodor Reik (1957) has argued, the dynamic of what in our culture paradigmatically passes for romantic love (and we perhaps more perspicuously refer to sometimes as infatuation) depends precisely on conferring upon the loved person qualities that one lacks and that originate in an ideal self one desperately wishes to be. (Hence our deep dismay when that person turns out not to possess these qualities, a dismay that usually leads to anger at the self for duping itself and, on the ground of having been deceived, a corresponding aggression toward that other who was before an object of such admiration.) Nor will we find so rare that (chronically) defensive person who has a "chip on her shoulder" yet is simultaneously all too eager to provoke its being knocked off to thus prove that it is really others' agressivity that justifies responding in kind. These types of deception, wherein the agent's way of behaving motivates and is contributive of precisely the kinds of responses that confirm her (anticipated) appraisal of the situation, will in their vicious circularity be particularly difficult to overcome.[4]

Under *rationalization* we group yet another intuitively recognized and prevalent form of deception. Its strategy consists of persuading ourselves that a suspect emotional engagement or reaction of ours is actually justified. The original motives that led to its inception are either left unexamined or just denied. In their stead we offer after-the-fact evidence that transforms the engagement into something grounded in perfectly acceptable and legitimate reasons. Thus a dishonest, greed-motivated business transaction becomes justified by my claims that it was played by the rules of market competition everyone accepts as fair, that others would have committed the same act were they in my shoes, that indeed it was pure chance that I was not done-in first. At the height of my insincerity, I may even insist that I brought about a good, having taught a valuable lesson to the victim, whose interests are henceforth served by the acquisition of skills more likely to ensure future success. And is this not—on the premise of the market's "invisible hand" steering competition to issue in the greatest common benefit—indeed a contribution to the good of all? Thus I silence my anguished conscience.

Rationalization has a proximate cousin: emotional detachment. Whereas rationalization neutralizes the troublesome nature of an emotional engagement by (re)anchoring the latter in different, more noble motives and thereby effecting a closure of any further investigation, the success of detachment lies in convincing ourselves that the engagement is not that integral to us after all. Initially this may involve blocking or freezing certain second-order emotions about the seriousnessness of what we are trying to dismiss, a process whose forced nature may reveal itself in such bodily symptoms as a tense posture and constricted breathing or in the nervous quality of humor and laughter designed precisely to make light of the engagement in question. In time, however, we can become very proficient and successful at detachment, admitting to our vices but (often with the aid of endless qualifications that prevents a definitive pronouncement on the engagement that would force a stand toward it) doing so only on a purely intellectual level.

Here the deception lies in fooling ourselves that the capacity for profound insights into our shortcomings is both a measure of and a sufficient condition for proving our moral self-worth, one that buttressed by the fact that reflection itself is traditionally for us a substantive good, an esteem-bestowing virtue, simultaneously dispenses us from any obligation to change ourselves concretely. The chances of falling into this trap will be greatly enhanced if there are cultural views that discount in principle all guilt and insist that we should not be too hard on ourselves. The supporting complicity between a publicly enunciated ideology of this sort and personal needs is obvious. In these circumstances, however disengaged, reflection will always serve to exonerate by the mere fact of being pursued; the more relent-lessly, of course, the better. But such intellectualization will have vir-tually no "heartfelt" consequences worth speaking of, bringing at once to our attention the fact that the relationship between an aspira-tion to self-honesty and self-deception itself has the potential to be an ideal target for self-deception (Martin 1986, 132).

This last point is further driven home by opposite situations, wherein reflection on a personal shortcoming *is* sufficiently engaged to induce feelings of guilt or regret but is pursued (as by Dostoyevski's underground man) out of self-abuse and solely for the "satisfactions" these feelings bring. For our being relentlessly hard on ourselves can be a mask for wanting to feel sorry for ourselves, to be victim and mar-tyr, to seek recognition and valuation from others through the pity our (intentional) victimhood evokes in them. (Hence, in the social sphere, we should also be suspicious of any individual's excessive demands for sincerity, serving, as these frequently do, as a means of degrading others.)

To pursue a bit further the socially generated aspect of decep-tions, some mention must be made of the role of those conventional views that are *directly* about emotions. For to the extent that these "metalevel" attitudes either promote a misunderstanding of our emo-tions or circumscribe the range of potential corrective measures, they bear directly on the issue of self-deception. Again, the enormous vari-ations in our second-order beliefs about emotions and how they actu-ally engage the contents of our (first-order) experiences will allow few (if any) generalizations, and whatever these are, caution is re-quired when advancing them.

Some deceptions arise, as de Sousa (1980) notes, from disregard-ing that the content of individuals' "same" emotional experience (e.g., anger) can vary a great deal owing to their particular tempera-ments and the specific details of their emotion-learning situations in infancy. Particularly amplified in our culture by gender socialization, such variations often generate misunderstandings between men and women in identifying emotions and what can or should be done to resolve an emotional conflict. In fact, the experiential differences re-garding the "same" emotion may be such that acting as if they did not exist will lead only to further conflict and mystification. To take jeal-ousy as an example, if a woman understands its elimination in "male" terms (i.e., as overcoming possessiveness), her very stance of in-creased independence will frequently lead to *his* possessiveness and jealousy (de Sousa 1980, 292). Thus adopting and acting on a single perspective turns out to be perilous to their relationship. His belief and perhaps urging (that she is like him and ought to act like him) is, as provocative of his insecurities, particularly irrational. She in turn is bound to be vexed and disoriented by his apparent double standard. Both are fooled by expectations of reciprocity, brought on by the homonomy of "jealousy," in the elimination of the unwanted emotion that *means* something essentially different to each (292).[5]

On a far more general level, perhaps the most pernicious of all conventional assumptions about emotions is a belief in their intrinsic ineducability, either because they are reduced to merely (biologically determined) somatic phenomena (i.e., feelings, sensations) or, if seen as learned, because such learning is assumed to be irredeemably fixed in early socialization patterns. What this view accomplishes in offering blanket excuses and disempowering us from taking a more responsible and active stance toward the persons we are and our emotions is all too obvious to be labored here.

But it may also function in ways that go beyond mere excuse concocting, being in fact a coconspirator in many refusals to give up (and even spiral escalations of) an emotion in spite of evidence against the empirical basis on which that emotion is putatively based. For although officially emotions, certainly in their interpretation as subjective proprioceptive states, do not have the exalted status of rational thought that relates to objective states of affairs, most of us privately sense that they are somehow central in our lives and in our assessments of the world. Thus many an angry person takes her feelings as precisely proof that whomever they are upset with must be guilty, this being typically reinforced by such spontaneous and seemingly innocuous yet responsibility-absolving locutions as "X *made* me angry" or "X *caused* my anger." And yet, despite the apparent admission of some link between emotion and world, when asked to consider whether his anger is warranted by the objective situation the angry agent may become ever more indignant, the demand for reconsideration being perceived as an implication that this is all in his mind. But this escalation should not surprise us since any assessment of the emotion in terms of the above-mentioned link is unlikely, crowded out as it is in the agent's mind by the official metaview. As proprioceptive states, emotions are by definition not the sort of things that can be (re)appraised. Why talk of warrants if emotions are just "feelings"? Here we have the "best of possible worlds": amplifying an emotion that we likely need to sustain meaning in our lives, feeling certain of the correctness of our judgments about the world, and keeping both safely immune from criticism and change.

This, looking at the flipside of the issue, is of course not to forget that there are many deceptions generated by a contrary belief—that emotions are completely under the control of our wills and thus independent of any determining factors pertinent to psychosexual development in specific social and historical settings. As many proponents of free-love communes found out in the not so distant past, such "ideals" were radically mistaken, demanding as they often did denials of aspects of personality that needed to be expressed and integrated. Much the same, with the deception occuring on a far grander scale, can be said of utopian Marxism's denial of attachment emotions constitutive of human property relations.

Many more examples of how socially engendered beliefs contribute to our being (sometimes massively) deceived in and about emotions could be brought forth to amplify this theme. By way of ending what is already a somewhat sprawling account, however, I want to touch on some items in two dimensions of self-deception so far neglected: the epistemic and the motivational. Both also throw light on why (at least some) self-deception is not just a possible but perhaps even a likely feature of everyday life.

Although "deception" in the compound self-deception may lead us to believe that the latter involves some serious breach of rationality, the ubiquity, subtlety, ellusiveness, and recalcitrance of the phenomenon suggest otherwise. There is, as de Sousa (1980, 138) notes, seldom a sharp mistake in logic of which the self-deceiver can be accused. Indeed, such must be the nature of the evidence that is the object of our attempts to reject (or accept) as relevant for our identities that it must permit the possibility of reinterpretation, coloring, adjustment, and manipulation while still allowing us to lead our lives more or less as before (i.e., preserving the psychological status quo). In self-deception we are not likely to disavow or bend basic rules of thinking (e.g., the principle of noncontradiction) nor attempt to deny self-evident, intuitive truths like "I am human" or "I have a mind," or basic perceptual judgments that orient us successfully in the physical world. Denials in the former category mean derangement, hallucinations, or serious perceptual impairement in cases of the latter—but not self-deception (Szabados 1985, 12–16). Rather, what self-deception most often exploits is our reflective awareness that the overwhelming majority of beliefs and descriptions by which we orient our lives (and are constitutive of our emotions) are inductive in character and that as such they always remain to some extent underdetermined by the experiential evidence on which they rest.

This contingent quality of our beliefs, as Sartre so brilliantly demonstrates in his account of self-deception, is precisely what allows for suspending the standards of critical, dispassionate inquiry when examining matters important to us. How easily, on the assumption that no investigative effort will prove a belief airtight, beyond doubt, do we slip into adopting it on flimsy evidence, exonerated from demanding too much and being satisfied when barely persuaded (Sartre 1966, 113). That same belief, when inconvenient, could very well be rejected by setting up a "realism of nonpersuasiveness," by insisting that this time it is its underdetermination that *really* counts. In Sartre's formulation, "Bad faith apprehends evidence but it is resigned in advance to not being fulfilled by [it]" (113). Even when the facts appear to point inescapably to some obvious conclusion, we can, using this skeptical strategy to the hilt, refuse to draw it by clutching at the slim (indeed perhaps no more than merely logical) possibility that this particular constellation of facts is merely coincidental, so warrants no strong judgments concerning it. And from this it is but a very short distance to considering beliefs as mere projections or "pure subjective determination[s] without external correlative" (114).

But the point to be reiterated and kept in mind is that these various orientations toward belief and evidence all retain their *plausibility*.[6] In Terry Warner's apt description, self-deception is not a matter of concealment in a sense of believing falsely but of avoiding a truth through believing "perversely" (1986, 164). That is, we believe in a manner contrary to conventional understandings of a "best" way to establish truth. Our inferences seem still supported by the facts but not in the most direct or comprehensive way; they are not, to use a familiar expression, inferences to the best explanation. But it is precisely the absence of patent falsehoods, along with the fact that any reflective effort considered as a form of emotional engagement (and now serving as a datum) is itself open to the ambiguities of play on belief and evidence, that coconstitute the conditions for our deceptions to remain hidden from us, regardless of what order reflection is carried to. Naturally, the further we get from the original facts to be avoided while exploiting the skeptical possibilities inherent in progressive reflection, the more difficult it will be to break out of our dissimulating tactics.

Now, I have touched on these "epistemic" features because while they are a point of concern for only some of the various orientations or traditions of approach to self-deception,[7] I believe that these features are fundamentally operative in all deceptions about what belongs and what does not as part of our identities. And specifically concerning the emotions, they merit highlighting on two counts. First, beliefs (in their usual understanding as statable propositions), although not identifiable with emotions, are nonetheless intrinsic to them. Beliefs constitute and sustain emotions by providing focal crystallizations for patterns of what we attend to and what is salient for us. Second, it is by means of these "more conventionally cognitive premises" that *transitions* between emotions are effected (de Sousa 1980, 146). In short, if beliefs are, to borrow Solomon's (1988) metaphor, the "skeleton" of our emotional lives, it seems important to know the structural basis for less than perfect inferential strategies among them as this may be exploited in avoiding the truth about our emotions and ourselves.

But if the fundamental "discrepancy" between our beliefs and sustaining evidence is what provides the escape hatch when we sense that certain admissions about ourselves would jeopardize our psychological well-being, it is equally necessary to remember that this discrepancy lies at the very heart of certain dimensions of human life critical for sustaining that life as *meaningful.* For in what often turns out (on the evidence) to be a less than satisfactory world, it is precisely our capacity for going *beyond* that evidence in such emotional engagements as hope, love, or faith that enables us to endure that world and endow it with significance. Which is to say at the same time that those incapable of self-deception would likely be also incapable of these latter modes of existing and receiving the "goods" provided through them and that, correspondingly therefore, any thought that self-deception can be eliminated is naive because that would entail a price we would almost certainly be unwilling to pay.

Moreover, in recognizing in our lives the legitimacy of at least some emotions, we undermine any assumptions about all emotions as states that are intrinsically deceptive and therefore something to be done away with,[8] as, for example, the Stoics believed. It is undeniably often difficult to attain a measure of objectivity vis-à-vis our emotions, this being especially so with the vital engagements of the sort just mentioned, precisely because of their import for us but also because to experience an emotion is essentially to be *within* a certain dramatic structure that displaces a publicly available correction-affording outlook.[9] The import's magnitude also ensures that this is an area where errors will carry potentially devastating consequences of deep dismay, disappointment, fragile integrity, loss of meaning. But this is something we simply have to resign ourselves to. Save for a complete retooling of ourselves as human beings, there appears to be no way of avoiding the condition that attendant with attaining our greatest goods is the potential for our greatest failures.

Self-deception is thus here to stay, so to speak, and for reasons additional to the "structural" ones adduced in considering its epistemic aspects and implications. Notwithstanding the uncompromising condemnation of all avoidance of the evidence by such advocates of authenticity as Kirekegaard and Sartre, in a harsh world a measure of self-deception is often necessary and perhaps even salutary. Consider, for example, a person who fails to admit to herself (and blocks out the awareness of any emotions bearing on) the fact of her poor health because, failing alternatives, she must continue working to support her family. As serving vital needs, denials pertinent to her state surely cannot be condemned as irrational or morally impermissible, even if such self-deception is not the highest state of human integrity, and especially since it is not infrequent that we ourselves support self-deception in others just to "avoid the difficulty in providing more substantial help that the truth, offered in the right way, would bring" (Martin 1986, 124). There may "objectively" be much less at stake, the truly tragic dimensions of life not being implicated, and this will bear importantly on the conventional moral assessments of self-deceivers. But for all that, we cannot neglect the basic fact of our subjective psychological reality—how harrowing it can be for the self to face itself squarely. When used in this context, as it often is, the common enjoinment to drop one's anxieties because "there is nothing to be afraid of" is no more than a pathetic gloss over the measure of personal courage the demand for self-honesty may actually require.

Aside from the unrealistic prospects of its elimination, the impulse for any blanket condemnation of self-deception should be tempered by realizing that denying significant truths that bear on our identity presupposes a measure of personal integrity. Almost always, as Fingarette notes, what is threatened is an aspect of integrity "rooted in moral concern; [t]he less integrity the less is there motive to enter into self-deception" (Fingarette 1969, 140). From this vantage point, self-deception is properly understandable only if seen as a mask for one's good faith being jeopardized. In short, it indicates both a capacity for and an appreciation of a higher moral vision, in much the same way that overt hypocrisy (proverbially "the homage that vice pays to virtue") points toward moral progress.

To say all this, on the other hand, is by no means to condone self-deception or to suggest that we should spare efforts to overcome it. And indeed there is much that each of us can accomplish in that direction. Once again, our capacities for reflection are the key. But owing to how easily they can connive at our being deceived, as the discussion of rationalization and intellectualization showed, a little more needs to be said about just what constitutes authentic or engaged reflection.

Above all, it is vital not to confuse reflection with self-consciousness. Whereas the former provides us with a sense of *perspective* on ourselves that is the precondition of any change, the latter is no more than the self's quantitative compilation of *information* about itself. The excessive pursuit of such compilation—regardless of whether the facts gathered are observed behaviors or data of introspective peerings into our stream of consciousness—typically does little except create a screen for the self to conceal its true character. Genuine self-knowledge, on the other hand, has two principal features. First, it requires that we look outward to the full intersubjective context that gives meaning to our acts (Martin 1986, 136). Second, as Socrates and Plato argued through their insistence that our really knowing a moral truth is tantamount to our expressing it in our way of life, genuine self-understanding is predicated upon a *commitment* to change ourselves when this is deemed neccessary. Barring such a commitment, insight gained from reflection is at best partial.

Of course, this deeper, more substantive sort of reflection does not come easily. Often what blocks it conceptually and psychologically is our failure to distinguish confidence (i.e., being sure of our beliefs) from security (i.e., the ability to leave even our most cherished beliefs open to revision). The former dupes us into relaxing the demand for further probing. It does so, however, not solely by itself but in complicity with what virtually all writers touching on self-deception recognize as self-deception's underlying generic motive: the need for self-esteem.

This returns us to the social dimension. For that, efforts aimed at concealing unpleasant truths about ourselves are rooted in this fundamental human concern means also that self-deception, as a ubiquitous symptom of personal defensiveness and lack of self-acceptance, is in a very real sense a product of *failed intersubjectivity*.[10] In this perspective, overcoming self-deception requires not just personal courage and a modicum of intellectual ability but also moral and cognitive support from others, and in turn social arrangements conducive to that support. We may be sure that as long as self-consciousness (in a neutral sense of being conscious of oneself as a self) and self-identity are principally a function of intersubjective relationships, and as long as it remains our (frequently insidious) habit to compare ourselves with others—a condition made more acute by increasing formal equality concomitant with pervasive social inequities of status, power, and income—self-deception will be with us. My intention is by no means to argue for some postcapitalist, non-self-alienating utopia. I merely wish to reiterate from yet another perspective the truth that self-deception is not something intrinsic to emotions but an aspect of the human predicament more broadly construed.

Much more, of course, could be said here. However, we also need to attend to a set of issues that self-deception implicitly brings onto the agenda to the extent that they are precisely what motivates considering it as more than just a tangential or secondary problem. Our point of departure here is a simple experiential fact: our intuitively believing that there is some intrinsic connection between emotions and the realm of values we live our lives by, and that indeed the former are perhaps *the* mode of "access" to the latter and hence the constitutive pivot of moral agency. Our coming to terms with values and being moral agents in turn will obviously be distorted or undermined by self-deception. In the final chapter of this essay, then, I shall look at the relationship between ethics, values, and emotions to see exactly what it is that can potentially be so easily subverted.

8

ETHICS, EMOTIONS, AND VALUES

" *'Tis not* contrary to reason to prefer the destruction of the whole world to the scratching of my finger," Hume (1888, 416) tells us, encapsulating in dramatic (if somewhat perverse) fashion his argument that our emotions ought to guide not just reason but ethical conduct in general. Hume thus harks back to the powerful tradition of the ancients who insisted that our emotions are essential to morality. While Plato (at least in the psychology developed in the *Republic*) claimed that the good life as expressed in the harmony of the soul required the satisfaction of those desires specific to the latter's emotional or spirited part (*thumos*), Aristotle saw moral formation as essentially constituted by the education of our emotions. But Hume's hunches can also be seen as very much confirmed by certain important contemporary currents in theories of moral psychology. I have in mind Carol Gilligan's (1982) "care" ethics, a powerful feminist challenge to the notion that right action is primarily, if not solely, informed by principles of will and rationality. For Gilligan, on the contrary, an appropriate response in any human situation is predicated on understanding others and being connected to them in ways that explicitly engage our emotions.

Our ordinary intuitions tell us there is something right about any such Hume-like position, at least concerning its general intent of securing in a positive manner the centrality of emotions for human conduct—taken in the generic sense as activity guided by norms and values—if not necessarily regarding the priority over reason he assigns to them. For what we feel about persons, objects, and events in our environment is generally a reflection of how we assess and value them, and this not just in a strictly subjectivistic or (particular) person-relative sense but as in feelings of "moral" indignation or approbation, a sense that has its roots in a *concern* for the general interpersonal welfare, is binding (we think) on us all, and hence reflects the "moral point of view" as standardly construed, that is, a view from a general and steady perspective. Thus, as our loves, prides, and admirations concern what we formally consider good, what we fear, are ashamed of, or disgusted by is directed at what is thought bad. Conversely, a "value" is by definition something important in our lives, something that *moves* us.

It is this very simple and basic observation that compels us to assume an intrinsic connection between emotions and values; the former, it seems, sustain (and perhaps are nothing but) apprehensions of the latter. And aside from any strictly epistemic connection between values and emotions, do we not typically take the strength of feelings and the sincerity with which they are held and expressed as a natural index that a value truly engages us? That a norm is adhered to with seriousness and commitment and not passing fancy is precisely what allows the stance to be dignified with the term *moral* (Williams 1973, 219). The connection between expressing an evaluative judgment in a speech-act and experiencing particular emotions is, of course, not a logical or conceptual one, and so defeasible on a *particular* occasion. Nevertheless, it is sufficiently strong and generally holding to call it a natural connection, one exhibiting a sort of basic experiential datum of ordinary (prephilosophical) life.[1] Then too, grasping the emotional structure of a person is often the indispensable background for grouping his (apparently) disparate behaviors into some kind of an intelligible set or unity, without which unity an explicitly moral assessment of them would seem precluded (222). Finally, emotions taken as *acts* are direct candidates for evaluations. Shame, for example, is in some sense an act of admitting reponsibility. In context, its presence can be viewed as commendable as its lack deplorable.

Still, we are at once reluctant to give unqualified assent to the notion that morality is grounded in emotions, and here paradoxically Hume himself has a major, if indirect, responsibility for our hesitations. For what Hume, as a good modern inspired by a nascent natural science, looks at is a neutral universe shorn of entities grasped through *functional* concepts, that is, concepts that define objects and organisms in terms of a purpose or function *intrinsic* to them and thus make impossible their apprehension independently of our understanding of what the paradigm, exemplar, or simply best instantiation of such objects or organisms would be. If the ancients and the medievals considered values as real facts in the world precisely because everything either instantiated a movement toward a telos (and hence was good) or away from it (and thus was bad), the strictly calculative and procedural reason of the moderns that comprehends no essential natures or transitions from potentiality to act (MacIntyre 1984, 54) has no such powers of value discernment. The former conceptions of health, normalcy, pathology, and so on, involving normative standards that are real and supplied by the world, simply vanish.

Here is the background that at once explains Hume's empiricist view of reason as a faculty that makes judgments concerning no more than matters of fact and conceptual relations and his famous general principle of the strict separation between the factual and the normative and the impossibility of drawing any conclusions of the latter kind on the basis of facts. As naturally "man" ceased to be a functional concept as well, thereby effecting a cleavage between "man" and "good man," Hume found himself unable to fulfill a key demand imposed by the Enlightenment—to justify (in the sense of offering *reasons* for) morality itself. In what is obviously a precursor of G. E. Moore's famous "open-question" argument, which exploits the fact that it is certainly not an *analytic* truth that certain worldly properties are good, Hume challenges us to come up with "that matter of fact, or real existence, which [we] call *vice*" (1888, 468). He finds instead only the introspectively gained empirical data of our psychology, that is, our passions, motives, volitions, and thoughts. There are no other matters of fact in the case except those that lie solely within us. They are emphatically not in the objective situation itself, so that any assessment of the latter is completely *extraneous* to it. Thus virtue is more or less whatever evokes in us the agreeable sentiments of approbation (vice being the contrary). Hume gives more concrete content to this general scheme by invoking a number of qualities likely to engender approbation in us. These reflect the common sense of his times and include discretion, caution, enterprise, prudence, and discernment, as well as (what he took to be) the more universally recognized positive qualities of patience, sobriety, temperance, considerateness, and presence of mind.

Hume realizes the threat of subjectivism and relativism as attendant to his system, especially if it is (mis)interpreted by emphasizing its quasi-hedonistic aspects. But adhering consistently to his profound epistemological pessimism, which motivates the commitment to emotions in moral matters in the first place, he believes that objectivity of ethics can be secured by appealing to yet another emotion: sympathy. Fellow-feeling can perform this important function because it is, Hume thinks, both universally shared and a most general principle of human nature, so that it is capable of countering reasons flowing from our more particular self-centered, fluctuating, and circumstances-governed desires and interests (MacIntyre 1984, 49).

Kant, as is well known, unequivocally rejects this manner of grounding the objectivity of ethics. In the process of elaborating what remains to this day the most dominant system of moral thinking, he also successfully manages to obsure for us the critical role of emotions for the question of how we ought to live. Kant apparently shared with Hume the assumption that morality must be a function exclusively either of reason *or* of the emotions (MacIntyre 1984, 49). But in a move that is the exact reverse of Hume's estimation of the limits of reason to motivate us and his consequent turning to emotions, Kant's very low opinion of the latter compels him to seek the grounds of morality in reason alone. (The only emotion that does make its way into his scheme—respect—is carefully denied any sui generis status. It is only a *product,* and more precisely an accompanying consciousness of, and not the motivation behind, the law's or rational concept's unconditional impinging on the rational will [Kant 1987, 26].)

Coming out of the Protestant tradition that puts a premium on duty, will, and autonomous deliberation but also considers these defining features of personhood as ever-endangered by (and in conflict with) the emotions, Kant must anchor our obligations and interpersonal dealings in the sturdier medium of reason. Only the latter can induce action that is consistent, reliable, principled, and not arbitrary, therefore capable by virtue of these qualities to trump unconditionally motivations from any other source. There is another important consideration. As Williams (1973, 228) points out, Kant's ambition is a consistent working out of the essentially Christian idea that moral worth is to be assessed completely independently of any natural advantages whatsoever and so must have its locus *outside* the empirically conditioned self.

But the emotions are clearly part of the self so conditioned. Indeed, that is precisely what makes them in Kant's judgment disruptive, weak, capricious, passively experienced (and thus undermining of personal autonomy), and above all in this context fortuitously distributed; and thus not amenable either to that requisite test of ethical objectivity: universalizability. On pain of scandal, though, that objectivity could not be in jeopardy for Kant, and it is not. It exists because morality is (potentially) everywhere the same, built into those structures of the human mind that constitute the faculty of pure practical reason. Actual objectivity that transcends the gap between individual subjectivities and universally binding norms can be secured through a proper cultivation of that faculty by each person. Each one of us, left to her own rational wits, will come up with the same morally relevant conclusions, will "legislate" the same ends of action. We will do so, however, only on condition that the emotions play no part in the process.

For a romantic enthusiast about emotions (even a sober one), it is all too easy to be dismissive of Kant for this extreme position. But we must guard against such a move since there are important truths to acknowledge here. Our concrete responses to situations are typically a product of both context-specific factors that engage features of individual character *as well as* general principles, and we would surely find life precarious if it were informed solely by how one felt at the moment and without any imput of the disengaged and impartial perspective that Kantianism emphasizes. An elaboration of formal principles of conduct is properly dispensed with in the sphere of intimate relationships, as Aristotle observed in his discussion of friendship in the *Ethics*. But that sphere makes up only a minor portion of a life of a typical citizen in highly rationalized, bureaucratized societies like ours wherein interpersonal relationships are necessarily structured to be at arm's length. Moreover, in an increasingly interconnected world it is unavoidable that ever more of our actions at the micro-level have an impact on others we shall have no occasion to meet and develop first-hand ties of identification with; but because of such impact they must surely be considered in any moral equation. In this context, formal rules and principles and universally proclaimed declarations (e.g., human rights) that make a strong appeal to "reason" seem indispensable. Here we appreciate the practical value of Kant's push for a rationally grounded ethical objectivity.

Admitting all this, and as admirable as the motives of Kant's project may be, we nevertheless rightly remain skeptical about its viability. Sympathy, at least in its role of carrying out the Herculean task assigned to it by Hume, may indeed be a "philosophical fiction," trying to bridge a gap between types of action-grounding reasons that are logically incommensurable (MacIntyre 1984, 49). (Only by stretching the notion far beyond recognizable application could I claim that that is what moved me to keep a promise or not to tell a lie in circumstances that had no bearing on my self-interest *and* had no further negative consequences.) But the outright rejection of emotions from morality cuts too deeply against our intuitions. To keep with the strong sense of the orientation-to-others that explicitly informs the formulation of Kantian maxims of conduct, in the absence of emotionally grounded personal attachments, a charity that "begins at home," no respect for humans in general (and strangers in particular) and no principles codifying them as ends-in-themselves and hence as beings worthy of respect would psychologically be possible.

These general rules of conduct are ultimately developmentally rooted in the mushy (for Kant) soil of the emotion-infused empirical self; any elementary textbook on psycho- or sociopathology can tell us that. Less dramatically, as both Williams (1973) and Stocker (1976) argue, is it not the case that what matters to us most in many a situation, what in fact is a mark of a proper moral response (i.e., one that caters to our true needs as humans), is that we are addressed in the particularity of our individuality and *not* as members of a category that attains the status of a candidate for such a response by virtue of some formal derivation. Only "insanity," in Williams's strong formulation, could make us consistently prefer the ministrations of the Kantian moral man over the spontaneous human gesture, the "truth" of which as a moral response lies precisely in the *mode* of its conveyance and not on the correct recognition of (abstract) propositions about the situation. From this angle, emotions are, as it were, the essential *medium* of moral interaction.

Emotions, it seems, then, must be factored into elaborating a viable ethics. Strictly from the standpoint of their power to motivate specifically moral actions, however, not all emotions will be fit candidates for this inclusion. At the same time, the historical and cultural diversity of traits that make up good character as well as the radically dissimilar experiential *contents* of terminologically identical traits located in different contexts and cultures allow only the most cautious generalizations. Any brief comparison between two of the Occident's best-known lists of virtues—Aristotle's and Christ's—quickly drives this point home. For example, the anger that Aristotle found (in the appropriate measure) an eminently rational and good response turns up as a serious vice on the Christian account. On the other hand the humility propagated by the latter would be found pathetic by any self-respecting Athenian who cared little for its egalitarian inspiration. The Athenian's "natural" pride in turn becomes the deadliest of sins in the Christian ethos. Spanning yet greater gaps between forms of life, we can be sure of Humean sympathy as having no chance of warrant among Homeric warriors.

But even when the cultural distances are apparently not as great as this, important experiential differences need to be noted. The boisterous courage of those Homeric warriors is not the same (and thus cannot function in morality in the same way) as the measured incurring of risk to physical and psychological well-being that is the mean between foolishness and cowardice that Aristotle has in mind just a few hundred years later. Closer to home, Locke-inspired strong feelings about possession of property can be held by a community considering itself no less Christian than another that, less threatened by arbitrary power and infused by a more communitarian spirit, finds such feelings utterly repugnant and not at all ennobled by some abstract (individualistic) aspiration to autonomy. To provide one more example, shame, a virtue not that long in the past, seems to be passing out of style in our "therapeutic" culture, frequently interpreted away as unjustified guilt, a useless passion, a hang-up that stands in the way of happiness and self-realization.

One could go on here, but the point, I think, has been made. We must remember, as MacIntyre (1984) insists, that those traits submitted as virtues are goods or excellences intrinsic to specific practices and ways of life contextualized by geography and history. (Which of course is not to say that they are all equally valid.) And the reasonable conclusion here, it seems to me, is that we can be sure of perhaps only very few, clearly negative emotions that are ethically worthless. There is nothing in such obviously self-absorbing and self-degrading emotions as envy, resentment, or despair, for example, that conceivably leads to another's good. (Envy in particular, because it is so destructive of the social fabric, seems to have been universally recognized as an unequivocal evil, as evidenced by taboos against it in all known cultures [see Schoeck 1966].)

Now, the above remarks concerned those emotions that are directly motivational of interpersonal action, and this seems obviously correct as a dominant focus insofar as—given especially the Kantian and traditional Christian (and to some extent even utilitarian) insistence on duty—the first connotation of the notion of the moral is that it involves action that bears on others in some type of an "ought" relationship to them. But on a broader conception of the ethical, one that takes its inspiration from the Aristotelian notion of thriving or self-realization (though far less aristocratic than his), there are good grounds to include a whole range of emotions and interests that are strictly speaking self-related and from a deontological perspective at least, and at best tangentially linked to morality. Again, I do not mean to refer to just those emotions and interests that are the *obvious* psychological preconditions of developing moral motives such as those mentioned above in discussing presuppositions of (Kantian) respect for persons. Rather, we must attend to the vast range of things that can actually constitute a person's "ground projects" (Williams 1976), that is, basic commitments that are central to character and self-esteem and give meaning to people's lives and provide reasons for their wanting to go on living, and from which thus everything starts. Occasionally even something as trivial (from an outside perspective) as a pursuit of a hobby can fulfill this function, which cannot therefore be dogmatically restricted only to such noble (other-oriented) desires as that for universal justice.

Typically, it is the "intermediate" goals of perfecting a skill, being a good professional or a good family person, *and the emotions generated with these goals,* that do the job. In her arguments against an overly abstract conception of the person in our most influential moral theories, Susan Wolf (1982) makes much the same point somewhat more dramatically. Engaging in a speculation about a contemporarily preferred "moral saint," she paints a picture of a dull and deficient human being, one whose incessant preoccupation with helping others necessarily leads to excluding intellectual inquiry, art, sport, or other such clearly life-enhancing activities. The moral saint ends up as a thoroughly unattractive if not downright repugnant figure. While not many are willing to employ the extreme tactic of logically reducing our moral theories to absurdity, the relevant issue posed has to be faced: we are much in need of moral ideals that will be worth aspiring to, partly because they reflect real-life possibilities of self-enhancement and not the self-immolation ultimately pointed to by any rationalistic rejection of emotions. As intrinsically valuable experiences, emotions cannot (and at the level of ethical theory should not) be done away with.

Of course, this admission of the overall need for emotion in ethics, construed more broadly than in the deontological perspective, says nothing yet about the comparative value of various emotions and interests. Surely not all "ground projects" are on a par. Within the space afforded here, however, I am able only to gesture in the direction of how this very complex issue is to be pursued.

Most obviously, the level of our admittedly general and abstract observations needs to be quickly supplanted by a full-blown theory of human nature in conjunction with detailed empirical studies of whether the various specific interests and emotions found *in particular contexts* promote that theory's view of self-realization. Of course, that theory itself will have normative presuppositions, will not be value-neutral, and here we run into an apparently huge problem of (noncircularly) justifying it and its vision of human thriving without being able to prescind completely from the concrete evaluative intuitions about life and character that it affords us.[2] Perhaps the least controversial directive—because it synchronizes with the prevailing pluralism of notions of human good—that can be given that theory is that it should minimally set out the experiential conditions for the development of a *cohesive sense of self* since this is a prerequisite for humanity[3] (one in fact articulated a long time ago in the ancients' insistence on the harmony of the soul and freedom from conflict). This will need the development of desires that are "relevantly consistent" and allow for deep-seated dispositions to reflect a general unity in what the person values. A further condition would be that a person *recognizes* her unity of character as an individual self, and this is secured by a personal narrative that enables us to see our lives as unified wholes. The narrative both depends on and creates the psychological conditions for experiencing the activities and events of a life as natural concomitants of our characters rather than random and disparate intrusions alien to our natures. Finally, cohesive selfhood can endure only with internal requisites to act on the dispositions that make us cohesive, that is, with "the practical wisdom to figure out what kinds of means suit one's ends and the self-control to act when it is practically feasible" (Conly 1988, 89–90).

Arguably, this still remains too general—a delineation of a sense of a suitable background, but compatible with too many kinds of dispositions, projects, attachments, ambitions, and so on, hence too broad to inform adequately the normative exclusions and inclusions of experiences that would lead to good character and moral virtue. Thus our empirical studies of the functions of specific emotions in particular contexts will appear, if not arbitrary, at least unlikely as a source of any strong generalizable conclusions—or so it will seem to those who emphasize diversity in ways of life, their contingency, their embeddedness in and structuring by differing conceptual systems.

But this predicament, I believe, can be avoided. We need not subscribe to the opposite but untenable supposition that there is some uninterpreted bedrock "human nature" the knowledge of which would found and license all evaluative claims. We merely have to acknowledge that beyond the obvious diversities in how life expresses itself there are basic (family-resembling) spheres of needs and desires that by virtue of their relatively greater universality deserve to be considered essential for any good human (see Nussbaum 1988b; Maslow 1968). We should not concede to relativism and incommesurabilism too quickly just because particular emotions—anger or romantic love, for example—are not everywhere present. Consider romantic love; it surely is a vital good for *us* because as a form of attachment (ideologically) oriented to the uniqueness of individual qualities of character, it *integrates and enhances* selves socialized to interpret themselves as constituted by these qualities.[4] Of course, it is incomprehensible and not a good in a society of persons-as-social-roles, wherein marriages are arranged by an official "destiny" or perhaps economic necessity.

But just as surely, its specifity as a phenomenon of the modern West should not obscure recognition that it is a species of a generic human desire for affiliation and reflective of our commonality as social animals.

The examples could be multiplied, but the simple point is that "differences notwithstanding, we are more human than otherwise . . . [that indeed] there are ways in which every human being is almost exactly like every other human being that has ever lived: in his feelings of fear and insecurity, of inadequacy and aggression, of lust and loneliness" (Smith 1988, 285–86). Specifics of upbringing, history, context, and genetics, all *do* count. But is the anxiety about death or loss of loved ones so different the world over that it lies beyond any common experiential horizon? Why should we not take experiences clustering around (and promoting or hindering the resolution of) problems brought forth by such focal human concerns as a basis for evaluating differential contributions of ways of living and specific emotions to the overall goal of integration, the honest coming to grips with our condition in all of its happy and tragic dimensions?

I will not pursue these considerations further. Rather, and for the remainder of the present discussion, I wish to turn to a broader axiological issue, namely, what I have very briefly identified at the outset of this chapter as the epistemic connection between emotions and values. For in a sense it is the assumption of emotions as epistemologically important human capacities that is really critical for their relevance in ethics. Indeed it stands as a premise of any differential assessment of emotions of the kind discussed above and appraisal of people in general. For when we admire a person's character, that is, his having specific emotions, this is precisely because he possesses certain capacities to take in reality and orient himself in ways we find worthy of attention and not merely because he happens to be good company. If emotions were just somatic agitations or self-enclosed feelings or impressions, assessing character would be an unintelligible activity, and asking which emotions are "better" would make as much sense as trying to figure out whether digestion is superior to blood circulation. Attempting such an evaluative comparison has no point, is irrational, because its terms are not fit candidates for anything like a process of comparing. On the other hand, if there is something like a learning and cultivating of emotions, whether other-oriented or more immediately self-interested, with a view of having certain ones constitute our characters, this implies a capacity to grasp certain imports or significances on the basis of which these emotions can be sustained, modified, or abandoned. This would at once also license calling emotions rational in at least one dominant sense of rationality, namely, the sense derivative of something being a mode of cognition.

Yet however convinced we may be about our ordinary intuitions that emotions open us to a world of values, to theoretically defend this is contemporarily extremely problematic. The fact-value dichotomy has by now attained the status of a "cultural institution" (Putnam 1981, 127), a received posture strongly immune to rational reappraisal— the background combination of scientism and relativism having given rise to some powerful skeptical queries. Can we rationally confirm our value judgments? Do values exist? And even if they do, how reliable can our emotions be in apprehending them?

The contemporary followers of Hume gave a negative answer to the first question. Following G. E. Moore's "open-question" argument (to the effect that value judgments cannot be substantiated by fact) but rejecting his intuitionism of some nonnatural property of goodness, the emotivists insisted that ethics has no cognitive content. Value claims as nonfactual and so not fit for truth-functional assessment simply cannot be accommodated in the standard empiricist understanding of knowledge. To be sure, on the emotivist picture, the emotions strongly figure in ethics, indeed constitute it; but ethics is severely discounted as rationally unjustifiable and having only a pragmatic function of expressing or inducing emotions, which themselves end up as more or less inert nonassessible states. They are certainly not a mode of cognition. For the emotivist, there is nothing to *argue* about with regard to ethics or the emotions. In de Sousa's (1987, 304) apt criticism, emotivism simply fails to take both seriously; it also runs directly against our ordinary evaluative practices.

But emotivism is not alone in generating skepticism about the cognitive capacities of emotion. That skepticism is also strongly supported by a relativism that gets its raison d'être from the fact that the objects we value and feel strongly about may be completely out of line with their real worth, the emotions' cognitivity becoming undermined here simply because they do not seem always (or necessarily) to put us in contact with values in a *reliable* manner; the assessments we make may be unwarranted or just plain wrong. This is a point driven home especially by Nietzsche's (1956) devastating critique of traditional morality. Focusing in his genealogy on the motives behind certain value frameworks held as objectively true, he argues that these motives are in fact diametrically opposed to the publicly enunciated reasons that ostensibly ground those frameworks. Rather than being the embodiment of our most profound spiritual and moral insights, the value judgments held out as objectively true are no more than arbitrary expressions of a will to power and self-assertion, "morality" being erected in particular by the weak to exact a revenge on those who are psychologically stronger and superior in social status.

Now, this gets us close to a final sort of rejection of any cognitivity of emotion, one accomplished simply by denying that the conventionally assumed referent of emotion has any ontological status. For in effect, though their ontologies may differ, the Nietzschean construal of morality and values is in essence the same as that of certain empiricists who see all values as *projections* onto a neutral world. Thus John Mackie denies the existence of values on the grounds that it would require the admission of "entities or qualities or relations of a very strange sort, utterly different from anything else in the universe" (1977, 40). The obvious standard of normalcy that licenses this negation of these "queer" entities and qualities is the one set by the physicalistic ontology of natural science. And commonsense ethical systems become for Mackie "error theories" (35) because they (falsely) impute values as properties inhering in objects themselves, much as we (falsely) believe that such secondary properties as color inhere independently in the world and are not relative to our perceptual apparatus. In this picture, there is nothing "out there" with prescriptive force that enjoins us to do anything.

To meet such skepticisms head-on, we must first deny the rational supportability of the fact-value dichotomy. In this context, one certainly relevant consideration pertains to the manner of presenting each term of the distinction (Putnam 1981, 139). If, as is typically done to establish it, "facts" are described by a physicalistic or bureaucratic jargon while "values" are referred to with the most abstract categories of "good" and "bad," the independence of the latter from the former will be seen as obvious and psychologically all but impossible to deny, with antirealism about values ensuing as a coherent metaphysical stance. But this (already value-laden) choice of descriptions neglects the pervasive use in our daily discourse of what Bernard Williams has called substantive or "thick" concepts, concepts that at once provide reasons for action *and* say something factual in the sense that their application is from the start "guided by the world" (1985, 140). This is not to deny that such concepts—*coward, lie, brutality, considerate, gratitude,* etc.—can and often do function in strictly causal accounts that seek to explain or predict behaviour (e.g., doing something "out of gratitude"). But this neutral usage is secondary to and derivative of their more original meaning, wherein the abstraction and subsequent independence of a factual component (e.g., that someone lies) and a normative one (e.g., lying ought to be condemned) is very difficult if not impossible to sustain. And we would have no idea to begin with how to apply these concepts in a diversity of contexts unless we understood the evaluative perspective from which each one of them draws its point (141). What this suggests is that the fact-value distinction is not something that arises on the basis of our vocabulary; rather, it seems more of an imposition of philosophical reflection on everyday language and as such does not license any firm ontological conclusions about values.

Nor should we so easily concede the validity of the empiricist-scientific realist argumentation about the queerness of values. First, as the Gestalt-inspired research has especially shown, what we experience in visual perception far outstrips (and sometimes directly contradicts) the "raw" data posited from a more disengaged, analytical perspective. The objectively parallel lines look crooked; the instrument-measured equal-length segments are taken in as uneven; the two concentric circles superimposed over a straight line plausibly represent a sombrero-clad bicycle rider (see Hanson 1969). In none of such cases can the experiential content be strictly accounted for by the visual data and independently of our minds' capacities actively to organize and interpret what we observe. But is this sufficient reason to say that the qualities of, say, oddness, symmetry, or magnitude that we are "taking in" are therefore not real, "not part of the fabric of the world" (Mackie 1977, 15)? If so, there are also devastating consequences here for many of our currently favored scientific theories. For these, as it has become so common to assert, are also radically underdetermined by the evidence, positing all sorts of strange entities whose existence we are committed to in spite of having no powers to discern them. To be sure, we do this to enhance the coherence and explanatory power of the theories, but as the history of science makes abundantly clear, the success in fulfilling these requirements gives no *absolute* guarantees that these things really exist.

The empiricist-inspired skeptic about values will no doubt remain unperturbed. She will not deny the involvement of our pragmatic and speculative intelligence in positing strange entities but insist that the lack of direct evidence for them indicates merely a limitation of our current apparatus, and that given the perfectibility of the latter, the entities in question will turn out as real as anything and completely independent of any theory about them. For after all, though they are presently unknowable, we are still talking about nothing but *natural* phenomena that are all part of (and cohering with all other known phenomena of the same kind) in "*the* one world." And if this exhausts the sense of what is real because the only other ontological alternative is some version of an untenable Platonism of ideal entities, then the only viable explanation for the nonsensible qualities we think we encounter and call values is that they are our projections and not real. Besides, something like our above appeal to "thick" concepts is an illegitimate loading of the dice in favor of positing values; a choice of less agent-relative notions would point to no such things. Or so goes the argument.

In formulating a denial of this position, a simple thought-experiment proves most helpful. Considering a range of different "objects" (e.g., the computer I am writing on, someone's ideas, a number, a friendship, a recent headache, molasses, electrons, the theory of relativity) and assigning a numerical value to reflect each thing's status as real[5] shows easily how value-laden and commitment-infused are our *general* notions of objectivity and reality. And proceeding more radically in this direction, we can see how value presuppositions show themselves up even in the (apparently) simplest and most neutral of perceptual facts. For example, our taking in the proverbial cat on the mat, as Hilary Putnam (1981) cogently demonstrates, depends on our powers to employ a variety of categories without which there would be no such "fact" before us. It is because we *care* to distinguish the animate from the inanimate, artifacts with purpose from natural objects, spatial relations (as grasped by the category *on*), that the situation is described in just the terms used and that this description is accepted by oneself and others as adequate and perspicuous, or just plain true. And the critical point here, of course, is that to a mind lacking dispositions to regard the above-mentioned categories as *relevant,* the banal assertion of a cat's presence on a mat would be completely irrational in the sense of being unintelligible; it would not be saying anything "about the world." In Putnam's radical summary, "A being with no values (i.e., criteria of relevance) would have no facts either" (1981, 201).

Surely if this is true of our encountering such "natural kinds" as cats, it holds even more of more complex objects. The critical issue can be stated in several mutually implicating ways, all grounded in the essentially Kantian intuition that denies we can know anything of the world beyond what is structured by our concepts. For instance, Putnam (1981, chap. 3), echoing some vital phenomenological themes, insists that the only viable realism is of an "internalist" variety wherein what is denied is of course not the existence of extramental reality but the possibility of meaningfully raising ontological questions—what objects the world consists of—outside any theory about (or general description of) the world.[6] The "one real world" asserted in opposition to the plurality of our beliefs, which is to make them true by virtue of their correspondence to it, is simply an objectivist myth and untenable for the skeptical conclusions Hume so brilliantly demonstrated.

Without access to God's perspective, objectivity can mean only objectivity-for-us, that is, an objectivity that is relative to beings with our physiological and psychological constitution. We can still maintain the intuitively necessary notion of correspondence to facts as a criterion of truth provided that we do not forget that it is we who (collectively) set up the world of those facts and the correspondences that are to obtain within it. Our original prereflective situation, as Hegel (1977) and Heidegger (1962) have especially insisted, is one wherein experientially there is no mind-world division and no issue of correspondence of the former to the latter; on the contrary, there is just a simple *identity:* the world-as-experienced. And far from being the starting point, the very capacity to entertain objects (in the sense of mind-independent entities that are clearly recognized as such) is psychologically very much a developmental *accomplishment* (see Keller 1978).

But once we accept that the only viable notions of reality, objectivity, truth, and so on are those internal to our activities and capacities as human agents, there are no a priori grounds to accept the claims of a physicalistic ontology as exclusively valid. The fact that the latter meshes with the dominant and by some lights hugely successful worldview is surely insufficient. Once, that is—and this I believe puts the issue in the clearest way, given our concerns here—we realize that there are *no* objects we know of in *our* world without some, however minimal, psychological qualifications, then any notion of a massive or general projecting of such qualities onto a neutral world (as would have to be asserted for the pervasive experiencing of colors and values) is non-sensical to begin with, useful only in pathological contexts, and a consequence of an ontological anxiety fueled by the straw-man alternative of Platonism.

The argument for projection and value antirealism loses its force because the sense of what is real required to carry it through is simply untenable. Of course, it would be absurd to claim on the other hand that values could exist independently of beings like us. They are essentially agent-relative properties or qualities constituted by a specific form of life with particular powers of discernment and caring, yet no less real for that reason; we can go on only on the basis of what we have, and what we have are, following Locke's distinction, only secondary (i.e., agent-relative) properties. From this point on in our understanding, our ontology—if indeed we must concern ourselves with it; it seems perhaps more profitable to forget it altogether given the impasses of never-ending dialectics of realism-antirealism such concerns typically lead to[7]—has to be set and justified by our experiences. That experience argues for the reality of values. Just as in ordinary object-perceptions we sense that these are *caused* by the very object encountered—and this self-referential causality appears to be part of the *mental content* gained in reflecting on those perceptions (see Searle 1983, chap. 2)—so it is a phenomenological feature of our value-experiencing that we are moved by something in itself valuable rather than that thing accruing value just because we are reacting to it in this particular manner. Put differently, our emotions are not inferential evidence for a subsequent value judgement; we do not conclude that something is valuable on the basis of an occurrence of certain feelings within us. Rather, in directing us to what is valuable, our emotions point to what we take to be real features of the world, part of its fabric as *we* find it.

But values are also real in the deeper pragmatic sense of being necessary or inescapable for beings like us. If there are no extensional equivalents for the meanings-for-us we call values that will figure in an account that makes as good or better sense of our experience[8] and how we actually lead our lives, then values are real; they cannot be denied as viable explanatory factors. As Charles Taylor expresses it in his most recent book, "What is real is what [we] have to deal with, what won't go away just because it does not fit with [our] prejudices. . . . What [we] can't help having recourse to in life is real, or as near to reality as [we] can get a grasp of at present. [Our] general metaphysical picture of 'values' and their place in 'reality' ought to be based on what [we] find real in this way. It couldn't conceivably be the basis of an *objection* to its reality" (1989, 59).

At the same time, while making use of the notion of agent-relative properties to argue for value realism, it is critical not to assimilate or conflate the various species the notion subsumes. If in drawing above on the idea of self-referential causality found in ordinary perception and value experiencing I inadvertently gave the impression of such conflation, this must be immediately corrected. For there is a (phenomenologically discernible) crucial *disanalogy* between values and other agent-relative properties such as colors. Whereas the latter are felt as simply causing the color-experience, the former, over and above eliciting a particular response, are considered also as justifying or *meriting* it (McDowell 1985, 118). But this is possible only if there are certain intersubjectively shared norms or standards that bear on the form of life we lead and the practices that take place within it and that thus stipulate what is or is not an appropriate response in relation to specific objects or situations. In this sense, values contain something intrinsically reflexive for which there is no comparable equivalent in the case of colors. The latter, relative only to a well-functioning mode of perception, depend solely on there being certain sensory experiences the capacity for which is universally distributed among us. What they do not require is the grasping of the evaluative point, the standards by which persons live and define themselves, of the culture they are experienced in.

At this juncture, I believe, a number of significant conclusions offer themselves, and I should like to point these out. First, we have here grounds for second thoughts about the overall usefulness of perceptual parallels in accounting for value experience, especially if they are relied on too heavily. Scheler (1973), for instance, seems to be guilty of the latter move, insisting that we take in values via emotions in just the way we perceive colors and sounds. The danger is that in failing to note the disanalogy, we are also very easily led to thinking that emotions are some sort of special organs or faculty that we can train and improve as we do perceptual skills. This would be just plain wrong. For while emotions are surely critical for value experiencing, it is now clear that the "organ" of value apprehension is not some discrete faculty but our whole minds-as-they-are-emotionally-attuned-to-the-world.

For similar reasons, but this time attending to the object-pole of experience, we might do better to reject talk of value properties (which gets some of us scurrying around looking for mysterious discrete entities as the putative formal objects of the special faculty of feeling) in favor of simply considering them as motivating *reasons* that animate our experience of the world. For some highly engaged individuals, perhaps even for entire communities (e.g., a zealous religious sect), value apprehension and perception are indeed experientially indistinguishable. Their world is continually charged with emotional tone and not informed at all by any distancing second-order perspective.

For many of us, though, given the empiricist baggage accrued to our ordinary conception of perception and the extent to which scientifically oriented, highly rationalized settings pervade our lives and neutralize the world, to say that we perceive values seems strange, perhaps even totally unintelligible. The proposed reformulation of values in terms of reasons makes the issue less contentious and at the same time has the virtue of expressly keeping with the "internalist" sense of reality we had arrived at, the sense delimited by what is "there to be experienced" by beings like us. Value cognition is simply an emotion-grounded recognition of actual and potential reasons to act occasioned by our interaction with the world.

There is no veridical feeling of a value as there is a veridical seeing of something in front of us. Rather, the cognitivity of emotions appears to be much like the cognitivity of literature and art. It functions through enlarged sensibilities and repertoires of meaning and metaphor as well as enhanced modes of expression and self-realization. All these open us on progressively more nuanced aspects of experience or "objects" with potential to move us. Needless to say, it will make even less sense here than in the case of perception to speak of the truth of value apprehensions within the narrow parameters of the standard epistemic notion of truth (i.e., as a matching of transcendent reality). What we need is closer to the quasi-pragmatic Hegelian idea of truth as a property satisfying the intrinsic standards or point of each activity, form of consciousness, or desire; truth in relation to emotions and values can mean only their potential for fulfilling the aim of human life (whatever that may be).

Now, just as we have come to a more sophisticated understanding of what it means to be aware of values, so correspondingly we must modify our thinking about their objectivity. For a further aspect of the disanalogy between paradigmatic secondary qualities like colors and values, one that is really the complement of the objects of emotion meriting particular responses, is the contentiousness that usually surrounds values, a contentiousness that in turn undermines claims of their objectivity and of the cognitivity of emotions. Implicating standards as an integral feature of an emotion's directedness to something valuable readily explains this contentiousness. For the standards in question are essentially *interpretations,* hence almost always in dispute, or at least in principle disputable. Thus we can appreciate too how skewed motivations can parade under the banners of what is good and noble while not being recognized for what they are, even by those who have them. This is not a domain where things stand out on their own as black and white for our recognition.

Yet that a worthless emotion (e.g., resentment) can motivate a value judgment is no reason to discount emotions as grounding value judgments in general. Pathological cases (e.g., of deficiency or excess) can be found for any emotion, including the most edifying (Moore 1987, 191). We must distinguish between the overall structuring of situations because of emotional valences on the one hand and the confusing or distracting roles emotions can play on any particular occasion on the other (see Mandelbaum 1955, chap. 5).

Once we understand all this, it seems absurd to demand of values the sort of objectivity that is held as paradigmatic and that science provides and to discount them because they cannot attain such objectivity. For the convergence or agreement on what science provides is possible principally because its "facts" are relative on the one hand to the universally shared features of our perceptual apparatus and on the other hand to certain constructions of thought that by virtue of their abstractness and analyticity are difficult if not impossible for human reason to deny.[9] But value discernment demands something quite the opposite because its objects are relative to factors of culture and life history. It demands being part of, or at least empathically understanding, the actual way of life in which given values are affirmed or negated.

To spell this out a bit more, it involves a multidimensional "emotional competence" that is perhaps best delineated negatively by some obvious characteristics that can block it: prejudice; lack of experience, education, skill; coarseness, insensibility, callousness; holding false, misleading, one-sided, or scanty beliefs about the objects of one's emotions; lacking familiarity with the objects of emotions that "comes through acting in social contexts, exercising skills and performing tasks, laboring, creating and enjoying works of art, playing games, physical enjoyments and sufferings, and so on" (Kerner 1971, 187). Only when we have removed from our emotions such impediments can we claim objectivity in our valuations.

Are there any "true" universal values, that is, reasons that would constitute "a series of possible steps in the development of human motivation which would improve the way we lead our lives, whether or not we actually take them?" (Nagel 1986, 140). I do not know. Yet I am quite certain that there is no a priori answer to the question. As in everything else, there is no standard of truth for values outside human life itself. The "ultimate goodness of fit" (Putnam 1981, 64) of any particular value with life can be determined only empirically and within a continually unfolding historical perspective that allows for assessment of gains and losses. The here and now is both the starting point as well as the foundation of this process. In any event, the possibility of necessary ("wired in") universal values is left entirely open, as is the further question of whether these are conducive to human thriving.

NOTES

CHAPTER 1

1. For a more detailed discussion of drives, see Heller (1979, pt. 1, chap. 2).

2. One way to see this shift is as a movement away from the understanding of rationality that we predominantly accept and receive from the Latin *ratio* (to deliberate or reckon) and toward the older Greek-inspired idea of reason as tied to speech and articulation in general.

CHAPTER 2

1. For two very good discussions of Hume's difficulties, see Gardiner (1963) and Solomon (1979). The most telling point against Hume's nonintentional analysis is that—the relation of emotion to object remaining causal and hence *contingent*—it allows for such experiential absurdities as being proud of something that bears no relation to oneself or afraid of something taken simultaneously as harmless.

2. I am indebted here to Strasser's (1977, chap. 3) account of the Gestalt school.

3. Even later, in the transition to genetic phenomenology, Husserl's "existentialist turn" is limited. Fearing that the flux of consciousness would submerge us, "he never undertakes to consider the creativity of consciousness unless led by a 'transcendental guide,' the object . . . an egology must make a detour through a theory of the *cogitatum*" (Ricoeur 1967, 99–100).

4. This is what should lie, it seems to me, behind Solomon's provocative claim that bodily feelings are not essential to emotion (Solomon 1976, 158) or not even components of emotion (178). That is, their presence is so pervasive, obvious, and unexceptional that they can be taken for granted. Instead, Solomon bases his argument on the fact that for many "calm" passions there is apparently little bodily involvement. But we cannot abstract from the body *completely.* I think his argument would be more successful if he claimed the obverse by showing that even the most "cerebral" states involve some feelings and so make the latter inconsequential for analyzing that which allegedly

distinguishes emotion. For other criticisms of Solomon on this as well as a general discussion of the issue, see the very good essay by Koch (1987b).

5. Sartre, of course, is able to arrive at his view because even though emotions are for him *reactions* to situations in which we are impotent, those responses are essentially set (as all acts of consciousness are) in the context of *action*. He thus takes an important step toward denying the orthodox view that emotions are passive phenomena, or at least toward undermining the validity of the active-passive distinction that has informed so much thinking about emotions and whose users feel somehow compelled to opt for either of its poles. Put differently, the cognitive aspect of emotion is understood by Sartre as an activity in a sufficiently strong sense to counterbalance the obvious passivity, usually considered emotions' defining feature, that ensues from the involvement in emotion of many autonomous self-affecting responses over which we have little control. Likewise, even if he does not develop a full-blown theory of emotions, Paul Ricoeur's (1965; 1966) views hold interest precisely because he sees emotions as occupying an intermediate, if not indeed ambiguous, ground between the voluntary and the involuntary. Like Sartre, Ricoeur is interested in the *whole* phenomenon and is thus unwilling to commit himself to either pole; in his view, emotion arises from the complementarity of the voluntary and the involuntary rather than from their dichotomic relation.

6. From a methodological perspective, this last point seems to me especially significant in the light of something like Husserl's ambition to describe experience (including emotions) by means of a transcendental reduction, that is, by appealing only to the internal features of our intentional states while systematically abstracting from any empirical beliefs we may hold about them or about the objects to which they are directed. Recently John Searle (1983) appears also to take this approach but in contrast to Husserl, and very much in line with Heidegger's views, he suggests that meaning and intentionality are possible at all only against a nonintentional background of shared skills and practices. The latter are the "enabling conditions" that allow intentional states to have the sense that they do; in fact Searle's description of how they function is pretty much in line with the dispositional picture of consciousness. But this was precisely the point of contention between Husserl and Heidegger who attacked the methodology of transcendental reduction on the basis that the internalist approach to consciousness and experience could not be maintained if indeed intentionality is conditional upon such a background of skills and practices. And the issue being raised here is that the compatibility of the thesis of the background and the methodology of transcendental reduction turns on whether the skills and practices in question have any appropriately "mental" (i.e., "internal") component (McIntyre 1984, 12n). As long as this issue is not settled in the affirmative—Searle himself does not seem to sufficiently appreciate it—a serious consideration of consciousness as dispositional precludes, in my judgment, a strictly transcendental approach to experience, and *a fortiori* to emotions.

7. For an excellent discussion of various strategies and problems involved in cognitivist attempts to square "emotion" and "belief," see Calhoun (1984).

CHAPTER 3

1. Which is not to suggest that there is a typical identity between our psychological states and our brainstates. In fact, the emergent research points in the opposite direction; identical mind-states may be realized in *several different* brainstates.

2. This also means that there are no animal analogues for our emotions. However anthropomorphically we may be inclined, the similarity of behavioral postures of some animals and ours cannot mean a similarity of emotions; our possession of language ensures that appearances notwithstanding, our experience must be radically different.

CHAPTER 4

1. An interesting parallel suggests itself here with Sartre's treatment of shame as an instantiation of man's radically social nature. Aristotle's shrewd observations suggest that in "proving" the existence of others via a phenomenological ontology of affective states, one need not confine oneself to the examination of such obvious other-dependent candidates as shame or love. In fact, I am prepared to argue that any emotion will do.

2. The usual counterexamples to this definition (or perhaps more accurately to its claim to comprehensiveness) point to our aggressive actions toward *objects* which it would be wholly absurd to accuse of malicious intent and transgressions of norms. But when I curse at or even kick that flat tire—it being surely the immediate object or target of my wrath—I do so because I have *personalized* it, because it embodies poor workmanship by those who should have produced a better product, or simply because I don't deserve this fate and the world "owes me better." In all these instances my adversary is an "agent." To be sure, as Sabini and Silver (1982, chap. 9) note, the Aristotelian account clearly reflects more the *measured* (i.e., reason-motivated) response of a civilized Athenian than the spontaneous and irrational outbursts that *we* typically associate with anger in particular and emotions in general. But then, this in large part is what the definitional battle is all about: what instances of an "emotion" will we accept as paradigmatic.

3. Of course, should we generally interpret emotions in mechanical or hydraulic terms (e.g., as releases or overflows of pent-up substances or energies), then any direct reference to moral distinctions and cultural norms will be suppressed. Anger serves here as a particularly fruitful example because it is overwhelmingly thought of as no more than an automatic consequence of, perhaps indeed a reflex response to, frustration and restrictions. Now, the latter can (and often do) issue in violence and agression, the response we consider typical of anger. But this, as a matter of empirical fact, cannot be universalized. For often frustrations (e.g., the need for food, clothing, shelter, etc.) just as likely lead to despair, helplessness, and submission rather than anger unless—and this is the key—such frustrations are perceived to be caused by a transgression as opposed to some objective and impersonal factors (Sabini and Silver 1987, 182). (Nor, to take the opposite view, do transgressions automatically lead to anger and/or violence.) But if the strictly mechanical account holds (thus collapsing any distinctions between aggres-

sion as produced by frustration and anger as caused by transgression), then we cannot distinguish those frustrations to which we ought to respond from those we should accept. We thus end up with an immature and narrow world-view. In such a context it would of course become nonsensical to inquire in general about the appropriateness of emotions about given objects and vice versa; we would be reduced, as in emotivism, to talking in neutral-descriptive terms about nothing more than subjective preferences presumed a priori as not amenable to more broadly based evaluations .

4. The rapidity with which the natural responses of the infant are taken up and developed (or suppressed simply by virtue of neglect) within a cultural scheme, as well as the necessity of this cultural amplification for the continued existence of the original response—e.g., a lack of visual reinforcement of the child's innate smile will ensue in its losing the capacity to smile—support further the notion of emotions as interpretative, socially constructed stances, insofar as the differentiation and development of *all* of our experience seems initially conditional on the interpretations of *others*. This does not mean that we should reject data from neurophysiology and early-motor-development theory, which delineate principles of perceptual salience and sensitivity thresholds relevant for natural responses. But the extent to which these will be seen as more "explanatory" than intentional and interpretive accounts will depend on negotiating or establishing precise boundaries of the extent to which early development can be reasonably considered as individualistic, as opposed to dyadic or social. A related issue here clearly is that of the gradation of intentionality of psychological attitudes. For how such gradation itself engenders ambiguities for attempts to account for genesis of emotions, see A. Rorty (1980) esp. pp. 111–14.

5. As may happen when a child encounters an (objectively) harmless object at just the instance of reacting strongly to something else, e.g., being frightened by a loud noise. He or she thereby subsequently associates strongly the latter with the former and develops a kind of a nameless or belief-free dread, reactivated each time that sort of object is met again (Peters 1974).

6. In any event, seizing on the differences in the systems of thought and feeling among different peoples may yet pay better dividends in our self-understanding and have superior explanatory value than focusing on the similarities. We have not done too well with the latter option, which we have espoused mainly on the (noncritical) belief that it is the only alternative to unrestrained relativism. The point, of course, is not analogously to err in the opposite direction and stipulate that there are no essential commonalities among peoples but, to reiterate once more, that an in-depth appreciation of what these commonalities may be can come only through an exhaustive look at the differences. What is required, then, is a methodology that will self-consciously prioritize—to adopt the existentialist formulation—experience and existence over essence, regardless of which human sciences (e.g., anthropology, sociology, psychology) inform its perspective.

7. No doubt we would be very much tempted to replace biology-inspired universalization with an intellectualistic counterpart; so much have we become collectively absorbed by a certain formalistic understanding of mind and intentionality, whose ultimate expression can be seen in contemporary

efforts to understand the mind as nothing more than a sophisticated computing device, i.e., one whose essential features pertain only to syntax. But this understanding trades on forgetting something about the background assumptions that (at least in part) inform it, namely, that such accepted differentiations as those between sense and reference (Frege) or act and content (Husserl) were strategic—i.e., intended principally, especially in Husserl, to counter empiricist psychologism by safeguarding the internal features of mental acts as crucial to psychological explanations—and not absolute. If and when they do appear as such, and thus encourage a formalistic approach to the mind, this is so to the extent that objects or contents are propositionally captured and then precisely because only propositions are sufficiently abstract *not* to make any difference in *how* we experience something. (Hence the same proposition can form [part of] the content of several and qualitatively different mental acts.) But this is clearly untenable for emotions if the notion of their acquisition through scenarios is even remotely close to the mark—the quality of the experience as well as *what* it is directed toward being inextricably bound together in an action context and subject moreover to the exigencies of holism of mental life. (Incidentally, this cashes out in more concrete terms what was previously stated from the predominantly linguistic perspective [Chapter 3], namely, how exactly it happens that the meaning of the object or referent of an emotion will be dependent on and cannot be prized apart from, the sense of the experiential act itself.)

8. The standard view of knowledge associated with Kantianism is thus never denied or even questioned here; all experience remains informed by concepts, except that the latter, even the basic ones such as causality, are metaphorically structured. The details of this position, with a wealth of concrete examples, are worked out by Johnson and Lakoff (1980). The key lies in abandoning the categories as unanalyzable primitives in favour of a genetic account of their formation. For "causation," the view postulates a prototypical and directly emergent *experiential gestalt* "direct manipulation" (itself composed of indefinitely analyzable simultaneously occurring properties) that serves as the core subsequently elaborated by metaphor to yield the broad category (of "causation") that covers so many special cases in our experience (chap. 14). For an excellent account of the manner in which metaphors are "cognitive," see Yoos (1971).

9. Writing about metaphor in dialogical contexts, Cohen (1979) seizes on metaphor's power to create a certain intimacy of understanding between participating interlocutors. Something analogously similar, it seems to me, occurs in our emotional self-understanding. Metaphor engages emotion precisely because of its capacity to address what is experientially close to the self in terms with which that self is already familiar. It draws us in by making us at home, as it were, with the contents of our (initially vague) experiences of engagement.

10. Thus I cannot agree with Harré's view that members of cultures that refer to or identify their emotions via bodily organs (e.g., the Chempoy or the Maori)—and for whom thus the social-moral component of emotions' causality apparently does not exist—just "do not have emotions" (Harré 1984, 126). Not only does this view assume that such identifications are univocal and not

metaphorical (which they may very well be) but also that for having emotions one must be able to distinguish between their phenomenal and intentional features, between "feelings" and "meaning." But as I have already suggested on several occasions, this is an illegitimate distinction consequent of an all too thin idea of intentionality, i.e., one discounting the constitutive role of behavioral knowhow in the generation of meaning. Besides, ultimately those peoples' "insides" may be as public and part of the cosmological order—indeed they probably are—as ours are individual and private. If anything, it is *we* who are the more likely candidates for being emotionless.

11. For a detailed discussion on the differences between men and women in the experience of anger, see Averill (1982, chap. 13).

CHAPTER 5

1. Henceforth I shall be using *self* and *person* interchangeably to avoid any "homuncular" interpretation of the former. This may appear evasive, shifting a problem that ultimately has to be faced as long as we recognize some, if only minimal, distinction between organic and psychological life. From wondering whether persons are coextensive with selves we come to questions about the equivalence of person with "human being," with the former now threatening to become analogously the new inner little man. But if person (or self) is understood functionally, i.e., as a structured and hierarchical system of (psychological) capacities, the inner little man can take a rest. Whether all human beings are persons can then be treated empirically: does the being in question possess the relevant capacities or not? Still, *what* constitutes personal capacities is a *conceptual* issue demanding negotiation among those to be affected by the arrived-at self-understanding. Thus what persons and selves are terminates as an inescapably *moral* question.

2. That notion, however underplayed in the history of philosophy because of an exaggerated emphasis on reason, is of course not new and with a home in diverse (and often surprising) quarters. Contemporarily, it belongs perhaps to Scheler (1973) to have presented its strongest version. On Scheler's account, persons are "value essences" whose identity is constituted by the hierarchical structure of their emotional (i.e., value-oriented) acts, or what he also calls the person's *ordo amoris,* "order of love."

3. The contrast itself as well as the possible content of these beliefs is suggested by Stephen Lukes (1985, 285–86).

4. This urgency for expression-recognition can perhaps best and prototypically be witnessed in the passion with which children attempt to stand out and be acknowledged, and this quite often prior to any elaborately (i.e., propositionally) developed consciousness of being single and "alone."

5. As in fact anyone who has been labeled an *in*valid, which is a common term designating those with impaired mobility, may be expected to feel.

6. Here I believe we also glimpse the reason why, try hard as he did to "alienate" the body from the mind by identifying it with pure extension, Descartes nevertheless held out for a more than merely accidental relation between the two, as if sensing that without the body his own reflexivity would furnish indeed nothing but a "ghost" existence.

7. Thus I could not disagree more with de Sousa's (1978) claim (against

Sartre and Solomon in particular) that self-esteem cannot motivate our emotions because it is "too abstract." What, one is tempted to ask, could be more concrete?

CHAPTER 6

1. The issue of justification being particularily poignant in regard to such "retributive" emotions as anger because any ensuing punishment is all too often energized by mixed, including the basest, motives (e.g., resentment, envy, sadism).

2. Typically, we naively assume that being good and having the "right" emotions is mostly a function of grace or good fortune rather than discipline, effort, and occasionally even great sorrow.

3. Additionally, there is a problem of generalizing about capacities for self-intervention; such capacities, as W. and H. Mischel suggest (1977), appear to be highly idiosyncratic.

4. The analogy of perceptual and emotional passivity is suggested in de Sousa (1987, 43).

5. A similar distinction is insisted on by Merleau-Ponty, who, following Husserl, differentiates between "intentionality of act" contained in our judgments and voluntary taking a position, and "operative intentionality" as that which governs the "natural and antepredicative unity of the world" (Merleau-Ponty 1962, xviii).

6. An analogous situation exists for "beliefs." We may voluntarily attend to different sorts of (especially new) evidence that ground them, but once on the "path of discovery," we can hardly choose to reject what we learn, except for reasons *extrinsic* to the process of belief formation itself. There is a legitimate sense, then, in which beliefs in their obviousness can be said to "force" themselves onto us—i.e., barring standing the world on its head we just cannot think otherwise, this being especially so for perceptual knowledge (Clarke 1986).

7. One possible response to the issue of "unchosen" negative characteristics is to treat them as objects of aesthetic-type judgments (see Sabini and Silver 1987). On this picture, we avoid repugnant persons on account of their simply *being* that way and independently of how they have *become* such. This approach allows for abstaining from such strong measures as punishing someone for their character while still providing justification for withdrawing from them, warning friends against them, and hoping our children do not turn out like that (174). While attractive in its apparent disposal of serious difficulties, my sense is that for the approach to stand up, we would need a far stronger link between the ethical and the aesthetic than is currently in vogue. In other words, we need something more robust than "merely" aesthetic judgments to ground acts that even if they are not punishable, are nonetheless of a very serious nature.

8. This is a point essentially tied to intentionality; as with any other "object," the choice of the evaluative description of an emotion will open on the range of "premises" available to us on the basis of which we can orient ourselves to it now and in the future. It also makes us appreciate how immensely correct Sartre is in the general linking of consciousness to freedom, even if he

misses its "mechanism" and so makes the link for the wrong reasons. For it is not that consciousness freely chooses wholly independently of any causal determinants but that the descriptions it provides allow for alternative perspectives and distance that partially deactualize the immediacy of the present moment and the constraints that follow from this immediacy.

9. For some excellent descriptions of this process of self-transformation as informed by a second-order norm (i.e., an ethical ideal) as well as the experiential place of "will" and "choice" within it, see "The Idea of Perfection" in Murdoch (1970).

10. Another way of making the same point is to point out the logical impossibility of any distinction between truth and falsehood were we implanted in falsehood to begin with. Yet another way is hinted by the colloquialism, "We could be fooled most of the time but not *all* of the time."

11. There will of course be huge differences among the competing informing perspectives. For example, orthodox Freudians' "child as father to the adult" motto will contrast sharply with a humanistic-existential vision more optimistic about the capacities of the self to change.

12. This "intuition" must be tempered, however, by the fact that the idea of childhood as a cognitively and morally rudimentary stage of human life is a "relatively recent cultural innovation" (Harré 1984, 22). It is one of the more unfortunate results of the darker side of our religious heritage that we regard children as far less generous and moral than they are actually capable of being.

CHAPTER 7

1. These alternative "neutral" perspectives on the possibilities of being mistaken about ourselves do not minimize Freud's contribution. Even if Freud overgeneralizes that being so mistaken is *always* motivated (in the strong sense of motivation) and indeed to some extent pathological, or even if he has his finger on the wrong sort of motivation or treats it in unacceptably mechanistic terms, his insistence that self-deception is *motivated* is nevertheless precisely the salient point to be gathered from him. For it is through this emphasis on motivation that I believe Freud succeeds at least in establishing the criterion that allows us to mark off the relevant and interesting instances of self-deception, regardless of our view of human nature, and this in itself is an outstanding accomplishment.

2. This also makes intelligible the complaint of certain existentially oriented psychotherapists (e.g., Rollo May) that psychoanalysis is a systematic training in indecision. Without a clear assertion of personal agency and responsibility, the active steps a patient can take to get better get postponed by the endless regressive search for the various determinants of one's psychology.

3. Hence, his most famous examples concentrate on that form of self-deception enacted in personal claims to sincerity on the basis of a perfect congruence of intentions and behavior—irrespective of any other evaluation one may bring on them—claims which thereby deny humans' transcendence (i.e., their "not being what they are").

4. The case mentioned belongs to the most familiar. There are, however, far more subtle variants within this type of deception, not all of which have

conflict and accusation as a premise. By taking advantage of "self-presentational feedback loops," we can also manipulate in Gofmanesque fashion the interpersonal environment in such a way that others will see us in just the positive light we wish to be seen by ourselves (see Gilbert and Cooper 1985).

5. Examples such as this one make it all the clearer just why grasping emotional deception demands looking at many concrete cases. Differently socialized emotions will, it seems, have their own specific patterns of generating misunderstandings in different individuals, groups, epochs, etc. There are also different metaviews about *individual* emotions that need to be considered. Not all emotions are given the same evaluation regarding their ethical and cognitive dimensions; some (e.g., love) are regarded as intrinsically blind, others as somewhat more perspicuous. These evaluations engender different potentials for deceiving ourselves about emotions.

6. This is an insight that Kant articulated perhaps most clearly in delineating the famous antinomies of reason. In considering something that involved going beyond the certainties offered by experience (e.g., the nature of the cosmos, the existence of God or the self), opposite conclusions regarding it could *rationally* still be asserted.

7. On this, see Martin (1986). I have chiefly in mind here the "authenticity" tradition of Sartre and Kierkegaard. Both most strongly insist on the autonomy of shaping our characters by refusing to ossify any evidence that may in turn lead to passive acceptance of conventionally established roles or of the past as wholly definitive of our identity.

8. Another way to state this point is to insist that it is not emotions *as such* that are rational or irrational. That evaluation can be made only with respect to *persons*. That is, it is people who on particular occasions are rational or irrational in being frightened, grieving, jealous, etc. (Rorty 1985, 344).

9. Hence also the frequent futility of settling emotional arguments by "the evidence." For a good (and humorous) example of such failure, see de Sousa (1987, chap. 10).

10. Without identifying self-deception with neurosis, my thinking here is along the lines of such neo-Freudians as Karen Horney (1950), who considers neurosis as grounded in a disturbance in our relation to others.

CHAPTER 8

1. What is needed to pin down this connection are some criteria for *authentically* holding emotions. I shall mention just two that seem minimally required. One, related to the emotions' motivational aspect, is that given recurring opportunities for action, we must at least occasionally do what an emotion motivates us to do; otherwise, it turns out to be just a species of self-indulgence (de Sousa 1987, 320)—"entertaining" the emotion (as in sentimentality) for the satisfactions feeling it brings (e.g., because we look good in the eyes of another) and not for any reasons grounded in the objective situation. Another criterion of authenticity is whether it survives the "test of reflection," that is, whether it engages our core as persons and is not a mere passing fancy.

2. The problem is merely apparent because ultimately *all* our evaluations are from within a certain perspective; we cannot leave our skins. Thus

the theory's justification lies simply in the conviction that it is the "best" theory we have so far, one that in a spirit of fallibilism we maintain as subject to revision by future experience and insight.

3. I am relying here on Sarah Conly's (1988) summary of a "broad conception of flourishing," as espoused by such writers as Williams and MacIntyre.

4. Which is not automatically to say that it is good that we pay such inordinate attention to it. Our culture's skewed "ecology" of emotions, wherein love is burdened with being a solution to all of one's problems, may perhaps be more symptomatic of some deep lacunae in other dimensions of our life.

5. I have adopted this excellent exercise from Solomon (1990, 82–83). It is of course, in essence, the same exercise Plato gives us in his allegory of the cave.

6. This sort of realism is, I take it, the key ontological assumption of Husserl's device of bracketing any beliefs about the existence or nature of the actual referents of experience—one in fact that sustains the viability of a phenomenologist's procedure as a method that gives access to what is real.

7. Much the same thought is expressed by Bruner: "It is far more important, for appreciating the human condition, to understand the ways human beings construct their worlds than it is to establish the ontological status of the products of these processes" (Bruner 1986, 46).

8. Since we can't even find such equivalents for colors, this is an unlikely prospect. No physiological or psychological description of vision can tell us whether we are seeing certain colors "correctly." That is only ascertained in relation to what *others* (idealized as the "standard observer under standard observing conditions") refer to.

9. Once again, this position is different from an objectivism that would insist that convergence is a consequence of the way the world is acting on us. That may be the best possible explanation for convergence, but prior to explanation there is experience. It is because of the regularity and similarity of an experience of "seeing X" in conjunction with no evidence of any agency acting upon X that I can assert its identity over time and existence independent of my seeing it. Only then comes the conviction that I am having the same experience because I am seeing the *same* thing.

REFERENCES

Aristotle. 1953. *Nicomachean Ethics,* trans. J. A. K. Thomson. Baltimore: Penguin.

Armon-Jones, C. 1985. "Prescription, Explication, and the Social Construction of Emotion." *Journal for the Theory of Social Behaviour* 15: 122.

Averill, J. 1974. "An Analysis of Psychophysiological Symbolism and Its Influence on Theories of Emotion." *Journal for the Theory of Social Behaviour* 4: 147–90.

Averill, J. 1982. *Anger and Aggression: An Essay on Emotion.* New York: Springer-Verlag.

Baier, A. 1985. *Postures of the Mind.* Minneapolis: University of Minnesota Press.

Baier, A. 1987. "Getting in Touch with Our Own Feelings." *Topoi* 6: 89–97.

Bedford, E. 1962. "Emotions." In *The Philosophy of Mind,* ed. V. Chappell. Englewood Cliffs, N.J.: Prentice-Hall.

Belenky, M., et al. 1986. *Women's Ways of Knowing: The Development of Self, Voice, and Mind.* New York: Basic Books.

Berger, P. 1985. "Western Individuality: Liberation and Loneliness." *Partisan Review* 52: 323–36.

Bernstein, R. 1971. *Praxis and Action.* Philadelphia: University of Pennsylvania Press.

Bernstein, R. 1983. *Beyond Subjectivism and Objectivism.* Philadelphia: University of Pennsylvania Press.

Blankenburg, W. 1972. "The Cognitive Aspects of Love." In *Facets of Eros: Phenomenological Essays,* ed. F. J. Smith and E. Eng. The Hague: M. Nijhoff.

Briggs, J. L. 1970. *Never in Anger.* Cambridge, Mass.: Harvard University Press.

Bruner, J. 1986. *Actual Minds, Possible Worlds.* Cambridge: Cambridge University Press.

Calhoun, C. 1984. "Cognitive Emotions?" In Calhoun and Solomon 1984.

Calhoun, C., and Solomon, R. C., eds. 1984. *What Is an Emotion: Classic Readings in Philosophical Psychology*. New York: Oxford University Press.

Cannon, W. 1929. *Bodily Changes in Pain, Hunger, Fear and Rage*. 2nd ed. New York: Appleton.

Cannon, W. 1971. "The James-Lange Theory of Emotions: A Critical Examination and an Alternative Theory." In *The Nature of Emotion*, ed. M. Arnold. Baltimore: Penguin.

Carr, D. 1986. *Time, Narrative, and History*. Bloomington: Indiana University Press.

Clarke, M. 1986. "Doxastic Voluntarism and Forced Belief." *Philosophical Studies* 50: 39–51.

Cohen, T. 1979. "Metaphor and the Cultivation of Intimacy." In *On Metaphor*, ed. S. Sacks. Chicago: University of Chicago Press.

Conly, S. 1988. "Flourishing and the Failure of the Ethics of Virtue." *Midwest Studies in Philosophy* 13: 83–96.

Darwin, C. 1896. *The Expression of the Emotions in Man and Animals*. New York: Appleton Press.

Descartes, R. 1911. *The Philosophical Works of Descartes,* trans. E. Haldane and G. Ross, vol. 1. Cambridge: Cambridge University Press.

de Sousa, R. 1978. "Critical Notice of *The Passions*." *Canadian Journal of Philosophy* 9: 335–50.

de Sousa, R. 1980. "The Rationality of Emotions." In Rorty 1980.

de Sousa, R. 1987. *The Rationality of Emotion*. Cambridge, Mass.: MIT Press.

Dorr, A. 1985. "Contexts for Experience with Emotion, with Special Attention to Television." In *The Socialization of Emotion,* ed. M. Lewis and C. Saarni. New York: Plenum Press.

Dworkin, G. 1987. "Intention, Foreseeability, and Responsibility." In Schoeman 1987.

Edie, J. 1976. *Speaking and Meaning*. Bloomington: Indiana University Press.

Elster, J. 1985. "Sadder but Wiser? Rationality and the Emotions." *Social Science Information* 24: 375–406.

Fell, J. 1965. *Emotion in the Thought of Sartre*. New York: Columbia University Press.

Fingarette, H. 1969. *Self-Deception*. London: Routledge & Kegan Paul.

Frankfurt, H. 1971. "Freedom of the Will and the Concept of a Person." *Journal of Philosophy* 68: 5–20.

Frankfurt, H. 1976. "Identification and Externality." In *The Identities of Persons*, ed. A. O. Rorty. Berkeley: University of California Press.

Freud, S. 1957. *The Standard Edition of the Complete Psychological Works of Sigmund Freud*, ed. J. Strachey, vol. 14. London: Hogarth Press.

Frings, M. 1978. "Husserl and Scheler: Two Views on Intersubjectivity." *Journal of the British Society for Phenomenology* 9: 143–49.

Gardiner, P. 1963. "Hume's Theory of the Passions." In *David Hume: A Symposium*, ed. D. Pears. London: Macmillan.

Gastaldi, S. 1987. "*Pathe* and *Polis*: Aristotle's Theory of Passions in the *Rhetoric* and the *Ethics*." *Topoi* 6: 105–10.

Gaylin, W. 1986. *Rediscovering Love*. New York: Viking, Penguin.

Geertz, C. 1973. *The Interpretation of Cultures*. New York: Basic Books.

Gilbert, D., and Cooper, J. 1985. "Social Psychological Strategies of Self-Deception." In Martin 1985.

Gilligan, C. 1982. *In a Different Voice: Psychological Theory and Women's Development*. Cambridge, Mass.: Harvard University Press.

Gordon, R. 1986. "The Passivity of Emotions." *Philosophical Review* 95: 371–92.

Griffiths, M. 1988. "Feminism, Feelings, and Philosophy." In *Feminist Perspectives in Philosophy*, ed. M. Griffiths and M. Whitford. Bloomington: Indiana University Press.

Hanson, R. 1969. *Perception and Discovery*. San Francisco: Freeman, Cooper.

Harré, R, 1984, *Personal Being*. Cambridge, Mass.: Harvard University Press.

Harré, R., ed. 1986. *The Social Construction of Emotions*. Oxford: Basil Blackwell.

Harré, R., and Finlay-Jones, R. 1986. "Emotion Talk across Times." In Harré 1986.

Heelas, P. 1986. "Emotion Talk across Cultures." In Harré 1986.

Hegel, G. W. F. 1977. *Phenomenology of Spirit*, trans. A. Miller. Oxford: Clarendon Press.

Heidegger, M. 1962. *Being and Time*, trans. J. Macquarrie and E. Robinson. New York: Harper & Row.

Heller, A. 1979. *A Theory of Feelings*. Assen: Van Gorcum.

Heller, A. 1982. "Habermas and Marxism." In *Habermas: Critical Debates*, ed. J. B. Thompson and D. Held. Cambridge, Mass.: MIT Press.

Herder, J. 1966. *Essay on the Origin of Language*, trans. J. Moran and A. Gode. Chicago: University of Chicago Press.

Hobbes, T. 1948. *Leviathan,* ed. M. Oakeshott. Oxford: Basil Blackwell.

Hochschild, A. 1979. "Emotion Work, Feeling Rules, and Social Structure." *American Journal of Sociology* 85: 551–75.

Horney, K. 1950. *Neurosis and Human Growth.* New York: W. W. Norton.

Hume, D. 1888. *A Treatise of Human Nature,* ed. L. A. Selby-Bigge. Oxford: Clarendon Press.

Husserl, E. 1970. *Logical Investigations,* trans. J. N. Findlay. New York: Humanities Press.

Ihde, D. 1969. "Language and Experience." In *New Essays in Phenomenology,* ed. J. Edie. Chicago: Quadrangle.

James, W. 1884. "What Is an Emotion." *Mind* 9: 188–204.

Johnson, M. 1987. *The Body in the Mind.* Chicago: University of Chicago Press.

Johnson, M., and Lakoff, G. 1980. *Metaphors We Live By.* Chicago: University of Chicago Press.

Kant, I. 1987. *Fundamental Principles of the Metaphysics of Morals,* trans. T. Abbott. Buffalo: Prometheus.

Kaye, K. 1982. "Organism, Apprentice, and Person." In *Social Interchange in Infancy: Affect, Cognition, and Communication,* ed. E. Tronick. Baltimore: University Park Press.

Keller, E. 1978. "Gender and Science." In *Psychoanalysis and Contemporary Thought,* ed. L. Goldberger. New York: International Universities Press.

Kenny, A. 1963. *Action, Emotion and Will.* New York: Humanities Press.

Kerner, G. 1971. "Passions and the Cognitive Foundation of Ethics." *Philosophy and Phenomenological Research* 31: 177–92.

Koch, P. 1987a. "Emotional Ambivalence." *Philosophy and Phenomenological Research* 47: 257–79.

Koch, P. 1987b. "Bodily Feeling in Emotion." *Dialogue* 26: 59–75.

Kosman, L. A. 1980. "Being Properly Affected: Virtues and Feelings in Aristotle's Ethics." In *Essays on Aristotle's Ethics,* ed. A. O. Rorty. Berkeley: University of California Press.

Lakoff, G. 1987. *Women, Fire, and Dangerous Things.* Chicago: University of Chicago Press.

Lakoff, G., and Kovesces, Z. 1983. *The Cognitive Model of Anger Inherent in American English.* Berkeley: Institute of Cognitive Studies, University of California.

Langer, S. 1962. *Philosophical Sketches.* Baltimore: Johns Hopkins Press.

Lasch, C. 1984. *The Minimal Self: Psychic Survival in Troubled Times.* New York: W. W. Norton.

Lukes, S. 1985. "Conclusion." In *The Category of the Person,* ed. M. Carrithers, S. Collins, and S. Lukes. Cambridge: Cambridge University Press.

Lyons, W. 1980. *Emotion.* Cambridge: Cambridge University Press.

McCormick, P. 1985. "Feelings and Fictions." *Journal of Aesthetics and Art Criticism* 43: 375-83.

McDowell, J. 1985. "Values and Secondary Qualities." In *Morality and Objectivity,* ed. T. Honderich. London: Routledge & Kegan Paul.

McGraw, J. 1986. "Personality and Its Ideal in K. Dabrowski's Theory of Positive Disintegration: A Philosophical Interpretation." *Dialectics and Humanism* 13: 211-37.

MacIntyre, A. 1984. *After Virtue.* Notre Dame, Ind.: University of Notre Dame Press.

McIntyre, R. 1984. "Searle on Intentionality." *Inquiry* 27: 468-83.

Mackie, J. 1977. *Ethics: Inventing Right and Wrong.* Harmondsworth: Penguin.

Mandelbaum, M. 1955. *The Phenomenology of Moral Experience.* Glencoe: Free Press.

Margolis, J. 1988. "Minds, Selves, and Persons." *Topoi* 7: 31-45.

Martin, M. 1977. "Immorality and Self-Deception: A Reply to Bela Szabados." *Dialogue* 16: 274-80.

Martin, M., ed. 1985. *Self-Deception and Self-Understanding: New Essays in Philosophy and Psychology.* Lawrence: University Press of Kansas.

Martin, M. 1986. *Self-Deception and Morality.* Lawrence: University Press of Kansas.

Maslow, A. 1968. *Toward a Psychology of Being.* Princeton, N.J.: Van Nostrand.

Merleau-Ponty, M. 1962. *Phenomenology of Perception,* trans. C. Smith. London: Routledge & Kegan Paul.

Mischel, W., and Mischel, H. 1977. "Self-control and the Self." In *The Self: Psychological and Philosophical Issues,* ed. T. Mischel. Oxford: Basil Blackwell.

Moore, M. 1987. "The Moral Worth of Retribution." In Schoeman 1987.

Morton, A. 1980. *Frames of Mind.* Oxford: Clarendon Press.

Murdoch, I. 1970. *The Sovereignty of Good.* London: Routledge & Kegan Paul.

Nagel, T. 1986. *The View from Nowhere.* Oxford: Clarendon Press.

Newson, J. 1979. "The Growth of Shared Understandings Between Infant and Caregiver." In *Before Speech: The Beginning of Interpersonal Communication,* ed. M. Bullowa. Cambridge: Cambridge University Press.

Nietzsche, F. 1956. *The Genealogy of Morals,* trans. F. Golffing. Garden City, N.Y.: Doubleday Anchor.

Nussbaum, M. 1988a. "Narrative Emotions: Beckett's Genealogy of Love." *Ethics* 98: 225–54.

Nussbaum, M. 1988b. "Non-Relative Virtues: An Aristotelian Approach." *Midwest Studies in Philosophy* 13: 32–53.

Peters, R. 1974. "Reason and Passion." In *Psychology and Ethical Development,* ed. R. Peters. London: Allen & Unwin.

Piaget, J. 1971. *Biology and Knowledge: An Essay on the Relations Between Organic Regulations and Cognitive Processes,* trans. B. Walsh. Chicago: University of Chicago Press.

Polkinghorne, D. 1988. *Narrative Knowing and the Human Sciences.* Albany: SUNY Press.

Pribram, K. 1980. "The Biology of Emotions and Other Feelings." In *Emotion Theory, Research, and Experience,* ed. R. Plutchik and H. Kellerman. New York: Academic Press.

Putnam, H. 1981. *Reason, Truth and History.* Cambridge: Cambridge University Press.

Radden, J. 1984. "Defining Self-Deception." *Dialogue* 23: 103–20.

Reik, T. 1957. *Of Love and Lust.* New York: Grove Press.

Ricoeur, P. 1965. *Fallible Man,* trans. C. Kelbley. Chicago: Regnery.

Ricoeur, P. 1966. *Freedom and Nature,* trans. E. Kohak. Evanston, Ill.: Northwestern University Press.

Ricoeur, P. 1967. *Husserl: An Analysis of His Phenomenology.* Evanston, Ill.: Northwestern University Press.

Ricoeur, P. 1970. *Freud and Philosophy: An Essay on Interpretation,* trans. D. Savage. New Haven, Conn.: Yale University Press.

Ricoeur, P. 1984, 1986. *Time and Narrative,* trans. K. McLaughlin and D. Pellauer. 2 vols. Chicago: University of Chicago Press.

Rorty, A. O., ed. 1976. *The Identities of Persons.* Berkeley: University of California Press.

Rorty, A. O., ed. 1980. *Explaining Emotions.* Berkeley: University of California Press.

Rorty, A. 1982. "From Passions to Emotions and Sentiments." *Philosophy* 57: 159–72.

Rorty, A. 1985. "Varieties of Rationality, Varieties of Emotion." *Social Science Information* 24: 343–53.

Rosaldo, M. 1984. "Toward an Anthropology of Self and Feeling." In Schweder and LeVine 1984.

Sabini, J., and Silver, M. 1982. *Moralities of Everyday Life.* Oxford: Oxford University Press.

Sabini, J., and Silver, M. 1987. "Emotions, Responsibility, and Character." In Schoeman 1987.

Sankowski, E. 1977. "Responsibility of Persons for Their Emotions." *Canadian Journal of Philosophy* 7: 829–40.

Sartre, J-P. 1948. *The Emotions: Outline of a Theory,* trans. B. Frechtman. New York: Philosophical Library.

Sartre, J-P. 1962. *Existential Psychoanalysis,* trans. H. Barnes. Chicago: Gateway.

Sartre, J-P. 1966. *Being and Nothingness,* trans. H. Barnes. New York: Washington Square Press.

Schachter, S., and Singer, J. 1962. "Cognitive Social, and Psychological Determinants of Emotional States." *Psychological Review* 69: 378–99.

Scheler, M. 1970. *The Nature of Sympathy,* trans. P. Heath, Hamden: Archon.

Scheler, M. 1972. *Ressentiment.* New York: Schocken.

Scheler, M. 1973. *Formalism in Ethics and Non-Formal Ethics of Values,* trans. M. Frings and R. Funk. Evanston, Ill.: Northwestern University Press.

Scheman, N. 1983. "Individualism and the Objects of Psychology." In *Discovering Reality: Feminist Perspectives on Epistemology, Metaphysics, Methodology, and Philosophy of Science,* ed. S. Harding and M. Hintikka. Dordrecht: D. Reidel.

Schoeck, H. 1966. *Envy.* New York: Harcourt, Brace & World.

Schoeman, F., ed. 1987. *Responsibility, Character, and the Emotions: New Essays in Moral Psychology.* Cambridge: Cambridge University Press.

Schrag, C. 1969. *Experience and Being.* Evanston: Northwestern University Press.

Schutz, A. 1962. *Collected Papers,* Vol. 1, *The Problem of Social Reality,* ed. M. Natanson. The Hague: M. Nijhoff.

Schweder, R., and LeVine, R. 1984. *Culture Theory: Essays on Mind, Self, and Emotion.* Cambridge, Mass.: Cambridge University Press.

Scruton, R. 1980. "Emotion, Practical Knowledge and Common Culture." In Rorty 1980.

Scruton, R. 1987. "Analytic Philosophy and Emotion. *Topoi* 6: 77–81.

Searle, J. 1983. *Intentionality: An Essay in the Philosophy of Mind.* Cambridge: Cambridge University Press.

Searle, J. 1984. *Minds, Brains, and Science.* London: British Broadcasting Corporation.

Shotter, J. 1976. "Acquired Powers: The Transformation of Natural into

Personal Powers." In *Personality,* ed. R. Harré. Oxford: Basil Blackwell.

Skillen, A. 1983. "Review of *Emotion.*" *Mind* 92: 310–11.

Smith, H. 1988. "Philosophy, Theology, and the Primordial Claim." *Cross Currents* 37: 276–88.

Snell, B. 1982. *The Discovery of the Mind in Greek Philosophy and Literature.* New York: Dover.

Solomon, R. C. 1976. *The Passions.* Notre Dame, Ind.: University of Notre Dame Press.

Solomon, R. C. 1977. "Husserl's Concept of the Noema." In *Husserl: Expositions and Appraisals,* ed. F. Elliston and P. McCormick. Notre Dame, Ind.: University of Notre Dame Press.

Solomon, R. C. 1979. "Nothing to Be Proud Of." In *Understanding Human Emotions: Bowling Green Studies in Applied Philosophy 1,* ed. F. Miller and T. Attig. Bowling Green, Ohio: Philosophy Documentation Center.

Solomon, R. C. 1981. "Sartre on Emotions." In *The Philosophy of Jean-Paul Sartre,* ed. P. A. Schilpp. La Salle, Ill.: Open Court.

Solomon, R. C. 1984. "Getting Angry: The Jamesian Theory of Emotion in Anthropology." In Schweder and LeVine 1984.

Solomon, R. C. 1988. "On Emotions as Judgments," *American Philosophical Quarterly* vol. 25, no. 2, April 1988.

Solomon, R. C. 1990. *The Big Questions: A Short Introduction to Philosophy.* New York: Harcourt Brace Jovanovich.

Stocker, M. 1976. "The Schizophrenia of Modern Ethical Theories." *Journal of Philosophy* 73: 453–66 .

Strasser, S. 1977. *Phenomenology of Feeling,* trans. R. E. Wood. Pittsburgh: Duquesne University Press.

Strawson, P. F. 1959. *Individuals.* London: Methuen.

Strawson, P. F. 1974. *Freedom and Resentment and Other Essays.* London: Methuen.

Sweeney, R. 1975. "The Affective 'A Priori.'" *Analecta Husserliana* 3: 80–97.

Szabados, B. 1985. "The Self, Its Passions, and Self-Deception." In Martin 1985.

Taylor, C. 1959. "Phenomenology and Linguistic Analysis." *The Aristotelian Society* 33: 93–110.

Taylor, C. 1970. "Explaining Action." *Inquiry* 13: 54–89.

Taylor, C. 1976. "Responsibility for Self." In *The Identities of Persons,* ed. A. O. Rorty. Berkeley: University of California Press.

Taylor, C. 1985. *Philosophical Papers,* Vol. 1, *Human Agency and Language.* Cambridge: Cambridge University Press.

Taylor, C. 1989. *Sources of the Self: The Making of the Modern Identity*. Cambridge, Mass.: Harvard University Press.

Vygotsky, L. 1986. *Thought and Language*. Cambridge, Mass.: MIT Press.

Warner, T. 1986. "Anger and Similar Delusions." In Harré 1986.

Williams, B. 1973. *Problems of the Self*. Cambridge: Cambridge University Press.

Williams, B. 1976. "Persons, Character, and Morality." In Rorty 1976.

Williams, B. 1985. *Ethics and the Limits of Philosophy*. Cambridge, Mass.: Harvard University Press.

Wilson, C. 1972. "Love as an Adventure in Mutual Freedom." In *Love Today: A New Exploration*, ed. H. Otto. New York: Association Press.

Wilson, T. 1985. "Self-Deception without Repression: Limits on Access to Mental States." In Martin 1985.

Wolf, S. 1982. "Moral Saints." *Journal of Philosophy* 79: 419–39.

Wolf, S. 1987. "Sanity and the Metaphysics of Responsibility." In Schoeman 1987.

Yoos, G. 1971. "A Phenomenological Look at Metaphor." *Philosophy and Phenomenological Research* 32: 77–88.

Zaner, R. 1981. *The Context of Self: A Phenomenological Inquiry Using Medicine as a Clue*. Athens: Ohio University Press.

INDEX

A Note About the Author

Born in Cracow, Poland, W. George Turski lectures in Philosophy at Concordia University in Montreal.